AF830561

Spatial Structure and Regional Development in China

Spatial Structure and Regional Development in China

An Interregional Input–Output Approach

Edited by

Nobuhiro Okamoto

and

Takeo Ihara

palgrave macmillan IDE-JETRO

© Institute of Developing Economies (IDE), JETRO 2005

All rights reserved. No reproduction, copy or transmission of this publication may be made without written permission.

No paragraph of this publication may be reproduced, copied or transmitted save with written permission or in accordance with the provisions of the Copyright, Designs and Patents Act 1988, or under the terms of any licence permitting limited copying issued by the Copyright Licensing Agency, 90 Tottenham Court Road, London W1T 4LP.

Any person who does any unauthorized act in relation to this publication may be liable to criminal prosecution and civil claims for damages.

The author has asserted his right to be identified as the author of this work in accordance with the Copyright, Designs and Patents Act 1988.

First published in 2005 by
PALGRAVE MACMILLAN
Houndmills, Basingstoke, Hampshire RG21 6XS and
175 Fifth Avenue, New York, N.Y. 10010
Companies and representatives throughout the world.

PALGRAVE MACMILLAN is the global academic imprint of the Palgrave Macmillan division of St. Martin's Press, LLC and of Palgrave Macmillan Ltd. Macmillan® is a registered trademark in the United States, United Kingdom and other countries. Palgrave is a registered trademark in the European Union and other countries.

ISBN-13: 978–1–4039–4348–4
ISBN-10: 1–4039–4348–6

This book is printed on paper suitable for recycling and made from fully managed and sustained forest sources.

A catalogue record for this book is available from the British Library.

Library of Congress Cataloging-in-Publication Data
Spatial structure and regional development in China : an interregional input–output approach / edited by Nobuhiro Okamoto and Takeo Ihara.
p. cm.
Rev. papers originally presented at an international workshop on 26th in Nov., 2003.
Includes bibliographical references and index.
ISBN 1–4039–4348–6 (cloth)
1. China – Economic conditions – 1976–2000 – Regional disparities. 2. China – Economic conditions – 2000 – Regional disparities. 3. China – Economic policy – 1976–2000 – Regional disparities. 4. China – Economic policy – 2000– 5. Regional planning – China. 6. Input–output analysis – China. I. Okamoto, Nobuhiro. II. Ihara, Takeo, 1940–
HC427.92.S697 2005
338.951—dc22 2005042143

10 9 8 7 6 5 4 3 2 1
14 13 12 11 10 09 08 07 06 05

Printed and bound in Great Britain by
Antony Rowe Ltd, Chippenham and Eastbourne

Contents

List of Figures and Tables

Figures

Tables

Preface

During the last two decades, the Chinese economy has continually attained high rates of economic growth. As a result, the influences of China on the global economy have increased rapidly, while the disparity of regional development has become a crucial topic not only for academic researchers but also for policy planners. In the literature of the studies on regional disparity in China, many researchers have been investigating not only the extent of this regional disparity, but also whether it diverges or converges. But, it should be noted, however, that there are very few studies from the aspects of 'Space Economy'. More specifically, even if one region is developing with the assumption that the development of other regions is still remained, the regional economic system may change, and, hence, this change may also have an impact on the economic activity of other regions through the interregional transactions between various industries.

In order to clarify the above-stated regional development problems in China, particularly from the spatial aspects, in 2001, the Institute of Developing Economies (IDE), the Japan External Trade Organization (JETRO) and the State Information Centre (SIC) in China launched a joint research project leading to the compilation of an *Interregional Input–Output Model for China*, and this result was published as *Multi-regional Input–Output Model for China 2000* from IDE–JETRO in 2003.

As an application of this input–output model, in 2003 a one-year research project was organized by IDE to explore the regional development problems from the spatial aspects in collaboration with SIC. Together we discussed which regional topics we would need to consider based on the input–output framework. This book, the result of the study, deals with two aspects: one is an attempt to understand regional development in China in a spatial context; and the other is to show how to apply an input–output analysis to considering such issues. We do hope that this book will play the role of a bridge between regional economists and input–output analysts. In the process of our joint research project, we held an international workshop on 26 November 2003. At this workshop, we presented and discussed the preliminary papers. We are grateful to all participants for their stimulating comments and contributions on that occasion.

Finally, we would like to express our thanks to Mr Yaxiong Zhang, who organized the special research group in China, and also to IDE, which gave us the opportunity to carry out this research.

NOBUHIRO OKAMOTO
TAKEO IHARA

Acknowledgements

The editors organized the research group on both the Japan and China sides – 'Spatial Structure and Regional Development in China' – starting in April 2003, and the research was completed in March 2004. Nobuhiro Okamoto wishes especially to express acknowledgement to the Institute of Developing Economies–JETRO for permitting and sponsoring the organization of this research group. We also wish to thank many people who contributed to publishing this book: Takao Tsuneishi and Yumiko Ishikawa, who are the director general and assistant director of Research Promotion Department, recommended that our research result be published by Palgrave Macmillan: thanks, too, to Keith Povey, who spent a significant amount of time restyling our initial typescript.

The editors and publishers are grateful to the following for granting permission for the use of copyright material: Blackwell Publishers Ltd for permission to reproduce Table 1 from Jane Golley (2002) 'Regional Patterns of Industrial Development during China's Economic Transition', *The Economics of Transition*, vol. 10, no. 3, 761–801. It appears as Table 7.1 in this book.

Notes on the Contributors

Shiro Hioki is Associate Professor, Faculty of Economics, Tohoku University.

Yongzhi Hou is Vice Director, Department of Development Strategy and Regional Economy, Development Research Centre of the State Council.

Takeo Ihara is Professor, Economics and Regional Science, Graduate School of the University of Kitakyushu.

Takaaki Kanazawa is Associate Professor, Faculty of Economics, Wakayama University.

Shantong Li is Director, Department of Development Strategy and Regional Economy, Development Research Centre of the State Council.

Qiyun Liu is Professor, School of Public Administration, Renmin (People's) University of China.

Nobuhiro Okamoto is Assistant Director, Micro Economic Analysis Group, Development Studies Centre, Institute of Developing Economies–JETRO.

Wenqing Pan is Lecturer, School of Economic Administration, Qinghua University.

Yaxiong Zhang is Chief and Associate Professor, Department of Economic Forecasting, State Information Centre.

Kun Zhao is Economist, Department of Economic Forecasting, State Information Centre.

1
Introduction

Nobuhiro Okamoto and Takeo Ihara

In 1999, the then Chinese President Jiang Zemin declared his policy of 'Western Area Development', which aimed to achieve economic development for the western region in China. This masked a substantial change in regional development policy in China. After the central government of China had implemented an 'open door' policy, China then applied the 'Step Ladder policy' for regional development. The intention of this policy was to start by developing the coastal region, and then to move on to the development of the interior regions. In practice, the coastal regions of China have developed rapidly, but the interior regions have been relatively underdeveloped. The regional disparities that have resulted have been one of the main concerns for policy planners at both national and regional levels as well as researchers both inside and outside China. This is the main reason why so many regional scientists or analysts have begun to study regional development in China.

In recent years, there have been a number of outcomes of study on regional development in China and on the economic disparities among Chinese regions. Earlier contributions came from Tsui (1991) and Lyons (1991), both of which measure the disparities in regional economies, and Tsui (1993) and Lee (2000), who decomposed the regional disparity into inter-provincial, intra-provincial and urban–rural disparities. Ying (1999) and Akita, Kawamura and Xie (1999) used the Theil index to examine the contents of regional disparities. From the viewpoint of new economic growth theory, Jian, Sachs and Warner (1996), Raiser (1998) and Yao and Zhang (2001) attempt to identify the mechanism of convergence and divergence of regional disparities. With the development of new economic geography or spatial economics in recent years, the concept of 'space' has been embraced keenly by a number of economists and applied to China's regional development problems. For example,

Chen (1996), Ding (1999), Cheng and Kwan (2000) and Belderbos and Carree (2002) have all discussed the location of foreign direct investment. Similarly, Golley (2002) discussed regional development, based upon the concept of 'cumulative causation hypothesis'. Furthermore, industrial agglomeration in a specific region has also become a focus of considerable attention. Marukawa (2001) tried to explain why there had been a process of industrial agglomeration in Shaoxing and Wenzhou, while Kimura (2003) analysed the relation between agglomeration and development as a whole, and Chen (2002) measured the extent of external economies of agglomeration. Spatial interaction has also been an important issue in interpreting interregional development: Zhang and Felmingham (2002) and Brun, Combes and Renard (2002) tried to measure the spillover effect from the coastal region to the interior region. However, this literature has yet to produce concrete conclusions and it should also be noted that there is a lack of acknowledgement of both inter-industrial linkages and its spatial interactions among the regions in these literatures.

In addition, the literature on regional development in China can be divided into the following two streams, according to the data which are used. One involves the analysis of regional inequalities, which focuses on the measurement of inequality by using such regional macro-data as production accounts, GDP, employment, and so on. The other uses regional micro-data, which can be derived from special survey on established agency or personal levels. Among others, interregional input–output data can be regarded as the combined data with macro and micro data. And hence, it can be seen as perhaps the best method to use in analysing such economic situations.

However, to date only two studies (Akita, Yue and Kawamura 1999; Ichimura and Wang 2003) have approached the situation from an interregional input–output context. Akita, Yue and Kawamura (1999) compiled a two-region model using non-survey methods. Ichimura and Wang (2003) constructed a seven-region model for the year 1987. It is still very important for us to capture regional economic developments from the viewpoint of spatial interaction. Clearly, this means that there might be great potential in these empirical studies, in which the regional development in China can be examined very carefully by using interregional input–output tables.

In this book, the chapters are organized as follows.

Part I, composed of two chapters, will discuss the methodology and data estimation of interregional input–output data, which have become the main tools used in analysing regional development in China. Chapter 2, entitled 'How to Utilize Interregional Input–Output Analysis in China', by Takeo Ihara, will consider the reason why the interregional input–output approach has not yet been fully developed in China, and will suggest the future development of application methods in this field. In Chapter 3, 'Non-Survey Methods for Estimating Regional and Interregional Input–Output Multipliers' by Nobuhiro Okamoto and Yaxiong Zhang in association with Kun Zhao, the estimation method of input–output multipliers with non-survey methods will be discussed reflecting the present situation in which it is not always easy to access regional data in China.

In contrast, Part II will focus on the analysis of various regional development problems by using an interregional input–output framework, specifically that developed as the Multi-regional Input–Output Model for China (CMRIO) (Institute of Developing Economies 2003). Chapter 4, 'Analysis of the Characteristics of Regional Development of the Society and Economy in China', by Shantong Li and Yongzhi Hou, focuses on the region's own characteristics or initial conditions for economic development and identifies its regional development process, then, in Chapter 5, 'The Differential Factors of Regional Development in China – a DPG Approach', by Takaaki Kanazawa, will explore the important factors of its economic development in each region. Spatial linkage between regions will be examined in Chapter 6, 'Spatial Linkages of the Chinese Economy', by Wenqing Pan and Qiyun Liu. According to the present situation of inequality of regional agglomeration, Chapter 7, 'Agglomeration, Intraregional and Interregional Linkages in China', by Nobuhiro Okamoto, tries to identify the linkage structures in the region where industrial agglomeration occurred. The final two chapters discuss the spread of economic development from the developed (core) region to the undeveloped (periphery) region based on the framework set out by Hirschman (1958) and Myrdal (1957). Chapter 8, 'The Magnitude of Interregional Input–Output Spillover Effects in China and its Implications for China's Uneven Regional Growth', by Shiro Hioki, discusses regional development policy from the viewpoint of the 'spread' or 'trickle-down' effect, according to the spatial repercussions of final demand, and Chapter 9, 'The Spillover and Feedback Effects between Coastal and Non-coastal Regions', by Yaxiong Zhang and Kun Zhao, measures the spillover and feedback effect between the regions. Finally we summarize our findings and clarify the achievements of this book.

The empirical analysis in Part II makes use of the same sector classification and regional definition of CMRIO. The 17 sector classification is used in most instances, except for Chapter 7, and eight regions are defined, except in Chapter 9 (see Table 1.1 and Figure 1.1).

Table 1.1 Sector classification

17 sectors		*Basic sector classification*	
1	Agriculture	1	Agriculture
2	Mining	2	Coal mining and processing
		3	Crude petroleum and natural gas products
		4	Metal ore mining
		5	Non-ferrous mineral mining
3	Food products	6	Manufacture of food products and tobacco processing
4	Textile and wearing apparel	7	Textile goods
		8	Wearing apparel, leather, furs and related products
5	Wooden products	9	Sawmills and furniture
6	Paper and printing	10	Paper and products, printing and record medium reproduction
7	Chemical products	11	Petroleum processing and coking
		12	Chemicals
8	Non-metallic mineral products	13	Nonmetal mineral products
9	Metal products	14	Metals smelting and pressing
		15	Metal products
10	Machinery	16	Machinery and equipment
11	Transport equipment	17	Transport equipment
12	Electronic products	18	Electric equipment and machinery
		19	Electric and telecommunications equipment
13	Other manufacturing products	20	Instruments, metres, cultural and office machinery
		21	Maintenance and repair of machinery and equipment
		22	Other manufacturing products
		23	Scrap and waste
14	Electricity, gas and water supply	24	Electricity, steam and hot water production and supply
		25	Gas production and supply
		26	Water production and supply
15	Construction	27	Construction
16	Trade and transport	28	Transport and warehousing
		29	Wholesale and retail trade
17	Services	30	Services

Source: Institute of Developing Economies–JETRO (2003, p. 24).

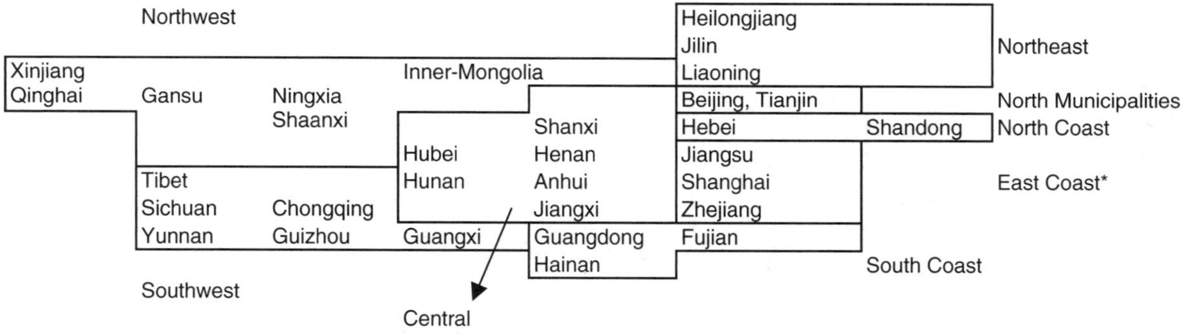

Figure 1.1 Regional definition

Note: * East Coast was named Central Coast in CMRIO (IDE 2003). However, we use 'East Coast' according to the usage of Chinese in this research.

References

Akita, T., K. Kawamura and B. Xie (1999) 'The Regional Economic Development of Northeast China: An Interregional Input–Output Analysis', *The Journal of Econometric Study of Northeast Asia*, 1(1), 53–78.

Akita, T., N. Yue and K. Kawamura (1999) 'Inter-provincial Income Inequality in China, 1985–1997: An Inequality Decomposition Analysis', *The Journal of Econometric Study of Northeast Asia*, 1(2), 55–71.

Belderbos, R. and M. Carree (2002) 'The Location of Japanese Investments in China: Agglomeration Effects, Keiretsu, and Firm Heterogeneity', *Journal of the Japanese and International Economies*, 16(2), 194–211.

Brun, J.F., J.L. Combes and M.F. Renard (2002) 'Are There Spillover Effects between Coastal and Noncoastal Regions in China?', *China Economic Review*, 13(2–3), 161–9.

Chen, C.H. (1996) 'Regional Determinants of Foreign Direct Investment in Mainland China', *Journal of Economic Studies*, 23(2), 18–30.

Chen, K. (2002) 'Chugoku no Chikukan Shotoku Kakusa to Shuseki no Keizai' (Regional Income Disparity and Economies of Agglomeration), *Kokumin Keizai Zasshi (Journal of Economics and Business Administration)*, 186(3), 41–51.

Cheng, L.K. and Y.K. Kwan (2000) 'What Are the Determinants of the Location of Foreign Direct Investment? The Chinese Experience', *Journal of International Economics*, 51(2), 379–400.

Ding, J.P. (1999) 'Agglomeration Effects in Manufacturing Location – Are There Any Country Preferences?', *Economia Internazionale*, 52(1), 59–78.

Golley, J. (2002) 'Regional Patterns of Industrial Development during China's Economic Transition', *Economic of Transition*, 10(3), 761–801.

Hirschman, A. (1958) *The Strategy of Economic Development*, New Haven: Yale University Press.

Ichimura, S. and H.J. Wang (eds) (2003) *Interregional Input–Output Analysis of the Chinese Economy*, Singapore: World Scientific.

Institute of Developing Economies–JETRO (2003) *Multi-Regional Input–Output Model for China 2000*, Statistical Data Series no. 86, Chiba: Institute of Developing Economies–JETRO.

Jian, T.L., J. Sachs and A. Warner (1996) 'Trends in Regional Inequality in China', *China Economic Review*, 7, 1–21.

Kimura, K. (2003) 'China's Regional Industrial Disparity from the Viewpoint of Industrial Agglomeration', in M. Kagami and M. Tsuji (eds), *Industrial Agglomeration: Facts and Lessons for Developing Countries*, Chiba: Institute of Developing Economies–JETRO, pp. 203–34.

Lee, J. (2000) 'Changes in the Source of China's Regional Inequality', *China Economic Review*, 11(3), 232–45.

Lyons, T. (1991) 'Interprovincial Disparities in China: Output and Consumption, 1952–1987', *Economic Development and Cultural Change*, 39, 471–506.

Marukawa, T. (2001) 'Chugoku no Sangyoshuseki-Sono Keizai Katei to Kozo-' (China's Industrial Agglomeration – its Formation and Structure), in M. Seki (ed.), *Ajia no Sangyoshuseki-Sono Hatten Katei to Kozo- (Industrial Agglomeration in Asia – its Formation and Structure)*, Chiba: Institute of Developing Economies–JETRO, pp. 29–60.

Myrdal, G. (1957) *Economic Theory and Underdeveloped Regions*, London: Gerald Duckworth.

Raiser, M. (1998) 'Subsidizing Inequality: Economic Reforms, Fiscal Transfers and Convergence across Chinese Provinces', *Journal of Development Studies*, 34(3), 1–26.

Tsui, K.Y. (1991) 'China's Regional Inequality, 1952–1985', *Journal of Comparative Economics*, 15, 1–21.

Tsui, K.Y. (1993) 'Decomposition of China's Regional Inequalities', *Journal of Comparative Economics*, 17, 600–27.

Yao, S. and Z.Y. Zhang (2001) 'Regional Growth in China Under Economic Reforms', *Journal of Development Studies*, 38(2), 167–86.

Ying, L.G. (1999) 'China's Changing Regional Disparities during the Reform Period', *Economic Geography*, 75(1), 59–70.

Zhang, Q. and B. Felmingham (2002) 'The Role of FDI, Exports and Spillover Effects in the Regional Development of China', *Journal of Development Studies*, 38(4), 157–78.

Part I

Effectiveness of an Interregional Input–Output Approach in China

2 How to Utilize Interregional Input–Output Analysis in China

Takeo Ihara

2.1 Introduction

The main aim of this chapter is to call for a full appreciation of the strengths and limitations of interregional input–output analysis and also to make readers familiar with how it can be used to obtain some clues about regional development in China.

1987 saw the first publication of an input–output table for China at the national level.[1] Since then, the 1990 table was also constructed as an extended form of the 1987 table. The 1992 table, which was based on the System of National Accounts, consisted of 118 sectors, including the scrap and waste sector. The 1995 table was again an extended form of the 1992 table. The latest input–output table for China at the national level is for the year 1997, and consists of 124 sectors.

After completing the time-consuming process of constructing national tables, we are now at the stage of utilizing a full-scale interregional input–output table in China for the year 2000.[2] This is because in March 2003 the Institute of Developing Economies (IDE), JETRO, finally released the Multi-Regional Input–Output Model for China 2000, a powerful analytical tool.[3] Therefore, we can now refine our own analytical skill in using input–output models and even point the way to developing a more sophisticated interregional input–output analysis for China from this day on.

But, in order to do so, it is extremely important for us to understand the *qualifications* and *limitations* of the basic input–output model. Judging from our past experience of a number of applications of interregional input–output models in China, we aim to clarify the relative advantages of an input–output model so as to consider some policy implications in applying its model to more complicated spatial interactions and/or interregional linkages. Therefore, in this chapter, we will refer to the following four comments in turn: First, the basic structure of an input–output model is to be explained. Secondly, the qualifications and limitations of an input–output model are to be clarified. Thirdly, a more sophisticated interregional input–output model is to be advanced. And, finally, some concluding remarks will give suggestions for further research.

2.2 Why use the input–output model?

It was Wassily W. Leontief who first compiled an input–output table for the USA in 1941 for the purposes of economic forecasting shortly after the Second World War.[4] Since that time, many applications of input–output models have been carried out across the world, mostly at the national level. More recently, however, interest in economic analysis at the regional level has led to modifications of an input–output model in order to deal with more complicated regional issues.[5]

The reasons why the input–output model has been so widely used *may* be due to its flexibility in handling quantitative measures. In other words, it could be regarded as the most fundamental and useful framework available to help grasp the reality of economic structures and to draw some meaningful policy implications from them.

However, it should be noted that an input–output model must be clearly defined, together with its underlying technical assumptions, before empirical implementations. In this sense, let us clarify the whole structure of an input–output model precisely, and then explain the technical assumptions which lie behind that model.

Formally speaking, an input–output model consists of the following three matrices: Firstly, the Input–Output Table (or the Transaction Matrix, i.e., $X = [x_{ij}]$ and/or Social Accounting Matrix, i.e., *SAM*), which might be regarded as a *descriptive device*, in an input–output model. This Input–Output Table (or the Transaction Matrix) is well characterized by the double-entry system. Namely, any entry seen from a row-wise view in this table shows the output (or sales) structure, while the same entry from a column-wise view simultaneously shows the input (or purchase) structure. Then, with the aid of this primitive Transaction Matrix, we can readily derive the Input Coefficient Matrix, i.e., $A = [a_{ij}]$, and also the Leontief Inverse Matrix, i.e., $B = [I - A]^{-1}$, which might be regarded as an *analytical tool*. Note that a_{ij} in A (i.e., the Input Coefficient Matrix) stands for the sector's input coefficient i in order to produce one unit of output in sector j. In addition, b_{ij} in $B = [I - A]^{-1}$ (i.e., the Leontief Inverse

Matrix) measures the direct and indirect requirements of sector i per unit of final demand for the output of sector j. In this sense, the Inverse Matrix (i.e., B) might be regarded as one of the expansions of the concept of a single *multiplier*, signifying the number by which the change in one variable must be multiplied in order to generate the resulting change in another variable.

Therefore, in a broad sense, an input–output model can be used not only as a *descriptive device* but also as an *analytical tool*. However, it should be noted that in order to convert the former Transaction Matrix (i.e., X) to the latter Leontief Inverse Matrix (i.e., B), very strong technical assumptions are conventionally introduced. They are explicitly stated as follows.

The first assumption is that of *Constant Returns to Scale*. This technical assumption signifies that each production function has the property of first-order homogeneity. Mathematically, it can be written as follows:

$$X_i = \min(x_{1i}/a_{1i}, x_{2i}/a_{2i}, \ldots, x_{ni}/a_{ni}, v_{0i}/a_{0i}); \quad i = 1, 2, \ldots, n$$

X_i is the gross output of sector i,
x_{ij} is the intermediate input of sector $i(i = 1, 2, \ldots, n)$ by sector j,
a_{ij} is the input coefficient of sector $i(i = 1, 2, \ldots, n, 0)$ in order to produce one unit of output in sector j,
V_{oj} is the primary input of value-added (i.e., sector $i = 0$) by sector j.

The second assumption is *Convexity of the Isoquant Surfaces*. This technical assumption tells us that, theoretically, the generalized law of decreasing returns always holds in an input–output model. Hence, if we denote the elasticity of substitution between each intermediate input by σ, then this assumption can be specified as follows:

$$\sigma = dlog(x_{jk}/x_{ik})/dlog(MP_{ik}/MP_{jk}) = 0$$

where MP_{ik} and MP_{jk} stand for the marginal productivity of intermediate inputs i and j by sector k, respectively.

The third assumption is the *Fixed Coefficients of Production*. This technical assumption signifies that the input coefficients of each sector, which can be derived from the following operation, are always constant over time, regardless of the input scale:

$$A = [a_{ij}] = [x_{ij}/X_j]; \quad i, j = 1, 2, \ldots, n$$

where a_{ij} is the input coefficient of sector i in order to produce 1 (one) unit of output in sector j $(i, j = 1, 2, \ldots, n)$
x_{ij} is the intermediate input of sector i by sector j $(i, j = 1, 2, \ldots, n)$
X_j is the gross output of sector j

Among those technical assumptions, most of the criticism so far has centred on the third assumption, namely, the *fixed coefficients of production*. Eventually, various viewpoints have emerged.

For further careful research work, let us classify the already revealed different viewpoints as follows.

The first group consists of researchers assert that the assumption is theoretically dubious, but that as the first approximation to analysis, its adoption might be permissible. The second group consists of those researchers who assert that the assumption has been empirically as well as statistically verified, hence the assumption might be approved. Finally, the third group consists of those economists who assert that the assumption has been verified by the *theorem on substitution*,[6] etc., hence they argue that the assumption should be positively adopted.

2.3 Qualifications and limitations of the input–output model

An input–output model has a great advantage as compared with other related models,[7] such as an econometric model, gravity-type model, and so on. Among other points, it should be emphasized that an input–output model has always offered the most fundamental and useful framework to date, which has stemmed from the general equilibrium theory.[8] In addition, an input–output model must be also qualified for its operation as well as manipulation with quantitative measure, although it depends upon the above-stated technical assumptions. Therefore, whenever we implement any empirical study by an input–output model, it is always necessary to check the validity and reliability of those technical assumptions. But it should be noted, however, that the introduction of such strong technical assumptions into an input–output model enables us to carry out an empirical study with its model.

Thus, we are required to recognize the full extent of the limitations of the input–output model, and hence, to keep on implementing positive practice and empirical studies by actively utilizing an input–output model on one hand. On the other hand, we must cope with the limitations imposed upon an input–output model in order to corroborate and develop further an analytical method based on an input–output model.

Methodologically, we can point out at least two ways in which we can corroborate a conventional input–output model. One is by *deepening* it, namely, the *intensive development*. The other is to *widen* it, namely, the *extensive development*. More specifically, the former involves decomposing the conventional Leontief Inverse Matrix, to measure inter-industrial linkages, and/or interregional feedback effects. The latter involves decomposed output growth, in order to carry out the so-called shift-share analysis, and/or to link to other econometric models. Therefore, when we are considering such interregional issues as income fluctuations, commodity flows, factor mobility, economic planning, and so on, then, a derivation from an input–output model at the national level to a more complicated interregional input–output model becomes inevitable. And this kind of elaboration of an input–output model might be classified into the former *intensive development*, which will be explained in more detail later on.

Prior to explaining an interregional input–output model, we must clarify some theoretical aspects of an input–output model in general, known as the relations of *duality*.[9]

Because of the above-stated technical assumptions imposed on an input–output model, the product-determining mechanism is completely independent of the price-determining mechanism in an input–output model, and vice versa. Mathematically, the former mechanism can be specified as $X = [I - A]^{-1}F$, where X and F are vectors of output and final demand, respectively, while the latter mechanism can be specified as $P = [I - A']^{-1}V$, where P and V are vectors of price and value-added, respectively.

If we consider the past applications of an input–output model, most of them turn out to be brought about by the former, i.e., the application of the product-determining mechanism. According to this logical reasoning, the equilibrium product level can be determined so as to meet the given level of final demand without any capacity constraints. In other words, if we are faced with some crucial capacity constraints, then we must take account of this kind of restrictions explicitly in our empirical study. There have been quite a few applications of the latter, i.e., the application of the price-determining mechanism. The underlying way of thinking on this mechanism is that the shadow price of each commodity can be determined so as to equalize it to the total costs of inputs. Judging from the recent move towards a market-oriented economic system in China, the issue of how to narrow the gap between the market price and its related shadow price might be considered to be one of the important policy issues, which might be partly resolved by applications of the dual aspect of an input–output model empirically.

In addition, we dare to admit that currently the input–output model has both fans *and* detractors. Generally, however, many of the detractors appear to have some qualms about the strong restrictions of an input–output model. Yet as has already been stated, many of these doubts arise from assumptions which were originally introduced by W.W. Leontief in developing a *practical version* of the general equilibrium theory advocated by Leon Walras. Many of the problems appear to have been addressed by the development of new practical modelling tools, such as a structural econometric model and also the Computable General Equilibrium (CGE) model.[10] Nonetheless, despite these developments, we must admit that an input–output technique is not yet complete, and we must always bear in mind some of the alternatives.

However, we should not overlook the fact that an input–output model is still characterized as a powerful *practical version* of the general equilibrium theory, whose advantage lies in its stress on interdependence, which shows how 'everything depends upon everything else' quantitatively.

2.4 On interregional input–output analysis

As part of the *intensive development* of an input–output model, we can readily extend it to the regional level, since this covers the range between extreme aggregation and complete disaggregation. If we need to clarify the regional differential and/or interregional linkages in more detail, an input–output table at the national level should be further disaggregated to the regional level in order to measure variables such as the interregional feedback effect.

Formally speaking, various types of an interregional input–output model have been proposed and empirically applied so far for different aims. Among others, the Isard-type model is the most primitive and fundamental one.[11] In this model, an *interregional input coefficient*, i.e., a_{ij}^{rs} in A is directly defined for any sector i in region r, and any sector j in region s, respectively. Therefore, a_{ij}^{rs} in A stands for an interregional input coefficient of sector i in region r in order to produce one unit of output of sector j in region $s(i, j = 1, 2, \ldots, n$: $r, s = 1, 2, \ldots, m)$. As a result, the Isard-type model requires detailed information of interregional transactions not only for supply-side but also for demand-side sectors. Thus, from the practical point of view, we are required to examine very carefully the stability as well as the reliability of those interregional input coefficients.

Another operational interregional input–output model has been proposed as a modification of the above-stated Isard-type model, which is called the Chenery–Moses-type model.[12] The relative advantage of this model lies in separating the input coefficients (i.e., a^s_{ij}), from the trade coefficients (i.e., t^{rs}_i). The former (i.e., a^s_{ij}) means the total inputs from sector i in order to produce one unit of output of sector j in region s, while the latter (i.e., t^{rs}_i) means the total amount of purchases from sector i in region r by region s. Mathematically, the relations between those coefficients in two different type models can be specified as follows:

$$t^{rs}_i a^s_{ij} = a^{rs}_{ij}; \quad i, j = 1, 2, \ldots, n: \ r, s = 1, 2, \ldots, m$$

where t^{rs}_i is the total amount of purchases from sector i in region r by region s

a^s_{ij} is the total inputs from sector i in order to produce one unit of output of sector j in region s

a^{rs}_{ij} is the interregional input coefficient of sector i in region r in order to produce one unit of output of sector j in region s

Therefore, so long as we stick to the Chenery–Moses-type model in our empirical implementation, we can readily carry out the impact studies in order to measure the different effects of the changes in production techniques and the changes in trading patterns, separately.

The last but not least interregional input–output model, which has been proposed by Leontief, is called the Balanced Regional model.[13] It differs from the former two-type models by classifying the goods under study into three categories, i.e., national goods, regional goods and local goods, respectively. The basic mathematical structure of this model is identical to that of the above-stated interregional input–output model, but the interpretation of each of the pieces of the model is rather different. It should be noted that the entire analytical structure of this model is based on the observation that in any national economy there are goods with different kinds of market areas. More specifically, there are some goods for which production and consumption balance at the national level. These are goods that have essentially a national market area. On the other hand, there are other sectors for which production and consumption tend to balance at a lower geographical level, i.e., which serve a regional or local rather than a national market. Therefore, we can easily point out that there is an entire spectrum of possibilities, from sectors that serve extremely small local markets to sectors that serve large national and international markets. This is the main reason why market-oriented goods classification (or the three-type industrial classification) has been undertaken explicitly in the Balanced Regional model.

Then, keeping those interregional input–output models in our minds, let us refer to some important remarks, which should be taken into account prior to various empirical implementations.

The most important issue is how to define regions precisely, which conform to the interregional input–output model. Naturally, the delimitation of the region is not an easy task. No matter how we use economic, administrative, historical or other criteria, there are as yet no satisfactory methodologies. Therefore, a certain compromise becomes inevitable.

Be that as it may, there are a few safe generalizations in defining regions. There is, of course, no unique definition, and hence, as a result, the choice must depend, to a large degree, upon the objectives underlying our inquiry and/or the subject of interest. For example, if regions are needed as a means of disaggregating national plans into interregional planning, then a small number of regions (perhaps 6 to 15) seems to be appropriate. In this case, the contiguity criterion becomes very important.[14] In other words, the regions of the system under study must not overlap, and combined they must cover the national territory. Therefore, an interregional system simply means the carving up of a national space into a limited number of adjacent regions. Incidentally, it should be noted that in the Multi-regional Input–Output Model for China 2000, eight regions[15] are defined based upon our careful considerations of the real economic situation in present-day China.

In addition, we must also take into account the fact that the difference between regions and nations has important implications for the content of regional economic analysis. Clearly, a region cannot be treated as a closed system, for *openness* is its essence. As a result, the key property of regional economics is their degree of *openness*. The assumption of a closed economy seems to be common to many macroeconomic models of the national economy, and hence these models cannot be used, unless they are drastically modified, for analysing sub-national regions. Therefore, so long as regions are open systems, key exogenous variables must be specified more carefully. Furthermore, the greater possibility of *disequilibria* in the process must be recognized, and then the models should be less deterministic, and regional economic projections must also be allowed to be more uncertain.

The third – and also very important – remark on utilizing an interregional input–output analysis alerts us to make clear distinctions between *intraregional* and *interregional* economic activities, or transactions. In a multi-regional setting of an input–output table, the former can be shown by a diagonal sub-matrix of a certain region, while the latter can be shown by off-diagonal sub-matrices of any two different regions. Therefore, if we are interested in formations of economic clusters and/or urban agglomerations, we must pay more attention to the former sub-matrices and examine them quantitatively. On the other hand, if we are more interested in the regional autonomy or the degree of openness of a particular region, then we must pay more attention to the latter sub-matrices and try to measure the interregional feedback effects and/or the degree of spatial linkages. But when we deal with the latter sub-matrices, i.e., interregional trade flow, we are often likely to face the cross-hauling phenomena, which might be ascribable to the way of aggregations. Thus, in utilizing interregional input–output analysis, it is very important to check this kind of aggregation problem as carefully as possible.

2.5 Some concluding remarks

In this chapter, we first explained the possibility of making use of a full-scale interregional input–output table in China for the year 2000, which was released by the Institute of Developing Economies, JETRO, in March 2003. As a result, we can now readily refine our analytical skills in using input–output models and can suggest future areas for research.

However, in order to do this, it is very important that we should understand the *qualifications* and *limitations* of the basic input–output model. Therefore, we have clarified the relative advantage of an input–output model so as to consider some policy implications in applying its model to more complicated spatial settings. More specifically, we first explained the basic structure of an input–output model in general. We then clarified the *qualifications* and *limitations* of an input–output model. Finally, as an example of the *intensive development* of an input–output model, we have carefully explained the structure of more sophisticated interregional input–output models.

As we have already clarified, an input–output model itself should not be regarded as a complete analytical tool yet, as compared with other alternatives, such as a structural econometric model, etc. But at the same time, an input–output model should be regarded as the most fundamental and useful framework for measuring real economic structures in a consistent way, and the qualifications could be found in its *operationality* and/or *manipulation* with some quantitative measures.

Therefore, all we have to do is to fully understand the technical assumptions which lie behind an input–output model, i.e., *Constant Returns to Scale, Convexity of the Isoquant Surfaces*, and *Fixed Coefficients of Production*, and also carry out the various empirical research works by actively making use of qualifications, i.e., an *operationality* and/or *manipulation* of an input–output model.

In addition, we have to make an effort to overcome any shortcomings, or limitations, which have been included in input–output models to date. For example, in this chapter, we have intentionally followed Leontief's traditional *demand-driven* input–output model. However, Ghosh has already proposed the adoption of a *supply-driven* input–output model[16] as an alternative to this Leontief-type model.

Therefore, in order to make a clear distinction between these two-type models, let us introduce Ghosh's viewpoints on a primitive input–output table by his following descriptions:

> An input–output transaction matrix may be conceived in terms of an equilibrium position of two sets of interacting forces. The broadest way in which we can define them is to denote one set of forces as technical factors expressed through production functions and the other set as a market factors expressed through allocation functions. Though technical factors influence production, it is widely recognized that there are various alternative technical combinations in any economy and under different market situations different combinations are actually taken up.
>
> An input–output matrix then represents an equilibrium solution for two sets of equations somewhat analogous to demand and supply functions.

Since then, some of the regional scientists have challenged to test whether the supply-driven input–output model might be plausible and/or reliable in empirical implementations.[17] At this stage, we should adopt Ghosh's proposal against the traditional Leontief-type model as one of the new challenges to expand the applicable scope for a flexible input–output model.

Finally, for further research works, let us summarize the contemporary frontiers on an input–output model. Firstly, how to analyse the structure of production over time and across regions has continued to be a focus of an input–output model. In order to find out the key sectors in an input–output model, the use of hypothetical extraction method[18] and/or the use of fields of influence[19] have been proposed on an *inter-industrial linkages*.

Secondly, how to measure the spatial interdependencies in an input–output model is another important task on *spatial structural analysis*. Miller's work, for example, has profound implications for studying regional economies, since he demonstrated the fact that interregional feedback effects are generally quite small, thus admitting the use of strictly intraregional models as opposed to multi-regional specifications.[20]

Thirdly, *Decomposition Techniques* have also developed remarkably quickly. The most commonly applied approach today is known as structural decomposition. The central idea behind this may be ascribable to the fact that change in an economic variable can be decomposed, commonly in an additive fashion, into changes in the constituent parts of this variable.[21]

Having established these fundamental properties of an input–output model, we are looking forward to making more researchers as well as practitioners enthusiastic contributors to the development of path-breaking input–output analysis in China.

Notes

1. Before the 1987 table, the 1973 and 1981 tables were compiled mainly by the State Planning Commission and Chinese Academy of Social Science respectively. See the detail to Polenske and Chen (eds) (1991) chapters 1, 2.
2. We can point to a few studies which have constructed interregional input–output models. One is the interregional input–output table in which Jiangsu province is divided into Subei (North Jiangsu) and Sunan (South Jiangsu) and compiled the table based on the sample survey result (Chen (ed.) (1988), pp. 170–80). The other is the interregional input–output table for the year of 1987 (Ichimura and Wang 2003).
3. See Institute of Developing Economies–JETRO (2003).
4. See Leontief (1941).
5. See Miller and Blair (1985), for example.
6. See Koopmans (ed.) (1951), for example.
7. For various techniques for analysing regional economies, see Richardson (1978), for example.
8. General equilibrium theory originates in Walras (1896).
9. See Leontief, Murgan, Polenske, Simpson and Tower (1965) or Dorfman, Samuelson and Solow (1958), for example.

10. See reviews by Shoven and Whalley (1984, 1992), and also Frietz, Westin and Suo (1994).
11. See Isard (1951).
12. See Chenery (1954) and also Moses (1955).
13. See Leontief (1965).
14. See Richardson (1978), for example.
15. Eight regions to be defined are as follows: Northeast, North Municipalities, North Coast, East Coast, South Coast, Central, Northwest and Southwest.
16. See Ghosh (1958).
17. See Oosterhaven (1988, 1989), and Dietzenbacher (1997), for example.
18. See Cella (1984), for example.
19. See Hewings et al. (1989), for example.
20. See Miller (1966), and also see Ihara (1999), for example.
21. See Lin and Polenske (1995), for example.

References

Cella, G. (1984) 'The Input–Output Measurement of Inter-industry Linkages', *Oxford Bulletin of Economics and Statistics*, 46, 73–84.

Chen, X. (ed.) (1988) *The Theory and Practice of Input–Output Analysis in China* (in Chinese), Beijing: China International Broadcast Press.

Chenery, H.B. (1954) 'Interregional and International Input–Output Analysis, the Structural Interdependence of the Economy', in T. Barna (ed.), *Proceedings of an International Conference on Input–Output Analysis*, New York: Milano, Giuffre.

Dietzenbacher, E. (1997) 'In Vindication of the Ghosh Model: A Reinterpretation as a Price Model', *Journal of Regional Science*, 37(4), 629–51.

Dorfman, R., P.A. Samuelson and R.M. Solow (1958) *Linear Programming and Economic Analysis*, New York: McGraw-Hill.

Frietz, T.L., L. Westin and Z. Suo (1994) 'A Spatial Computable General Equilibrium Model', *Umea Economic Studies*, 330, University of Umea.

Ghosh, A. (1958) 'Input–Output Approach in an Allocation System', *Economica*, 25(97), 58–64.

Hewings, G.J.D., M. Fonseca, J. Guihoto and M. Sonis (1989) 'Key Sectors and Structural Change in the Brazilian Economy, Comparison of an Alternative Approaches and Their Policy Implications', *Journal of Policy Modeling*, 11(1), 67–90.

Ichimura, S. and H.J. Wang (eds) (2003) *Interregional Input–Output Analysis of the Chinese Economy*, Singapore: World Scientific Publishing Co.

Ihara, T. (1999) 'Diagnosis and Therapy of Interregional Feedback Effects', in G.J.D. Hewings, M. Sonis, M. Madden and Y. Kimura (eds), *Understanding and Interpreting Economic Structure*, Heidelberg and New York: Springer, pp. 91–111.

Institute of Developing Economies–JETRO (2003) *Multi-Regional Input–Output Model for China 2000*, Statistical Data Series no. 86, Chiba: Institute of Developing Economies–JETRO.

Isard, W. (1951) 'Interregional Input–Output Analysis: A Model of Space Economy', *Review of Economics and Statistics*, 33(4), 318–28.

Koopmans, T.C. (ed.) (1951) *Activity Analysis of Production and Allocation*, New York: Wiley.

Leontief, W.W. (1941) *The Structure of American Economy 1919–1939: An Empirical Application of Equilibrium Analysis*, New York: International Arts and Sciences Press.

Leontief, W.W. (1986) *Input–Output Economics*, 2nd edition. New York: Oxford University Press.

Leontief, W.W., A. Morgan, K. Polenske, D. Simpson and E. Tower (1965) 'The Economic Impact – Industrial and Regional – of an Arms Cut', *Review of Economics and Statistics*, 47(3), 217–241.

Lin, X. and K.R. Polenske (1995) 'Input–Output Anatomy of China's Energy Use Changes in the 1980s', *Economic System Research*, 7, 67–84.

Miller, R.E. (1966) 'Interregional Feedback Effects in Input–Output Models: Some Preliminary Results', *Papers of the Regional Science Association*, 17, 105–25.

Miller, R.E. and P.D. Blair (1985) *Input–Output Analysis: Foundations and Extensions*, Englewood Cliffs, NJ: Prentice-Hall.

Moses, L.M. (1955) 'The Stability of Interregional Trading Patterns and Input–Output Analysis', *American Economic Review*, 45(5), 803–32.

Netherlands Economic Institute (ed.) (1953) *Input–Output Relations*, Leiden: H.E. Stenfert Kroese.

Oosterhaven, J. (1988) 'On the Plausibility of the Supply-Driven Input–Output Model', *Journal of Regional Science*, 28(2), 203–17.

Oosterhaven, J. (1989) 'The Supply-Driven Input–Output Model: A New Interpretation but Still Implausible', *Journal of Regional Science*, 29(3), 459–65.

Polenske, K.R. and X.K. Chen (eds) (1991) *Chinese Economic Planning and Input–Output Analysis*, Hong Kong: Oxford University Press.

Richardson, H.W. (1978) *Regional Economics*, Chicago: University of Illinois Press.

Shoven, J.B. and J. Whalley (1984) 'Applied General-Equilibrium Models of Taxation and International Trade: An Introduction and Survey', *Journal of Economic Literature*, 22(3), 1007–51.

Shoven, J.B. and J. Whalley (1992) *Applying General-Equilibrium*, New York: Cambridge University Press.

Walras, L. (1896) *Eléments d'économie Politique pure, ou Théorie de la richesse Sociale*. 3e ed. Lausanne: F. Rouge.

3

Non-Survey Methods for Estimating Regional and Interregional Input–Output Multipliers

Nobuhiro Okamoto and Yaxiong Zhang with Kun Zhao

3.1 Introduction

Many regional economists in China have only undertaken a descriptive analysis of the regional development problem when they approach this topic. One reason is that input–output analysis is not a popular method for studying regional economic features in China, and the other is that it is difficult for regional economic analysts to obtain regional input–output data. On the other hand, many input–output analysts in China have paid little attention to various kinds of regional development problems, and have used input–output frameworks only to understand the policy effects on the regional economy, rather than understanding regional economy in regional economics or in a regional science context. The two fields have barely communicated with one another. More precisely, regional economists cannot obtain the input–output data at the regional level and input–output economists have not provided a methodology to obtain input–output data at the regional level in China.

Input–output data at the provincial level[1] has been compiled in order to construct a national input–output table (Liu and Wu 1991, p. 159), and now the provincial statistical offices of 30 of the 31 provinces (with the exception of Tibet) have constructed regional input–output tables in conjunction with the national input–output compilation scheme. But these data are confidential so that regional economists in China or economists outside China[2] cannot usually gain access to the provincial tables.

Because of this limited access to regional input–output data for many economists both inside China and outside China, it is important to consider how to estimate regional input–output data from the existence of data. Although non-survey methods have been criticized (Round 1983) and hybrid methods or partial survey methods have become a main stream for constructing a regional input–output table (Lahr 1993, 2001), applying non-survey methods to China is useful as a first step of getting input–output data under the current situation in which provincial data are not available to the public.

In this regard, we have some questions: In the absence of any access to much regional input–output data for many analysts, how can we estimate an accurate regional input–output model? Is a non-survey technique effective for producing regional and interregional input–output data in China? If not, what kinds of problem are likely to arise? The purpose of this chapter is to consider these questions. It is hoped that this will be useful for regional economists or researchers outside China for applying input–output analysis to regional economic problems in the case of an absence of input–output data at the regional level.

The remainder of this chapter consist of four parts: first, we survey the literature in related to non-survey techniques and select appropriate techniques to fit the data situation in China. Secondly, the provincial input–output data estimated from national data by non-survey techniques will be compared with the original provincial input–output table. Thirdly, interregional input–output data will be also estimated by non-survey methods consistent with the technique above. Then, it will be compared with our model (Institute of Development Economies 2003). However, in conducting this study, only input the coefficient matrix[3] is estimated in these two sections, rather than, the estimated table as a whole, since the Leontief inverse matrix is at the heart of input–output analysis. In the final section of the chapter, the findings will be discussed and future issues will be considered.

3.2 Non-survey techniques and methodology

In this section, we discuss about the development of non-survey techniques, its variation and what technique will be applied in the case of China.

The development of non-survey techniques

Survey, non-survey and hybrid approaches

The construction of a regional and interregional input–output table can employ three methods: survey-based table, non-survey-based table and a hybrid approach-based table which is compiled using both survey data and non-survey techniques. Sometimes this last case is termed partial survey or semi-survey-based table and so on. Such an approach is ideal for conducting detailed survey of regional purchases, by sector, and of regional sales, by sector. In fact, most researchers do not have the time or money to allow this kind of data gathering. Even if we could conduct this kind of survey, the input data from the sectors for production and of outputs to the sectors will differ. We will need to reconcile row-wise and column-wise information in order to construct input–output data and sometimes there will be considerable difficulties in making this adjustment.

In reality, it is virtually impossible to conduct such surveys frequently, and regional economists do not usually able to have enough funds or the time to carry out such work. Therefore, a policy of using non-survey methods has been developed in many countries, including the United States, Japan and Australia. Although the non-survey method is very convenient in terms of saving time and money, its accuracy has been widely questioned. So at the very least, data obtained in this manner are generally combined with more reliable data, such as survey-based information, partial survey results, superior data from other reliable sources (both primary and secondary) and specialist (or expert) opinion. Since other reliable information would be added on the result of non-survey estimation, this hybrid approach has become popular among those conducting input–output studies. The type of approach applied in any particular estimation of regional input–output data might be dependent on the topics to be analysed, and also the funding and time available.

Variation of non-survey techniques

Non-survey methods have been developed because of the limitations of regional data during the 1960s and 1970s. There are three kinds of approach in non-survey technique (Round 1983). Yet here we will only consider two of them.[4] The first to be considered is the quotient approach, which involves adjusting the national input–output coefficient by the quotient. The second is the RAS approach, which is the application of the 'matrix balancing technique'. RAS was developed by Stone (1961) and is also used to update the table.

Many variations on the quotient approach have been developed and discussed, namely, Simple Location Quotient, Purchase-only Location Quotient, Cross industry Quotient, Supply–Demand Approach, Regional Purchase Coefficient and Fabrication Effect Approach and so on (Miller and Blair 1985). According to the empirical work in the USA, in general, the Simple Location Quotient method is the best among various location quotient techniques (Schaffer and Chu 1969; Morrison and Smith 1974; Sawyer and Miller 1983; Miller and Blair 1985, p. 302).

The RAS technique generates a coefficient matrix for a recent year, given the exogenous data on total outputs, total intermediate demand and total intermediate input for that year, and using an earlier coefficient matrix as a starting point. Instead of an earlier coefficient matrix, as a starting-point a national coefficient matrix is used (Schaffer and Chu 1969; McMenamin and Haring 1974; Morrison and Smith 1974; Sawyer and Miller 1983) and other regional coefficient matrix is borrowed (Hewings 1977; Thumann 1978; Hewings and Janson 1980) for estimating a certain regional input coefficient matrix with an iterative procedure. Using a RAS method, we require three times more data than that needed to use Location Quotient method, so it is natural that an RAS method achieves better estimation than a quotient approach. However, it is still critical for regional economists to gather data related to intermediate transaction totals (or final demand and value added) by sector, both row-wise and column-wise. Therefore, the quotient approach might be regarded as a pure non-survey method.[5]

However, this approach has limitations in that it only uses a quotient approach, and this method has been widely criticized the literature (Round 1983). In the recent literature, discussion has focused on the hybrid method, in which partial survey data or other superior data are added on the basis of regional input coefficient by non-survey estimation (West 1980; West, Morrison and Jensen 1984; Lahr 1993, 2001).

In the hybrid approach, it is important to identify the critical transaction (cell of the table) in the coefficient matrix. Jensen and West (1980) and West (1981) have discussed how to identify the important cells, those which affect the accuracy of the Leontief multiplier. And Lahr (2001) also advances a strategy of estimating a high accurate coefficient. If the critical cell or sector could be found, the survey should be conducted on that transaction or sector. In such circumstances, the holistic accuracy (Jensen 1980) would be guaranteed even if there were error estimations in any unimportant cell. Considering the inherent inaccuracies of non-survey models, the trend towards the hybrid approach is understandable. However, even though the hybrid approach is now the main method of producing an input coefficient, non-survey methods are used for the primary estimation of the coefficient as a starting point for constructing a hybrid approach model (West 1990; US Department of Commerce 1997). In this regard, it is still meaningful to investigate the application and to understand its limitation of non-survey methodology in the case of China.

The methodology for estimation

In this essay, only a coefficient matrix will be estimated. If we could obtain the data for an input coefficient matrix at the regional level, then we can calculate the Leontief multiplier. In the input–output model, the impact analysis or linkage analysis is the most common approach. Therefore, the Leontief multiplier, derived from the input coefficient, is most important for regional economic analysis.

Regional input coefficient

According to the literature, the quotient approach and the RAS approach are the main methodologies used in regionalizing national data. Here, we apply a simple Location Quotient (LQ) as the non-survey method in the case of China, because the data required is the lowest of all methods, and we can appreciate the limitation of this methodology under the worst conditions of data gathering.

LQ is a very popular concept in regional economics. We let:

X_i^R = output in sector i in a given region R
X^R = total output in region R
X_i^N = output in sector i in the nation
X^N = total output in the nation

We construct the ratio:

$$LQ_i^R = \frac{X_i^R/X^R}{X_i^N/X^N}$$

which is defined as the location quotient. This represents the percentage of the region's total output in activity compared to that for the nation. It also provides us with information on what industry the region has or does not have and the extent to which each industry is under- or over-represented in the region compared to the nation. From this ratio, we can see the situation which industries are agglomerated or concentrated in the region compared to the national average. This is very useful information for understanding the regional industrial development pattern.

The quotient approach regionalizes the representative industry technology matrix at the national level by using the quotient, which includes regional information. In general, the representative industrial technology matrix is used for the national input coefficient,[6] assuming that national industrial technology is showing the average technology over space. So the regional input coefficient is obtained by multiplying the national input coefficient by regional information. Here, let a_{ij}^N denote a matrix of input coefficient in the national table, a_{ij}^R represent the regional input coefficient and α_{ij}^R for the adjustment coefficient, which shows regional information.[7] In the non-survey method of LQ, LQ is regarded as the adjustment coefficient, showing the regional information.

LQ represents the trade pattern of that region. If it is larger than or equal to unity, that industry is concentrated in that region compared to the national average and it is considered that the supply of that commodity meets the demand for it within the region, and, further, that sector exports that commodity outside the region. If LQ is less than unity, it is viewed as being less concentrated in that region and less capable of satisfying the regional demand. As a result, that commodity is imported from outside the region in order to meet the regional demand for that commodity. Thus, it is assumed that the national coefficient will apply to the region and the regional surplus will be exported to the rest of the nation when LQ is greater than one. On the other hand, the national coefficient will be adjusted downwards in the case of an LQ of less than one, regional coefficient are estimated from the national coefficient by multiplying them by LQ. The general procedure for this adjustment is as follows:

$$\begin{array}{ll} LQ_i^R a_{ij}^N & \text{if } LQ_i^R < 1 \\ a_{ij}^N & \text{if } LQ_i^R \geq 1 \end{array}$$

Here we have to be careful of the meaning of the estimated regional input coefficient obtained by this procedure. As Miller and Blair (1985, p. 295) mentioned, this coefficient does not include imports from outside the region, it is the same as the coefficient calculated from a non-competitive import-type table. Thus, this term, the regional input coefficient, is the same as that used by Miller and Blair (1985).

Interregional input coefficient

As far as we know, there have been few applications of interregional input–output models in China. The first one is Jiangsu province is divided into Subei (North Jiangsu) and Sunan (South Jiangsu) and compiled the table based on the sample survey result (Chen (ed.) 1988, pp. 170–80). After that, Ichimura (Ichimura and Wang 2003) undertook a joint project of Japan and China. This produced an interregional input–output analysis in China from 1992 and constructed an interregional input–output table for the year of 1987, and was completed in 1995. This table is quite big with seven regions and 9 sectors and compiled by the National Bureau of Statistics (Li et al. 2003). Akita, Kawamura and Xie (1999) compiled an interregional model between the Northeast region and the rest of China by the LQ approach on non-survey basis. Following that, studies by Okamoto (Okamoto 2002, 2003; Liu and Okamoto 2003) focused on a three-region, 10-sector model which used a non-survey-based approach employing the framework of the Leontief–Strout-type Gravity model (Leontief and Strout 1966). This methodology was also applied to the compilation of the Multi-regional Input–Output model for China (Institute of Developing Economies 2003) as a primary estimation of the interregional commodity flow (for the details, see Okamoto and Zhang 2003).

With regard to the non-survey method of constructing an interregional input–output model, there are two kinds of approach in terms of estimating the interregional flows. The first is the Quotient approach (Round 1978a, 1978b; Akita, Kawamura and Xie 1999), and the second is the Gravity model approach (Okamoto 2002, 2003; Liu and Okamoto 2002). Under the data access limitation of regional input–output data, here, we consider the quotient approach, which is considered as consistency within framework of regional input coefficient estimation discussed in the previous parts.

Here, assuming that we have only two regions R and S in the nation, let a_{ij}^{RR} and a_{ij}^{SS} denote the regional input coefficients for R and S region respectively, and t_i^R and t_i^S for the self-sufficient ratio within the region for R and S, then, the regional input coefficient for each region are estimated from the national input coefficient as follows:

$$a_{ij}^{RR} = t_i^R a_{ij}^N$$
$$a_{ij}^{SS} = t_i^S a_{ij}^N$$

LQ will be used as a self-sufficient ratio, which presents the proportion of input requirements within the region, thus:

$$t_i^k = LQ_i^k \quad \text{if } LQ_i^R < 1$$
$$t_i^k = 1 \qquad \text{if } LQ_i^R \geq 1 \quad (k = R, S)$$

In the case of the R region, the proportion of imports that is not supplied in the region comes from the rest of the nation – that is, the S region in case of the two-region model. Therefore the input requirement from

S region for R region production are derived from the following equation:

$$a_{ij}^{SR} = (1 - t_i^R)a_{ij}^N$$

Similarly:

$$a_{ij}^{RS} = (1 - t_i^S)a_{ij}^N$$

Using the format of an interregional input matrix, the image of producing interregional input coefficients is as follows:

$a_{ij}^{RR} = t_i^R a_{ij}^N$	$a_{ij}^{RS} = (1 - t_i^S)a_{ij}^N$
$a_{ij}^{SR} = (1 - t_i^R)a_{ij}^N$	$a_{ij}^{SS} = t_i^S a_{ij}^N$

In this essay, we have only two kinds of data required for estimation of regional and interregional input coefficient – namely, total output[8] in the region and national input coefficient.

3.3 Empirical study

Data and comparison method

Provincial input–output data

In the execution of the China Multi-regional input–output project (Institute of Developing Economies 2003), we have collected all of the provincial input–output tables for 1997, except for Tibet,[9] using confidential data.[10] Most of the tables collected have the same sector classification as is used in the national table. However, some of them do not use the same sector classifications. Although full coverage surveys are carried out at the regional level in China, provincial statistical offices do not generally publish survey results and the construction methods used in the input–output data officially, besides it appears that they share little consistency with the national input–output data. And the quality of the provincial input–output data is very much dependent on the training levels of staff in the provincial statistical office, which appears to be a matter of some considerable concern.[11]

Our tables have a 40-sector classification as is used in the national table. And besides, the treatment of imports and exports in both foreign trade and in domestic trade also differs among provincial tables. All imports are put in the column vector in final demand items, in which imports are a negative figure. In other words, it is a competitive import type table. Yet, there are differences between the items of exports and imports. For example, some provinces have four vectors, export, outflow, import and inflow, in which foreign export and import, domestic outflow and inflow are presented in the table independently. Some have two vectors, export and import, regardless of foreign or domestic trade. The rest of the provincial tables have only one vector as net export, which shows the net amount of outflow minus inflow of the region.[12] In the comparison between the estimated coefficient matrix and the original one, we will use four-vector or two-vector tables, because we have to calculate the Leontief multiplier without imports and inflows, as will be shown below.

Despite the data collection of all provincial input–output data, we are unable to use all of them for comparison because of time limitation, doubts about data reliability and the import data availability mentioned above. In this chapter, we will focus on a few representative tables. When we consider the tables according to the rank of GDP size of the region, this means that the table reliability in any province might be increasing in line with the development of the individual regional economies.

From the viewpoint of basic statistical features,[13] regional dispersion and data reliability, the chosen tables are Guangdong (Max), Jiangxi (second max), Beijing (median), Sichuan (second quartile), Guangxi (near mean), Inner Mongolia (third quartile), Jilin (mode) and Qinghai (minimum).

Comparison method

When comparing input coefficients, it is not always obvious how best to compare sets of coefficients; for example, there are 40 times 40 = 1,600 coefficients even in the case of a 40-sector table. In general, then, summary measures of comparison are useful. In the input–output model, the techniques of comparison might be divided into two categories. One method might be the direct comparison of input coefficients by using some summary measurement. These indices have been developed in the context of non-survey vs survey-based table comparisons.

Another method to quantify in an aggregate way the effects of input coefficient change over time or over region is to use the Leontief inverse. This inverse embodies changes in structure in a more comprehensive way than input coefficient matrices. However, there are still a large number of coefficients in the Leontief inverse. Thus, in this chapter we also consider summary measurement.

In this chapter we apply the two summary indices to compare input coefficient as follows (see the detail of indices in Lahr 2001, Appendix 3):

Standardized Total Percentage Error (STPE)[14]

$$STPE = 100 \times \frac{\sum_j \sum_i |a_{ij} - a'_{ij}|}{\sum_j \sum_i a_{ij}}$$

Mean Absolute Difference (MEAD)[15]

$$MEAD = 100 \times \frac{\sum_j \sum_i |a_{ij} - a'_{ij}|}{n \times n} \quad (n = \text{number of sectors})$$

In comparison of the Leontief inverse, we use the average of output multipliers without respect to household.

Provincial level

Comparisons of coefficient matrix

First, we compare the national technical coefficient with the provincial, technical coefficient. In the China table, imports are treated as competitive type, where each transaction includes the imported or inflowed goods from the outside region.

Table 3.1 reports the result of comparison with two kinds of matrices. Clearly, the region with the larger GDP provides a very similar technical structure to the national one, with the exception of Guangdong and Guangxi, which have experienced a different development pattern from the other regions, with few state-owned enterprises have been established during the planned economy period and light industries having grown very rapidly in the 1980s. On the other hand, in Jiangsu and Sichuan, where the macro control of the regional economy was relatively strong throughout the planned and open economy, are relatively similar to the national structure. In general, the larger GDP is in the region, the more similar the technical coefficient is.

Secondly, we will compare the coefficient generated by non-survey methods, here, LQ approach, with provincial one. However, the estimated coefficient matrix by LQ excludes the inputs of imported goods from outside the region, as was seen earlier. The provincial table provides the data in the form of competitive import type, in which input structure includes both the inputs produced inside the region and imported goods produced outside the region. Thus, we cannot directly compare the LQ

Table 3.1 Measures of closeness between national and provincial technical coefficient

	STPE	*MEAD*
Guangdong	60.43	1.02
Jiangsu	52.07	0.84
Sichuan	58.77	0.86
Guanxi	71.58	1.05
Beijing	69.80	1.04
Jilin	67.11	1.05
Inner Mongolia	76.09	1.08
Qinghai	90.86	1.27

Source: Calculated from the SIC data base by Kun Zhao.

estimated coefficient with the provincial technical coefficient. Here, we calculate the regional input coefficient by the following formulae:

$$a_{ij}^{RR} = (1 - n_i)a_{ij}^{R}$$

here, a_{ij}^{RR} denotes the regional input coefficient, and n_i the regional import ratio, it is defined as:

$$n_i = \frac{m_i}{\sum_i a_{ij}^{R} x_i^{R} + f_i^{R}}$$

here, m_i is the total import and inflow and this is represented as the ratio of imports to total domestic demand. Then, $(1 - n_i)$ shows the domestic self-sufficient ratio.

Table 3.2 shows the results of the comparison between the LQ estimated coefficient matrix and the regional input coefficient. Compared with Table 3.1, STPE become larger, but MEAD shows better estimates. This means that the difference in each cell is small based on MEAD, but this small difference might become significant in the summation of a lot of cells. According to this result, it cannot be judged which is better; the difference between the national and provincial technical coefficients and the difference between the LQ estimated coefficient and regional input coefficients. This difference might be similar.

Comparison of regional input–output multiplier

Multipliers are also compared. Table 3.3 reports the differences between the national and provincial Leontief multiplier. The result supports the

Table 3.2 Measures of closeness between LQ estimated and provincial input coefficient ((*I* – *M*)*A* type)

	STPE	*MEAD*
Guangdong	66.27	0.78
Jiangsu	69.37	0.72
Sichuan	54.93	0.75
Guangxi	73.16	0.63
Beijing	68.50	0.72
Jilin	76.15	0.76
Inner Mongolia	82.80	0.89
Qinghai	147.44	1.37
cf. Sawyer and Miller (1983, Table 2)		
Washington		
28 sectors	76–78	
50 sectors	81–83	

Source: Calculated from the SIC data base by Kun Zhao.

Table 3.3 Measures of closeness between national and provincial Leontief multipliers

	STPE	*MEAD*
Guangdong	32.89	2.62
Jiangsu	28.23	2.11
Sichuan	29.02	1.77
Guangxi	40.05	2.62
Beijing	41.22	2.72
Jilin	32.40	2.29
Inner Mongolia	39.14	2.42
Qinghai	48.27	2.79

Source: Calculated from the SIC data base by Kun Zhao.

same general trend drawn from the comparison of coefficient matrices. For example, Jiangsu and Sichuan are very close to the national multiplier in terms of both STPE and MEAD, but Guangdong does not fit the national pattern, even though its GDP is the largest in the country. However, Jilin and Inner Mongolia have also both become close to the national. It seems that the inter-industrial linkage structure of Jilin and Inner Mongolia might be similar to the national, but the direct input structure is very different to the national.

Table 3.5 reports the differences in the average output multiplier. It seems that multipliers in coastal provinces will be higher than national multiplier, and the multiplier for interior provinces is opposite, with the

Table 3.4 Measures of closeness between LQ estimated and $(I-(I-M)A)^{-1}$ type multiplier

	STPE	*MEAD*
Guangdong	29.31	1.42
Jiangsu	40.45	1.76
Sichuan	24.49	1.36
Guangxi	24.94	0.97
Beijing	39.25	1.76
Jilin	28.37	1.19
Inner Mongolia	33.64	1.51
Qinghai	76.28	3.00
cf. Sawyer and Miller (1983, Table 2)		
Washington		
28 sectors	22.4	
50 sectors	23.9	

Source: Calculated from the SIC data base by Kun Zhao.

exception of Jilin. If we use the national multiplier instead of the regional one for regional analysis, the multiplier effect of the coastal provinces will be underestimated, while interior provinces might be overestimated.

Comparisons between the LQ estimated and the $(I-(I-M)A)^{-1}$ type multiplier are summarized in Table 3.4. This shows that all of STPE and MEAD become better compared with Table 3.3, as is confirmed by Table 3.5. Table 3.5 also reports that Jiangsu is overestimated and Sichuan is underestimated, with relatively large differences. It might be that the data reliability of the import and inflow vector in the provincial input–output table or the existence of product mix in this aggregated sector will affect the regional inflow estimated from LQ.

In summary, (1) the regional technical coefficient might be similar to the national one, and the regional input coefficient might also be similar to the LQ estimated input coefficient. Basically when the economic size of a region increases, estimated results would be better. (2) However, in terms of the multiplier, the LQ provides a better estimate than does using national figures.

Interregional level

In comparing the interregional model of non-survey and survey based, unlike Japan, there have been no survey-based data produced in China. In this situation, the accuracy of the non-survey method cannot be verified without the survey-based data. In this section, we use

Table 3.5 Differences in each multiplier

	Original	*NM*[1]	*Diff. (%)*
Guangdong	3.187	2.586	−23
Jiangsu	2.996	2.586	−16
Sichuan	2.439	2.586	6
Guangxi	2.614	2.586	−1
Beijing	2.637	2.586	−2
Jilin	2.827	2.586	−9
Inner Mongolia	2.470	2.586	5
Qinghai	2.311	2.586	11
	(I−M)AM[2]	*LQM*[3]	*Diff. (%)*
Guangdong	1.931	1.909	−1
Jiangsu	1.736	2.227	22
Sichuan	2.224	1.922	−16
Guangxi	1.548	1.712	10
Beijing	1.788	1.707	−5
Jilin	1.683	1.814	7
Inner Mongolia	1.797	1.706	−5
Qinghai	1.575	1.604	2
cf. US regional model			
Schaffer and Chu (1969, Appendix C)	1.365[a]	1.658	21
Morrison and Smith (1974, p. 12)			20
Sawyer and Miller (1983, Table 8)[b]			
28 sectors			20
50 sectors			18

Notes

1. NM is the Leontief multiplier of national table.
2. $(I - M)$AM is $(I - (I - M)A)^{-1}$ type Leontief multiplier.
3. LQM is the Leontief multiplier of LQ estimated coefficient.

[a] survey-based table.

[b] This figure is the mean percentage deviation.

Source: Calculated from the SIC data base by Kun Zhao.

Multi-regional input–output model for China (CMRIO) (Institute of Developing Economies 2003), which was compiled by hybrid approach, as the benchmark for the interregional input–output model in China. Since there is no established correct interregional input–output table in China, the accuracy of the non-survey methods can be judged only on their consistency with the real economy and on underlying data behaviour. The information obtained from this investigation might just be a preliminary result.

In order to estimate the interregional input–output model, we divided the country into two regions: the coastal region, which includes

Table 3.6 Differences of input coefficients between CMRIO and LQ estimated model

	STPE	*MEAD*
Input coefficient	44.49	0.49
Interregional		
A^{AB}	106.05	0.26
A^{BA}	145.35	0.30
Intraregional		
A^{AA}	36.61	0.75
A^{BB}	34.23	0.65
Leontief Inverse	34.48	1.34
Interregional		
B^{AB}	222.97	1.12
B^{BA}	116.77	0.93
Intraregional		
B^{AA}	24.33	1.83
B^{BB}	21.91	1.48

Notes: Supersubscript A means the coastal region, and B the interior region.

Source: Calculated from the SIC data base by Kun Zhao.

Beijing, Tianjin, Hebei, Shandong, Jiangsu, Shanghai, Zhejiang, Fujian, Guangdong and Hainan, and the interior region, which includes all other provinces in China. Using the definition of region in CMRIO, the coastal region consists of the North Municipalities, the North Coast, the East Coast and the South Coast, all other regions are classified as the interior region.

The sectoral classification used is also the same as the CMRIO, in which 30 sectors – most of the service sector – is aggregated.

Assuming that we could only use national input–output data and regional total output in the same way as in the case of regional input–output estimation. We estimate a two-region interregional input–output model that consists of interregional input coefficient and interregional Leontief multiplier.

First of all, all of the coefficients estimated by non-survey methods are investigated. Secondly, we check the regional input coefficients, which are in diagonal matrix (a^{RR}_{ij} and a^{SS}_{ij}) of interregional input–output model. Thirdly, trade coefficients in non-diagonal matrices are compared with the one of CMRIO. Table 3.6 reports the result of the comparison, and we will find that MEAD of the input coefficient is lower than in the

Table 3.7 Differences of total output

	CMRIO	*LQ*	*Diff.*	*(%)*
AA001	70,115,618	75,404,013	5,288,395	(7.5)
AA002	2,222,196	4,221,711	1,999,516	(90.0)
AA003	1,729,512	3,540,900	1,811,388	(104.7)
AA004	1,331,635	1,911,072	579,437	(43.5)
AA005	1,198,601	2,079,350	880,748	(73.5)
AA006	45,159,438	54,156,284	8,996,846	(19.9)
AA007	19,733,287	20,457,688	724,401	(3.7)
AA008	16,424,986	20,332,168	3,907,182	(23.8)
AA009	3,469,254	4,049,961	580,707	(16.7)
AA010	9,738,021	12,657,267	2,919,247	(30.0)
AA011	4,522,070	7,919,595	3,397,526	(75.1)
AA012	36,354,342	47,785,515	11,431,173	(31.4)
AA013	6,169,502	8,564,734	2,395,232	(38.8)
AA014	10,420,398	14,254,617	3,834,219	(36.8)
AA015	6,504,866	8,766,288	2,261,421	(34.8)
AA016	8,882,893	9,278,326	395,433	(4.5)
AA017	9,211,365	9,549,042	337,678	(3.7)
AA018	12,594,675	12,818,127	223,452	(1.8)
AA019	12,294,205	17,876,341	5,582,136	(45.4)
AA020	1,377,081	2,082,649	705,568	(51.2)
AA021	1,304,762	1,976,056	671,295	(51.4)
AA022	4,884,512	6,116,835	1,232,324	(25.2)
AA023	827,869	998,173	170,304	(20.6)
AA024	8,410,973	12,035,600	3,624,627	(43.1)
AA025	508,842	677,952	169,110	(33.2)
AA026	928,318	1,338,052	409,735	(44.1)
AA027	1,925,082	3,167,853	1,242,771	(64.6)
AA028	8,059,362	15,070,054	7,010,693	(87.0)
AA029	20,684,565	31,459,615	10,775,049	(52.1)
AA030	52,089,050	69,203,234	17,114,185	(32.9)
AB001	113,597,671	110,354,196	−3,243,474	(−2.9)
AB002	4,282,069	9,038,880	4,756,811	(111.1)
AB003	3,757,315	5,168,650	1,411,335	(37.6)
AB004	1,580,525	2,828,854	1,248,329	(79.0)
AB005	1,994,142	3,826,474	1,832,332	(91.9)
AB006	61,334,161	64,856,247	3,522,086	(5.7)
AB007	15,388,875	14,871,042	−517,833	(−3.4)
AB008	8,707,755	9,377,008	669,253	(7.7)
AB009	4,532,931	5,559,972	1,027,042	(22.7)
AB010	5,948,384	7,666,340	1,717,956	(28.9)
AB011	5,846,798	7,880,195	2,033,397	(34.8)
AB012	29,637,011	31,023,850	1,386,839	(4.7)
AB013	8,016,790	13,283,875	5,267,085	(65.7)
AB014	8,265,971	13,028,447	4,762,477	(57.6)

Continued

Table 3.7 Continued

	CMRIO	*LQ*	*Diff.*	*(%)*
AB015	4,860,126	5,997,845	1,137,719	(23.4)
AB016	6,706,038	6,199,094	−506,944	(−7.6)
AB017	6,806,192	6,665,740	−140,453	(−2.1)
AB018	4,940,137	5,140,324	200,187	(4.1)
AB019	4,512,152	4,057,623	−454,529	(−10.1)
AB020	626,733	886,501	259,768	(41.4)
AB021	1,421,650	1,931,806	510,155	(35.9)
AB022	3,947,566	5,105,154	1,157,589	(29.3)
AB023	584,854	878,138	293,284	(50.1)
AB024	8,247,183	10,657,887	2,410,704	(29.2)
AB025	331,273	409,814	78,541	(23.7)
AB026	737,717	1,018,676	280,959	(38.1)
AB027	1,955,130	1,855,919	−99,212	(−5.1)
AB028	8,701,018	15,667,272	6,966,254	(80.1)
AB029	22,922,338	29,557,220	6,634,882	(28.9)
AB030	48,296,717	54,803,445	6,506,728	(13.5)
Total	777,564,497	929,345,560	151,781,063	(19.5)

Source: Calculated from the SIC data base by Kun Zhao.

regional input–output case, but STPE is a little bit higher, compared to the regional input–output. In the case of the Leontief multiplier, this still seems to be a good result. However, the coefficient of interregional parts is not as good as the total result.

LQ method, estimating interregional flow, has some problem. Because it does not allow the cross-hauling between the regions. That is why there are relative large discrepancies between CMRIO and the LQ estimated model.

Table 3.7 represents the difference between the total output realized by the Leontief multiplier of CMRIO, multiplied by the consumption and total output estimated by using the Leontief multiplier from the LQ method. Overall, the total output estimated by the LQ method is higher than that of CMRIO. In particular, the mining sector, chemical sector and service sector in the coastal region are overestimated, while a few sectors related to machinery are underestimated in the interior region.

In summary, (1) if we use national IO coefficients to estimate interregional IO coefficients by the LQ method, the regional parts of the model will be better than the interregional one. LQ will underestimate interregional flow. (2) As discussed in the regional case, the national technical coefficient is higher than the regional one, thus, the total output estimated from the national technical coefficient by non-survey methods will be overestimated and the Mining and Service sector will not provide an accurate estimation.

3.4 Conclusion

In this chapter, we have tested the reliability of non-survey methods, by applying the provincial input–output model and interregional input–output model in China, and assuming that we have only published data, national input–output data and production accounts (total output).

The results of the investigation, suggest the following:

1. If we use the national technical coefficient to conduct our regional economic analysis, it might be reasonable when the regions concerned have a relatively large GDP. However, we should always bear in mind its development pattern, in comparison with the national economy.
2. When we wish to undertake an impact analysis of a particular region, the regional input coefficient should be estimated. According to the empirical results, the regional input coefficient, estimated by the LQ approach, may be relatively useful. Therefore the regional Leontief multiplier should be obtained from the regional input coefficient.
3. Compared with previous research, in which the US regional models were estimated by the same method, our estimated regional input–output model provides better results in terms of the average of the output multiplier. Thus, the non-survey method might be useful as a first step in estimating a regional input–output model in China.
4. The interregional model estimated by non-survey methods is not accurate – in particular, the computed interregional coefficients are underestimated. This is because of the limitation that LQ cannot estimate cross-hauling transactions between the regions. Furthermore, since the national multiplier is larger than the provincial one, the estimated total output would be larger than we expected.[16]
5. However, in a situation in which we do not have a survey-based interregional input–output model in China, the result above might still be tentative.

In estimating the regional and interregional input–output model, we consider the worst situation in which we cannot conduct a survey and can only obtain published data from the government. Considering this worst-case situation of data gathering, we can understand the worst limitation of this methodology. If we could do some survey, partial and crucial, or can get the superior data from some agency, needless to say, the accuracy of the estimated model would become higher.

Notes

1. Administrative regions in China are divided into four kinds: municipality, province, autonomous region and special administrative region. In this chapter, 'province' is used for all kinds of administrative regions. However, the Hong Kong and Macao special administrative regions and the Taiwanese provinces are not considered.
2. Provincial input–output data is kept strictly confidential, especially for foreigners. However, some economists outside China (for example, Naughton 2000; Poncet 2001) have gained access to the figures. It seems to us, however, that they did not examine the provincial input–output data carefully enough.
3. The term 'input coefficient matrix' is used for the various types of coefficients. It means the coefficient matrix whose intermediate transaction is divided by total input. According to the treatment of import, there are several coefficients, such as technical coefficient, regional input coefficient and so on. See Miller and Blair (1985).
4. Commodity balance approach is neglected here, because it is itself a technique for producing an input–output table. As we mentioned in the introduction, we concentrate here on the methodology of estimating the input coefficient matrix.
5. Miller and Blair (1985, p. 295) said: 'By purely nonsurvey techniques we mean those methods that estimate regional input coefficients through adjustment of national technical coefficients entirely on the basis of published information on regional employment, income, or output, by industry.'
6. This national input coefficient matrix should be of the competitive import type, which includes the import value in each cell and the import vector should be in the final demand item with a negative figure. If we say 'technology', it should be the input structure of both domestic and imported commodity. Please see the detailed discussion in Hewings and Jensen (1986).
7. This is also called the regional trade coefficient, which shows the geographical source of input supply within a region.
8. Employment data also can be used. But here we use total output.
9. Tibet has never compiled input–output data.
10. The Institute of Developing Economies (IDE) in Japan and the State Information Center (SIC) in China have conducted a joint project for constructing interregional input–output model in China for two years (April 2001–March 2003). In this project, SIC collected the provincial table as confidential data for this project; however, one of the authors, Nobuhiro Okamoto, cannot see the detailed data. The computation work is carried out by Yaxiong Zhang, in association with Kun Zhao.
11. We heard this from the officials of the National Bureau of Statistics.

12. The four-vector table included Beijing, Tianjin, Shanghai, Jiangsu, Guangdong, Guangxi, Ningxia and Xinjiang. The one-vectors table included Hebei, Heilongjiang, Anhui, Shandong, Chongqing, Guizhou and Gansu. The rest of the provinces are the two-vector table.
13. We made the frequency distribution table of provincial GDP size.
14. This measure is also called the mean absolute deviation as a percentage of the mean coefficient (MPMC) in Sawyer and Miller (1983).
15. According to the suggestion of Takeo Ihara, we do not use the term 'MAD' because it sounds strange.
16. Akita, Kawamura and Xie (1999) compiled an interregional input–output model using the LQ method. Therefore, there may be the same problems with their results.

References

Akita, T., K. Kawamura and B. Xie (1999) 'The Regional Economic Development of Northeast China an Interregional Input–Output Analysis', *The Journal of Econometric Study of Northeast Asia*, 1(1), 53–78.

Chen, X. (ed.) (1988) *Theory and Practice of Input–Output Analysis in China* (in Chinese), Beijing: China International Broadcast Press.

Hewings, G.J.D. (1977) 'Evaluating the Possibilities for Exchanging Regional Input–Output Coefficients', *Environment and Planning A*, 9(8), 927–44.

Hewings, G.J.D. and B.N. Janson (1980) 'Exchanging Regional Input–Output Coefficients: A Reply and Further Comments', *Environment and Planning A*, 12(7), 843–54.

Hewings, G.J.D. and R.C. Jensen (1986) 'Regional, Interregional and Multiregional Input–Output Analysis', in P. Nijkamp (eds), *Handbook of Regional and Urban Economics*, vol. I, New York: Elsevier, pp. 295–355.

Ichimura, S. and H. Wang (eds) (2003) *Interregional Input–Output Analysis of the Chinese Economy*, Singapore: World Scientific Publishing Co.

Institute of Developing Economies–JETRO (2003) *Multi-regional Input–Output Model for China 2000*, Statistical Data Series no. 86, Chiba: Institute of Developing Economies–JETRO.

Jensen, R.C. (1980) 'The Concept of Accuracy in Regional Input–Output Models', *International Regional Science Review*, 5, 139–54.

Jensen, R.C. and G.R. West (1980) 'The Effects of Relative Coefficient Size on Input–Output Multipliers', *Environment and Planning A*, 12, 659–70.

Lahr, M.L. (1993) 'A Review of the Literature Supporting the Hybrid Approach to Constructing Regional Input–Output Models', *Economic Systems Research*, 5, 277–93.

Lahr, M.L. (2001) 'A Strategy for Producing Hybrid Regional Input–Output Tables', in M.L. Lahr and E. Dietzenbacher (eds), *Input–Output Analysis: Frontiers and Extensions*, New York: Palgrave, pp. 211–42.

Leontief, W. and A. Strout (1963) 'Multiregional Input–Output Analysis', in T. Barna (ed.), *Structural Interdependence and Economic Development*, London: St Martin's Press.

Li, Q., S. Qi, T. Ito and E. Kusanagi (2002) 'Interregional IO Table of Chinese Economy in 1987', in S. Ichimura and H. Wang (eds), *Interregional Input–Output*

Analysis of The Chinese Economy, Singapore: World Scientific publishing 13–20.

Liu, Q. and N. Okamoto (2002) 'Zhongguo Diqujian Touruchanchu Moxing de Bianji ji Qiwenti' (Establishing an Interregional Input–Output Model of China and Its Problem), *Tongji Yanjiu (Statistical Research)*, no. 9 (Series no. 131), pp. 58–64.

Liu, S. and C. Wu (1991) 'Construction and Application of Regional Input–Output Tables', in K.R. Polenske and X. Chen (eds), *Chinese Economic Planning and Input–Output Analysis*, Hong Kong: Oxford University Press, pp. 159–66.

McMenamin, D.G. and J.E. Haring (1974) 'An Appraisal of Non-survey Techniques for Estimating Regional Input–Output Models', *Journal of Regional Science*, 14(2), 191–205.

Miller, R. and P.D. Blair (1985) *Input–Output Analysis: Foundations and Extensions*, Englewood Cliffs, NJ: Prentice-Hall.

Morrison, W.I. and P. Smith (1974) 'Nonsurvey Input–Output Techniques at the Small Area Level: An Evaluation', *Journal of Regional Science*, 14(1), 1–14.

Naughton, B. (2000) 'How Much Can Regional Integration Do to Unify China's Markets?', *Center for Research on Economic Development and Policy Reform Working Paper*, 58, 1–38.

Okamoto, N. (2002) 'Chugoku Chiikikan Sangyorenkanhyo no Suikeihouhou to sono Kento' (Discussion on the Estimation Methodology of Interregional IO Model for China), in N. Okamoto (ed.) *Chugoku no Chiikikan Sangyokozo-Chiikikan Sangyorenkan Bunseki(I) (Interregional Industrial Structure in China: Interregional Input–Output Analysis (I))*, Asian Input–Output Series no. 61, Chiba: Institute of Developing Economies–JETRO, pp. 1–20.

Okamoto, N. (ed.) (2002) *Chugoku no Chiikikan Sangyokozo-Chiikikan Sangyorenkan Bunseki(I) (Interregional Industrial Structure in China: Interregional Input–Output Analysis (I))*, Asian Input–Output Series no. 61, Chiba: Institute of Developing Economies–JETRO.

Okamoto, N. (ed.) (2003) *Chugoku no Chiikikan Sangyokozo-Chiikikan Sangyorenkan Bunseki(II) (Interregional Industrial Structure in China: Interregional Input-Output Analysis (II))*, Asian Input–Output Series no. 63, Chiba: Institute of Developing Economies–JETRO.

Okamoto, N. (2003) 'Chugoku Chiikikan Sangyorenkanhyo no Suikeihouhou to sono Kento: Saiko-non-survey hou ni yoru Chiikikan wo Chushin ni' (Discussion on the Estimation Methodology of Interregional IO Model for China: Revisited–on the Basis of Regionalization Method), in N. Okamoto (ed.), *Chugoku no Chiikikan Sangyokozo-Chiikikan sangyorenkan Bunseki(II) (Interregional Industrial Structure in China: Interregional Input–Output Analysis (II))*, Asian Input–Output Series no. 63, Chiba: Institute of Developing Economies–JETRO, pp. 32–75.

Okamoto, N. and Y. Zhang (2003) 'Compilation Procedure of Multi-regional Input–Output Model for China 2000', in Institute of Developing Economies, *Multi-regional Input–Output Model for China 2000*, Statistical Data Series no. 86, Chiba: Institute of Developing Economies–JETRO, pp. 9–20.

Poncet, S. (2001) 'The Magnitude of Chinese Provinces' Internal and Interregional Trade Integration: Is Chinese Provinces' Greater International Openness Threatening China's Domestic Market Integration?', paper presented at the 3rd International conference on the Chinese economy, *Has China Become a Market*

Economy? CERDI (le Centre d'études et de recherches sur le développement international), Clermont-Ferrand, France.

Round, J.I. (1978a) 'On Estimating Trade Flows in Interregional Input–Output Models', *Regional Science & Urban Economics*, 8, 289–302.

Round, J.I. (1978b) 'An Interregional Input–Output Approach to the Evaluation of Nonsurvey Methods', *Journal of Regional Science*, 18(2), 179–94.

Round, J.I. (1983) 'Nonsurvey Techniques: A Critical Review of the Theory and the Evidence', *International Regional Science Review*, 8(3), 189–212.

Sawyer, C.H. and R.E. Miller (1983) 'Experiments in Regionalization of a National Input–Output Table', *Environment and Planning A*, 15, 1501–20.

Schaffer, W. and K. Chu (1969) 'Nonsurvey Techniques for Constructing Regional Interindustry Models', *Papers, Regional Science Association*, 23, 83–101.

Stone, R. (1961) *Input–Output and National Accounts*, Paris: Office of European Economic Cooperation.

Thumann, R.G. (1978) 'A Comment on Evaluating the Possibilities for Exchanging Regional Input–Output Coefficients', *Environment and Planning A*, 10(3), 321–5.

US Department of Commerce (1997) *Regional Multipliers – A User Handbook for the Regional Input–Output Modeling System (RIMS II)*, third edition, Washington: US Government Printing Office.

West, G.R. (1980) 'Generation of Regional Input–Output Tables (GRIT): An Introspection', *Economic Analysis and Policy*, 10, 71–86.

West, G.R. (1981) 'An Efficient Approach to the Estimation of Regional Input–Output Multipliers', *Environment and Planning A*, 13, 857–67.

West, G.R. (1990) 'Regional Trade Estimation: A Hybrid Approach', *International Regional Science Review*, 13, 103–18.

West, G.R., J.B. Morrison and R.C. Jensen (1984) 'A Method for the Estimation of Hybrid Interregional Input–Output Tables', *Regional Studies*, 18, 413–22.

Part II

Regional Development in China by an Interregional Input–Output Approach

4
Analysis of the Characteristics of Regional Development of the Society and Economy in China

Shantong Li and Yongzhi Hou

4.1 China's regional division

China is a large country with a vast territory. Its land area totals 9.6 million square kilometres, and by 2001 its population stood at 1.28 billion. For a combination of historical and present-day reasons, the development level varies greatly across the different regions of China. For example, in 2001, the gross domestic product (GDP) of Shanghai averaged 37,382 yuan per capita and that in Guizhou province was 2,895 yuan per capita. A difference of 13 times was seen between the two provinces. Therefore, in order to study China's regional issues, it is necessary to divide China into a number of different regions.

The Chinese mainland was formerly divided into areas such as the coastal region and the interior region in the 1950s, and to 'Fronts' such as the First Front, the Second Front and the Third Front in the 1960s. Since China's national reforms and its opening to the outside world, researchers have coined a variety of different methods for dividing the regions of China:

(1) Three belts. This method divides China into the eastern, central and western belts. This has been applied to different provinces in different periods. In the early stages, when the concept of the three belts was being advanced, the Guangxi autonomous region was listed in the eastern belt and Inner Mongolia autonomous region in the central part. Later on, some objections were raised to this method of dividing the country. Following the implementation of the 'western development'

strategy, new 'three belts' are settled by central government. The Eastern belt consists of 11 provinces and municipalities: Beijing, Tianjin, Hebei, Liaoning, Shanghai, Jiangsu, Zhejiang, Fujian, Shandong, Guangdong and Hainan; the central belt includes the eight provinces of Shanxi, Jilin, Heilongjiang, Anhui, Jiangxi, Henan, Hubei and Hunan; and the western belt includes 12 provinces, an autonomous region and one municipality of Chongqing, Sichuan, Guizhou, Yunnan, Tibet, Shaanxi, Gansu, Qinghai, Ningxia, Xinjiang, Guangxi and Inner Mongolia.

(2) Six comprehensive economic regions. This involves classification as follows: the Northeast region, the middle and lower reaches of the Yellow River, the middle and lower reaches of the Yangtze River, the Southeast Coast, and the Southwest and Northwest regions.

(3) Seven economic regions. Northeast China (Liaoning, Jilin and Heilongjiang), Northwest China (Shaanxi, Gansu, Qinghai, Ningxia and Xinjiang), North China (Beijing, Tianjin, Hebei, Inner Mongolia and Shanxi), East China (Shandong, Shanghai, Jiangsu and Zhejiang), Central China (Henan, Anhui, Jiangxi, Hubei and Hunan), South China (Fujian, Guangdong, Guangxi and Hainan) and Southwest China (Sichuan, Guizhou, Yunnan and Tibet).

(4) Nine economic regions. This has resulted in two different methods of division. The first method of division includes Northeast China (Heilongjiang, Jilin, Liaoning and Inner Mongolia), the Bohai Rim Area (Beijing, Tianjin, Hebei and Shandong), the valley of the middle reaches of the Yellow River (Shanxi, Henan and central and west parts of Inner Mongolia), the Yangtze River delta (Shanghai, Jiangsu and Zhejiang), the middle reaches of the Yangtze River (Hubei, Hunan, Anhui and Jiangxi), the Southeast coastal area (Fujian, Guangdong, Guangxi and Hainan), the Northwest region (Shaanxi, Gansu, Qinghai, Ningxia and Xinjiang) and the Southwest region (Sichuan, Yunnan and Guizhou). The second way of division includes Northeast China (Heilongjiang, Jilin, Liaoning), the North Coast (Beijing, Tianjin, Hebei and Shandong), the North Interior (Shanxi, Shaanxi and Inner Mongolia), the East Coast (Shanghai, Jiangsu and Zhejiang), the East Interior (Henan, Anhui and Jiangxi), the Central Interior (Hunan and Hubei), the South Coast (Fujian, Guangdong, Guangxi and Hainan), the West Interior (Gansu, Qinghai, Ningxia, Xinjiang and Tibet) and the Southwest Interior (Sichuan, Yunnan and Guizhou).

(5) Nine 'metropolis economic circles'. This includes Shenda (Shenyang and Dalian), Jingjinji (Beijing, Tianjin, Tangshan, Qinhuangdao and Shijiazhuang), Jiqing (Jinan, Qingdao and Yantai), Dashanghai (Shanghai, Suzhou, Wuxi, Changzhou, Ningbo and

Hangzhou), the Pearl River delta (Guangzhou, Shenzhen, Zhuhai and Shantou), Jihei (Changchun and Harbin), Xiang'egan (Wuhan, Changsha and Nanchang) and Chengyu (Chengdu and Chongqing).

It is clear from the above that there are many different methods of classifying China into different regions. However, for a variety of reasons, the government could only accept the division into 'three belts' mentioned in (1) above.

In order to try and overcome the defects of the present methods of regional division, in this chapter we divide the Chinese mainland into eight regions based on the notion of the homogeneous region and the planning region, reflecting the real economic situation in China. It should be noted that the western regions of China are defined as planning regions, based on the definition of the central government, and the other regions are considered for their economic homogeneity. These eight regions are:

(1) The Northeast region, consisting of Liaoning, Jilin and Heilongjiang provinces, which covers a total of 790,000 square kilometres, and had a population of 106.96 million by the end of 2001. These areas share similar natural conditions and resource structures, and have close historical relations. At present, they are faced with many common issues such as exhausted resources and the upgrading of their industrial structure.

(2) The North Municipalities region consists of Beijing and Tianjin municipalities, covers 30,000 square kilometres, and had a population of 23.87 million by the end of 2001. Enjoying an ideal geographical location, this region has convenient transport facilities and is developing its scientific, educational and cultural infrastructure. This region has been benefited from the national reform and opening to the outside world.

(3) The North Coast region consists of Hebei and Shandong provinces, which cover 340,000 square kilometres and had a population of 157.40 million by the end of 2001.

(4) The East Coast region, consisting of Shanghai municipality and the Jiangsu and Zhejiang provinces, covers 210,000 square kilometres and had a population of 135.82 million by the end of 2001. This region had started modernization at an earlier stage, had close foreign economic ties in history, takes the lead in many fields of the national reform and opening to the outside world, and has abundant human capital and an obvious advantage in development.

(5) The South Coast region includes the Fujian, Guangdong and Henan provinces, covers 330,000 square kilometres and had a population of

120.19 million by the end of 2001. This region is located near to Hong Kong, Macao and Taiwan, and therefore has many overseas links.

(6) The Central region includes Shanxi, Henan, Anhui, Hubei, Hunan and Jiangxi provinces, covers 990,000 square kilometres and had a population of 359.12 million by the end of 2001. This region has abundant natural resources – coal in particular – and good farming conditions and is densely populated. It is located in a strategically important interior position. However, it has not yet opened its markets sufficiently to the outside world, and it faces a heavy burden in attempting to adjust its structure.

(7) The Northwest region consists of the Inner Mongolia autonomous region, Shaanxi, Gansu and Qinghai provinces, and Ningxia and Xinjiang autonomous regions, which covers 4.07 million square kilometres and had a population of 115.73 million by the end of 2001. The region is characterized by poor natural conditions, covers a vast territory, has scarce population and a limited market. However, it does have the potential to open up to other western countries.

(8) The Southwest region consists of the Yunnan, Guizhou and Sichuan provinces, the Chongqing municipality, and the Guangxi and Tibet autonomous regions. The region covers 2.54 million square kilometres and had a population of 248.74 million by the end of 2001. The region is located in a remote area with poor soil and an undereducated labour force. However, it is in an ideal situation to open up to Southeast Asia.

4.2 Comparison of the characteristics of social and economic development in China's regions in 2001

The analysis of the characteristics of social and economic development in China's regions can be undertaken in many different ways. This chapter concentrates on six different aspects: basic conditions, GDP and industrial structure, infrastructure, opening up to the outside world, market scale and residents' consumption, and development potential and economic activities.

Basic conditions

We can see from Table 4.1 that there is a great range in terms of the territory and population of different regions:

(1) In terms of territory, the Northwest region ranks largest, covering 4.07 million square kilometres, accounting for 42.35 per cent of the

Table 4.1 Basic conditions

	Territory (square kilometres)	*Proportion (%)*	*Population (million people)*	*Proportion (%)*
Northeast	790,000	8.23	106.96	8.38
North Municipalities	30,000	0.29	23.87	1.87
North Coast	340,000	3.54	157.4	12.33
East Coast	210,000	2.14	135.82	10.64
South Coast	330,000	3.48	120.19	9.42
Central	990,000	10.31	359.12	28.14
Northwest	4,070,000	42.35	115.73	9.07
Southwest	2,540,000	26.48	248.74	19.49

Note: These are 2001 figures, and data in the following tables come from the same source.
Source: 2002 *China Statistical Year Book*.

country, and the North Municipalities region is the smallest, covering 30,000 square kilometres, and accounting for 0.29 per cent of the total.

(2) With regard to population, the Central region is the most populous, with a population of 359.12 million by the end of 2001, accounting for 28.14 per cent of the national population, and the North Municipalities region has the lowest population, just 23.87 million the (1.87%).
(3) In terms of population density, the North Municipalities region ranks top with a density of 796 people per square kilometre; and Northwest region has the lowest density, at 29 people per square kilometre. The ratio of the former to the latter is 27.5.

GDP and industrial structure

GDP

We can observe from Table 4.2 that:

(1) The Central region has the largest gross domestic product (GDP) reaching 2,153.1 billion yuan in 2001, and accounting for 20.17 per cent of the national figure; and the North Municipalities region has the smallest GDP, amounting to 468.6 billion yuan, and accounting for 4.39 per cent. The former was 4.6 times larger than the latter.

Table 4.2 GDP

	GDP (billion yuan)	*Proportion (%)*	*Per capita GDP (yuan)*
Northeast	1,062.7	9.95	9,935
North Municipalities	468.6	4.39	19,630
North Coast	1,501.6	14.06	9,540
East Coast	2,121.1	19.87	15,617
South Coast	1,544.7	14.47	12,852
Central	2,153.1	20.17	5,996
Northwest	654.7	6.13	5,657
Southwest	11,701.0	10.96	4,704

(2) The North Municipalities region ranks first in per capita GDP, which was 19,630 yuan per capita in 2001 and Southwest region is the bottom with the per capita GDP averaging 4,704 yuan. The former is 4.2 times larger than the latter.
(3) The per capita GDP in five regions – Northeast, North Municipalities, North Coast, East Coast and South Coast – has surpassed the national average level and that in the other regions – Central, Southwest and Northwest – has lagged behind.
(4) There is an obvious difference between south and north in coastal areas. The per capita GDP in the East Coast region exceeded that in the North Coast region by 63.7 per cent in 2001.

Industrial structure, employment structure and distribution of urban and rural population

Tables 4.3 and 4.4 report the industrial structure, employment structure and the distribution of the urban and rural populations of different regions. Tables 4.3 and 4.4 show that:

(1) The proportion of primary industry is highest in the Southwest region and its value added accounted for 22.21 per cent of GDP in the region. By contrast, the proportion of secondary and tertiary industries is highest in the East Coast region with the respective value added in the region accounting for 50.55 per cent and 40.66 per cent of GDP.
(2) The proportion of employment in the primary industry is highest in the Southwest region, accounting for 62.84 per cent of gross employment in the region; that in the secondary industry in the North

Table 4.3 Composition of GDP (%)

	Primary industry	*Secondary industry*	*Tertiary industry*
Northeast	12.82	50.06	37.11
North Municipalities	3.67	41.29	55.04
North Coast	15.14	49.43	35.44
East Coast	8.78	50.55	40.66
South Coast	12.02	47.63	40.35
Central	19.41	44.90	35.69
Northwest	18.85	43.08	38.07
Southwest	22.21	39.40	38.39

Table 4.4 Employment structure and urbanization (%)

	Employment structure			
	Primary industry	*Secondary industry*	*Tertiary industry*	*Urbanization*
Northeast	44.80	22.03	33.17	52.1
North Municipalities	14.71	35.77	49.52	75.2
North Coast	51.17	24.54	24.28	32.9
East Coast	36.30	32.05	31.65	49.5
South Coast	40.73	29.25	30.02	50.2
Central	57.32	17.15	25.53	29.6
Northwest	56.56	15.28	28.16	32.9
Southwest	62.84	11.93	25.23	26.7

Municipalities region ranks top, accounting for 35.77 per cent, and that of tertiary industry is the highest, accounting for 33.16 per cent in the North Municipalities region.

(3) The value added of primary industries of all of the nation's regions is smallest, with a share of less than one-quarter. However, in terms of employment, primary industries still occupy the first place in all regions with a higher share than the secondary or tertiary industries. The value added of primary industry approaches or surpasses 50 per cent in four regions: the North Coast region, the Central region, the Southwest region and the Northwest region.

(4) The North Municipalities region is the most urbanized region, with a figure of 75.2 per cent in 2001, and the Southwest region lags behind with urbanization accounting for 26.7 per cent. The former was 48.5 percentage points higher than the latter.

(5) All of the major regions shoulder the heavy tasks of urbanization. There are only four regions which have an urbanization level either approaching or exceeding 50 per cent: the Northeast, the North Municipalities, the East Coast and the South Coast. The urbanization level of the rest of the regions is below 40 per cent and a few of them record levels, lower than 30 per cent.

Infrastructure

Transportation infrastructure

Table 4.5 shows that:

(1) The provision of railway transportation infrastructure is highest in the North Municipalities region with 62 kilometres per 1,000 square kilometres in the region in 2001; the North Coast, Central and Northeast regions rank next; and the Northwest and Southeast regions have the lowest level of provision, with only four kilometres of track per 1,000 square kilometres.
(2) In terms of highway infrastructure, the North Municipalities region is the best with 785 kilometres of roads per 1,000 square kilometres in 2001. The South Coast, East Coast and Central regions come next, with road density beyond 400 kilometres per 1,000 square kilometres. The Northwest region has the lowest road density, at only 67 kilometres per 1,000 square kilometres.
(3) The density of inland river waterways in the East Coast region is the highest with a water shipping density of 173 kilometres of inland river courses per 1,000 square kilometres. This is followed by the South Coast and Central regions.

Table 4.5 Infrastructure of transportation (kilometres per 1,000 square kilometres)

	Railway	*Highway*	*Inland river waterways*
Northeast	16	189	10
North Municipalities	62	785	15
North Coast	22	393	8
East Coast	11	519	173
South Coast	10	542	54
Central	16	409	31
Northwest	4	67	1
Southwest	4	169	8

(4) In general, transport conditions in the East Coast region are best, those in the South Coast region and North Municipalities region are good, and those in Northwest region are the least developed.

Urban infrastructure

According to Table 4.6:

(1) The percentage of people using tap water in the urban population in all of regions is not particularly high. The percentage of the population in the North Municipalities region using tap water is 81.89 per cent, ranking it first. This is followed by the economically developed North Coast, East Coast and South Coast regions, with 56.85 per cent, 61.71 per cent and 47.43 per cent respectively, and then the Southwest region (45.32%), which is the lowest region.
(2) The percentage of people using coal gas, natural and petroleum gas is low in all of the regions. The proportion is 79.89 per cent in the North Municipalities region, and the interior regions are less than 40 per cent, 39.53 per cent, 37.77 per cent, 31.85 per cent and 16.79 per cent in Central region, Northwest region and Southwest region, respectively.
(3) In relative terms, the burden of treating industrial waste water in the Northeast region, the East Coast region and the Central region is heavy and that in the South Coast region and the Northwest region is relatively light. With the exception of the South Coast and North Municipalities regions, the burden of waste industrial gas treatment plants in all regions is similar.

Table 4.6 Urban infrastructure

	Percentage of the number of people using tap water	*Percentage of the number of people using coal gas, natural and petroleum gas*	*Burden of treating industrial wastewater plants (10,000 tons per set)*	*Burden of waste industrial gas treatment plants (100 million standard cubic metres per set)*
Northeast	63.35	53.91	47	1.1919
North Municipalities	81.89	79.89	30	0.9456
North Coast	56.85	50.63	32	1.3847
East Coast	61.71	58.96	45	1.4843
South Coast	47.40	46.72	18	0.8972
Central	54.87	39.53	34	1.1165
Northwest	53.50	37.77	28	1.2944
Southwest	45.32	31.85	33	1.1255

(4) In conclusion, the urban infrastructure is underdeveloped throughout the nation, and considerable infrastructure construction is still required.

Opening to the outside world

According to Tables 4.7 and 4.8:

(1) South Coast region opens wider in terms of imports and exports and the utilization of overseas capital, and relies to a greater extent on the open door policy. In 2001, the import and export value of South Coast region accounted for 40.42 per cent of the country's

Table 4.7 Conditions of opening to the outside world (part 1, %)

	Percentage of imports and exports to the country's total	*Percentage of imports to the country's total*	*Percentage of exports to the country's total*	*Percentage of actual use of foreign capital to the country's total*	*Percentage of direct overseas investment to the country's total*
Northeast	5.62	5.43	5.82	6.61	6.89
North Municipalities	9.01	6.31	11.96	8.08	8.41
North coast	7.48	8.25	6.65	8.69	9.04
Central coast	29.84	30.25	29.38	27.77	28.94
South coast	40.42	41.80	38.90	37.30	35.19
Central	3.77	4.22	3.29	7.57	7.38
Northwest	1.77	1.51	2.05	1.26	1.31
Southwest	2.10	2.24	1.95	2.73	2.84

Table 4.8 Conditions of opening to the outside world (part 2, %)

	Import and export dependence	*Import dependence*	*Export dependence*	*Proportion of actually used foreign capital to fixed assets*	*Proportion of direct foreign capital to fixed assets*
Northeast	22.31	11.26	11.05	9.78	9.78
North Municipalities	81.09	29.65	51.45	17.07	17.07
North Coast	21.03	12.10	8.93	7.99	7.98
East Coast	59.36	31.42	27.94	16.36	16.36
South Coast	110.40	59.62	50.79	33.47	30.31
Central	7.39	4.32	3.08	5.41	5.06
Northwest	11.39	5.09	6.30	2.10	2.10
Southwest	7.57	4.21	3.36	2.93	2.93

total. Of this, the import value accounted for 41.80 per cent and the export value for 38.90 per cent. The actual use of foreign capital accounted for 37.30 per cent, and the actual use of direct overseas investment accounted for 35.19 per cent. The import and export dependence reached 110.44 per cent, made up of the import dependence (59.62%) and the export dependence (50.79%). The percentage of foreign capital actually used was 33.47 per cent of fixed assets, and that of actually used direct foreign capital was 30.31 per cent.

(2) The North Coast, East Coast and South Coast regions have opened themselves up to overseas markets to a greater extent than other regions. The South Coast region took the lead, followed by the East Coast region and then the North Coast region.

(3) With regard to the proportion of foreign trade and the use of foreign capital in the country, the Northwest region falls behind with import and export value accounting for only 1.77 per cent of the country's total and actually used capital is only 1.26 per cent, making a big difference from the figures for the South Coast region. In terms of import and export dependence, the Central region falls behind in opening to the outside world with 7.39 per cent of the dependence on foreign trade in 2001, 103.05 percentage points lower than the South Coast region. Included were the import dependence of 4.32 per cent and the export dependence of 3.08 per cent, 55.30 percentage points and 47.71 percentage points lower respectively.

Market scale and residents' consumption

Market scale

Table 4.9 shows that:

(1) The Central region is China's largest market in terms of social consumer goods retail sales value, which stood at 805.2 billion yuan in 2001, 21.42 per cent of the national total.

(2) The market scale of the three coastal regions is larger than the other regions. The East Coast region tops the South Coast region, which in turn heads the North Coast region.

(3) The scale of commerce and catering service in the Central region is the largest of its kind, with the number of employees in wholesale trade and catering service amounting 1.09 million in 2001, accounting for 22.59 per cent.

Table 4.9 Market scale

	Social consumer goods retail sales value (billion yuan)	*Number of employees in wholesales trade and catering service*	*Proportion of social consumer goods retail sales value to the nation's total (%)*	*Proportion of the number of employees in wholesales trade and catering service to the nation's total (%)*
Northeast	414.3	441,374	11.02	9.15
North Municipalities	242.6	391,518	6.45	8.11
North Coast	461.3	597,977	12.27	12.39
East Coast	728.6	913,982	19.38	18.94
South Coast	620.2	581,570	16.50	12.05
Central	805.2	1,089,853	21.42	22.59
Northwest	219.3	280,394	5.83	5.81
Southwest	439.8	528,657	11.70	10.96

Table 4.10 Residents' purchasing power (yuan)

	Disposable income of urban residents per capita	*Net income of rural residents per capita*	*Expenditure of urban residents per capita*	*Expenditure of rural residents per capita*
Northeast	5,549.90	2,364.50	4,410.00	1,690.20
North Municipalities	10,476.20	4,572.20	8,108.60	2,920.70
North Coast	6,626.00	2,719.00	4,923.60	1,702.70
East Coast	9,079.00	4,303.50	6,806.50	3,032.50
South Coast	9,510.50	3,556.20	7,255.90	2,556.90
Central	5,753.10	2,166.20	4,537.30	1,566.60
Northwest	5,639.40	1,648.70	4,546.80	1,337.50
Southwest	6,416.70	1,804.70	5,156.40	1,412.30

(4) The scale of market, commerce and catering services in the Northwest region is the smallest with social consumer goods retail sales value amounting to 219.3 billion yuan in 2001, accounting for 5.83 per cent of the nation's total and one-seventh less than in the East Coast region. It had 280,000 employees in wholesale trade and catering service, accounting for 5.81 per cent of the national total.

Residents' purchasing power

The following are shown in Table 4.10:

(1) The North Municipalities region is the strongest in terms of residents' purchasing power, followed by the South Coast region and the East Coast region, with the Northeast region being the weakest. In 2001, the average disposable income of urban residents in North

Municipalities region is 10,476.2 yuan per capita and the average expenditure is 8,108.6 yuan per capita. The disposable income of urban residents in the Northeast region is 5,549.9 yuan per capita on average and the expenditure is 4,410 yuan per capita on average, accounting, respectively, for 52.98 per cent and 54.39 per cent of the figures in the South Coast region.

(2) The North Municipalities region ranks first in terms of rural residents' purchasing power, followed by the East Coast region, the South Coast region, with the Northwest region being the weakest. The net income of rural residents is 4,572.2 yuan per capita in the North Municipalities region, and the expenditure is 2,920.7 yuan per capita in 2001. The net income of rural residents is 1,648.7 yuan per capita in Northwest region with the expenditure reaching 1,337.5 yuan per capita in this period, accounting for 36.06 per cent and 45.79 per cent of those in North Municipalities region respectively.

Possession of typical durables in urban and rural households

The standard of living of China's urban and rural residents has become relatively comfortable. Durable goods such as colour televisions, refrigerators and washing machines are popular in urban areas in all regions, but some of them have not been popular in rural areas. To reflect briefly the difference in the level of durable goods among the regions, the report has selected and made comparison study on the indexes of the possession of personal computers and mobile telephones in urban families and the possession of colour televisions and motorcycles in rural areas (see Table 4.11).

Table 4.11 Possession of typical consumer durables in urban and rural households (set per 100 households)

	Possession of computers in urban households	*Possession of handsets in urban households*	*Possession of colour televisions in rural households*	*Possession of motorcycles in rural households*
Northeast	7.9	27.2	69.7	22.4
North Municipalities	35.2	45.1	104.5	37.8
North Coast	11.4	28.6	62.8	41.3
East Coast	18.2	46.2	76.7	37.6
South Coast	27.5	76.4	76.9	57.4
Central	9.6	24.3	42.8	16.2
Northwest	7.3	22.8	50.3	19.8
Southwest	11.8	33.8	37.4	10.8

It can be seen from Table 4.11 that:

(1) The North Municipalities region and the South Coast region rank first in terms of the possession level of typical durable goods in urban and rural households. In 2001, there were 35.2 computers and 45.1 handsets for 100 urban households, and 104 colour televisions and 37.8 motorcycles for 100 rural families in the North Municipalities region.
(2) Generally speaking, household consumption of typical durable goods in three coastal regions is higher than other regions. Speaking of urban households, East Coast region is higher than North Coast region. In rural households, North Coast region is about the same as in East Coast region. On the one hand, the level of the possession of colour televisions in rural area of East Coast region is higher than in North Coast region, and on the other hand, the level of the possession of motorcycles in North Coast region is higher than East Coast region.
(3) In urban households, the level of possessing durable goods is the lowest in the Northwest region. In 2001, there were 7.3 computers per 100 urban families, 24.9 less than in the North Municipalities region and there were 22.8 handsets, 53.6 less than the South Coast region.
(4) In rural households, the level of possessing durable goods is lowest in the Southwest region. In 2001, there were 37.7 colour televisions per 100 rural families, 66.8 fewer than in the North Municipalities region and 10.8 motorcycles, 46.6 fewer than in the South Coast region.

Table 4.12 Living conditions

	Living space of urban residents per capita (square metres)	*Number of hospital beds of 10,000-people medical institutes*
Northeast	23.5	37
North Municipalities	30.8	48
North Coast	23.4	25
East Coast	22.3	27
South Coast	23.4	23
Central	24.2	23
Northwest	25.3	28
Southwest	22.5	20

Living conditions

Many different indexes are used to reflect residents' living standards. This report uses two measures for the purposes of comparison: the living space available to urban residents and the number of hospital beds per 10,000 people in each region (Table 4.12). According to the study, the findings are:

(1) Living space of urban residents in the North Municipalities region was the greatest, reaching 30.8 square metres per capita in 2001; and that in the East Coast region was the lowest, at 22.3 square metres, 8.5 metres less than the figure for the North Municipalities region.
(2) The North Municipalities region has the highest number of hospital beds per 10,000 people, with an average of 48 in 2001; and the Southwest region had the lowest, with 20 per 10,000 population.

Development potential and economic development

Investment and financial situation

Tables 4.13 and 4.14 show that:

(1) The East Coast region has the largest scale of investment in fixed assets. In the first eight months of 2000, 2001 and 2002, the scale of investment in fixed assets in the East Coast region was higher than that for other regions, accounting for 21.29 per cent, 22.23 per cent and 22.96 per cent respectively, of the national total. By contrast, that in the Northwest region is the lowest, accounting for 7.50 per cent, 7.84 per cent and 7.55 per cent of the national total for the corresponding periods.

Table 4.13 Proportion of investment in fixed assets to the nation's total (%)

	2000	*2001*	*2002 (Jan.–Aug.)*
Northeast	8.48	8.55	8.86
North Municipalities	5.93	6.15	7.58
North Coast	13.63	13.03	11.40
East Coast	21.29	21.23	22.96
South Coast	13.97	13.50	13.57
Central	17.55	17.72	16.06
Northwest	7.50	7.84	7.55
Southwest	11.66	11.99	12.02

Table 4.14 Comparison of the financial situation

	Proportion of local fiscal revenue to the nation's total (%)	*Proportion of local fiscal expenditure to the nation's total (%)*	*Per capita financial income (yuan)*	*Per capita financial expenditure (yuan)*
Northeast	9.04	10.96	659	1,346
North Municipalities	7.92	6.04	2,588	3,325
North Coast	10.98	9.65	544	806
East Coast	21.56	15.49	1,239	1,498
South Coast	18.95	13.50	1,230	1,476
Central	14.89	18.29	324	669
Northwest	5.74	10.38	387	1,178
Southwest	10.93	15.68	343	828

(2) According to the scale of fixed asset investment, three coastal regions have achieved greater investment capabilities than other regions. Its capacity in the East Coast region is larger than the South Coast region, which is better than the North Coast region.
(3) With regard to the financial situation, the East Coast region ranks first, with local fiscal revenue accounting for 21.56 per cent of the total. The per capita local fiscal revenue of the North Municipalities region is higher than other regions and it reached 2,588 yuan.
(4) Considering the proportion of local fiscal revenue in national fiscal revenue, the Northwest region is the smallest, reaching 5.74 per cent in 2001. With regard to per capita financial income level, the Central region is the lowest with per capita income of 324 yuan per capita on average, and is one-eighth of the North Municipalities region.
(5) Per capita fiscal income of all regions is smaller than per capita fiscal expenditure. This indicates that the central government has transferred fiscal aid to all regions. In per capita level, the Northwest region received more fiscal transfers, reaching 791 yuan per capita, and the South Coast region gained the least with 246 yuan per capita.

Development of technology

Table 4.15 shows that:

(1) The North Municipalities region and the East Coast region made the largest investments in research and development. In 2000, their respective spending on research and development accounted for 20.14 per cent and 20.11 per cent, or nearly 40 per cent of the total national amount. The South Coast region and the Central region also made considerable investment in this field. By contrast, the

Table 4.15 Development of technology, 2000

	Percentage of spending on research and development	*Percentage of students in colleges*	*Percentage of students in technical secondary schools*
Northeast	7.82	11.98	7.76
North Municipalities	20.14	6.82	4.34
North Coast	8.73	11.12	11.74
East Coast	20.11	16.11	14.55
South Coast	14.42	8.00	8.80
Central	13.06	24.58	28.00
Northwest	7.40	9.36	10.01
Southwest	8.33	12.01	14.79

Table 4.16 Industrial development, 1997 (%)

	Percentage in the mining sector	*Percentage of intermediate products*	*Percentage of consumer goods*	*Percentage of capital goods*
Northeast	21.18	7.20	11.36	8.76
North Municipalities	1.60	3.04	3.56	5.46
North Coast	8.31	14.22	15.88	12.59
East Coast	4.23	22.56	23.47	28.40
South Coast	7.03	15.68	10.65	16.43
Central	28.15	21.36	21.01	15.97
Northwest	11.03	3.91	5.60	3.49
Southwest	8.47	12.02	8.47	8.91

Source: Database in Development Research centre.

Northwest region had the lowest level of R&D funding, accounting for only 7.4 per cent in 2000.

(2) The North Municipalities, East Coast and Central regions have also paid attention to the training of their population. In 2001, the number of students in the colleges of the East Coast region (16%) and the Central region (24.5%) were comparatively high, whereas that for the North Municipalities region (6.82%) was fairly low. In the coastal regions, the South Coast region was also comparatively weak.

Industrial development

Table 4.16 shows that the Central region had the largest mining sector in 1997 in value added terms, accounting for 28.15 per cent of the country's total in terms of industrial capacity. And the East Coast region ranked first in the production of intermediary products, consumer goods and capital goods in value added terms, accounting for 22.56 per cent, 23.47 per cent and 28.10 per cent, respectively. The North Municipalities region had the smallest mining sector in value added terms (1.60%), and the Northwest region was the weakest region in producing intermediary products, consumer goods and capital goods in value added terms, accounting for 3.91 per cent, 5.60 per cent and 3.49 per cent respectively.

Transport mobility

Table 4.17 shows that:

(1) There are more frequent contacts among people in the Central region than in the North Municipalities region. In 2001, the passenger traffic in the Central region accounted for 27 per cent of the country's total, and that in the North Municipalities region, 1.78 per cent. The former was 25.22 percentage points higher than the latter.
(2) Freight transportation is highest in the East Coast region and lowest in the Southwest region. The volume of goods transport in the East Coast region accounted for 22.46 per cent of the country's total in 2001 and that in Southwest region, 6.35 per cent, a difference of 16.11 percentage points.
(3) The Central region has the highest level of ownership of civil motor vehicles. In 2001, the possession of civil motor vehicles in the Central region accounted for 18.14 per cent of the country's total; by contrast, the North Municipalities region accounted for 8.84 per cent.

Table 4.17 Situations of transport mobility (%)

	Percentage of passenger traffic	*Percentage of volume of freight transport*	*Percentage of possession of civil motor vehicles*
Northeast	9.18	7.61	10.29
North Municipalities	1.78	13.03	8.84
North Coast	12.12	17.49	13.74
East Coast	13.24	22.46	12.64
South Coast	12.65	10.28	13.14
Central	27.00	15.36	18.14
Northwest	9.26	7.41	9.45
Southwest	14.76	6.35	13.76

Table 4.18 Economic growth rates (1999 = 100)

	2000	*2001*
Northeast	108.7	109.2
North Municipalities	110.9	111.5
North Coast	110.1	109.5
East Coast	110.8	110.3
South Coast	110.4	109.4
Central	108.9	108.9
Northwest	109.0	109.2
Southwest	108.2	108.5

Economic development

Table 4.18 shows that:

(1) The North Municipalities region is the highest in terms of economic development, showing growth rates of 10.9 per cent and 11.5 per cent, in 2000 and 2001 respectively, and Southwest region is the lowest, with rates of 8.2 per cent and 8.5 per cent.
(2) Economic activity in the three coastal regions is more vigorous than in the other regions in the country. The economies of the North Coast, East Coast and South Coast regions also experienced high growth rates, at more than 10 per cent in 2000.

4.3 Summary and conclusion

(1) In order to overcome many problems in various methods to divide China's regions, which sometimes make it difficult to analyse regional differences thoroughly, this chapter has proposed a new method of dividing China's regions. It has divided China into eight regions: the Northeast, North Municipalities, North Coast, East Coast, South Coast, Central, Southwest and Northwest regions.

(2) The Northeast region has a good industrial foundation and infrastructure and a very high level of urbanization. It has a large number of talented people, in terms of its professionals and technicians. With the development of a new national strategy of the promotion of the Northeast region development, it could become a new growth pole for China.

(3) The North Municipalities region ranks first in per capita GDP, and has the best railway and highways infrastructure.

(4) The North Coast region is the upper-middle level development region in many respects.

(5) The East Coast region has enjoyed the highest levels of economic strength and industrial development and has the most promising market potential. It also ranks first in terms of transport conditions, investment in fixed assets, financial situation and R&D expenditure. East Coast region also ranks the top.

(6) The South Coast region has the most open markets and the highest level of imports and exports. It also enjoys the highest level utilization of overseas capital. It has a very good foundation for industrial development in both physical and social aspects. Now and for the foreseeable future it is likely to be a very dynamic region.

(7) The Central region has the largest GDP and domestic market in terms of durable goods retail sales value in China. This region abounds in natural resources – rich coal and natural gas resources in particular – and has good farming conditions and dense population.

(8) The length of road in Northwest region is the longest because it is a sparsely populated region. It is likely to suffer from having a very small local market and having few contacts with the outside world.

(9) The Southwest region was bottom in terms of both per capita GDP and growth rate. However, some of their industrial sectors have considerable potential. Because of their location, they have a comparative advantage in sub-regional cooperation with both Southeast Asia and South Asia.

(10) In terms of overall characteristics, the East Coast region is probably the most developed region in China at the start of the the twenty-first century.

References

National Bureau of Statistics of China (2000) *China Statistical Yearbook*, Beijing: China Statistics Press.

National Bureau of Statistics of China (2001) *China Statistical Yearbook*, Beijing: China Statistics Press.

National Bureau of Statistics of China (2002) *China Statistical Yearbook*, Beijing: China Statistics Press.

5

The Differential Factors of Regional Development in China: A DPG Approach

Takaaki Kanazawa

5.1 Introduction

Generally speaking, the economically active space is not a simple geometrical one, but is restricted in many ways. Among other restrictions, we can cite natural geography, human geography, historical and cultural conditions, institutions, and central and local government policies. The combinations of these factors determine disparities of economic activities between regions. This leads to different industrial structures being developed in different regions of the same country. We then need to consider what factors are important in explaining these regional differences in development and understanding what the differences indicate. In this chapter, using a deviation from proportional growth (DPG) model which is derived from structural decomposition techniques of input–output (IO) analysis,[1] we compare the differences in industrial structure of the eight regions in China. The data of the interregional China IO table of 2000 are compared, and based on these comparisons, we analyse its factors in each industrial sector from the point of view of the demand.

5.2 The methodological framework

DPG is an index which reflects the change of output share of each industrial sector among the total sectors. In reality, such an output share changes with time. In contrast, here, we assume a quasi situation in which there is no change in output share which remains constant throughout the same period. By using the DPG approach, we examine the gap between the real situation and the quasi situation.[2] In this chapter, a time series analysis is used with a cross-sectional one to assess the level and the causes of structural differentials among China's regions (North East, North Municipalities, North Coast, East Coast, South Coast, Central region, Northwest, and Southwest). That is, compared with the imaginary case in which each industry has the same differential as total output, we will know the factors of the differentials of intraregional industrial structures through estimating how far the real inter-industrial gap among regions is.

Following this, we will explain the linear algebraic extension of the DPG framework with IO matrix in order to realize the findings of China's cross-sectional comparisons shown in the next section. Here, we use the Chenery–Moses-type regional IO tables of eight regions derived from the Multi-regional Input–Output Model for China 2000 which is shaped as an Isard-type. As a benchmark, we take the arithmetic mean from the data of the total sum of every eight areas' Chenery–Moses-type IO tables, and let them regard the data as a quasi-national average.[3]

Let:

- I be identity matrix (diagonal)
- A_i be technical coefficients matrix at region *i*
- X_i be a total output column vector at region *i*
- $F_{(d)_i}$ be a regional domestic final demands column vector at region *i*
- Ex_i be an export column vector at region *i*
- Of_i be a domestic outflow column vector at region *i*
- $\hat{M}_i$ be a diagonal matrix of import coefficient at region *i*[4]
- $\hat{N}_i$ be a diagonal matrix of domestic inflow at region *i*

Then we can obtain the intraregional equilibrium output equation in region *i*; that means quantity of total output which is needed for satisfying final demands in region *i*, that is:

$$X_i = B_i[(I - (\hat{M}_i + \hat{N}_i))F_{(d)_i} + Ex_i + Of_i] \tag{5.1}$$

where $B_i = [I - (I - (\hat{M}_i + \hat{N}_i))A_i]^{-1}$ is the Leontief inverse matrix.

Based on this intraregional equilibrium output equation, intraregional comparisons can be revealed. On this comparison, we suppose a benchmark. Here, as a benchmark table, we calculate the arithmetic mean of each item of IO data from the total sum of eight regions Chenery–Moses-type table and let them be regarded as quasi-regions. Against this benchmark, let every eight regions regard as the object of comparison each by each. As for region i, let $i = 1$ be each region and let $i = 2$ be the benchmark region, fundamental equation on column vector of total DPG (δX) of region 1 from region 2 is expressed as follows:

$$\delta X = B_2[(I - \hat{M}_2 - \hat{N}_2)F_{(d)2} + Ex_2 + Of_2] - \alpha B_1[(I - \hat{M}_1 - \hat{N}_1)F_{(d)1} + Ex_1 + Of_1] \quad (5.2)$$

where α is the total output ratio of benchmark against each region $(\sum_j X_{j2}/\sum_j X_{j1})$. By the column vector of, we mean that from the assumption of the total sum of all sector output of the benchmark being equal to that of each region, findings on the unevenness of industrial structure and its factor analysis are reached. In other words, it would be checked how much the unevenness of each industry is in an arbitrary region. This equation indicates that when each column sectors are $\delta X > 0$, the sectors of each region have a smaller share than the benchmark, which are relatively regarded as under developed or non-accumulative industrial sectors. To the contrary, when sectors are $\delta X < 0$, each region's sectors have a larger share than benchmark, and are regarded as relatively developed or accumulative industrial sectors that have comparative advantages.[5]

Next to this, we are going to grasp the factors of deviation of proportional growth among industrial sectors from the dimension of each demand row.

First, let $(I - (\hat{M} + \hat{N}))F_{(d)} + Ex + Of$ be simply expressed as F,
Thus, equation (5.2) is simplified as:

$$\delta X = B_2F_2 - \alpha B_1F_1 \quad (5.2')$$

And, this equation can be transformed as:

$$\delta X = (B_2 - B_1)F_2 + B_1(F_2 - \alpha F_1) \quad (5.3)$$

in one way. From this equation on each component of F, let δX decompose into several factors as follows:

$$\begin{aligned}\delta X &= B_2(I - \hat{M}_2 - \hat{N}_2)(F_{(d)2} - \alpha F_{(d)1}) + B_2[(Ex_2 - \alpha Ex_1) + (Of_2 - \alpha Of_1)]\\&\quad + [B_2(I - \hat{M}_2 - \hat{N}_2) - B_1(I - \hat{M}_1 - \hat{N}_1)]\alpha F_{(d)1}\\&\quad + (B_2 - B_1)\alpha(Ex_1 + Of_1)\\&= B_2(I - \hat{M}_2 - \hat{N}_2)(F_{(d)2} - \alpha F_{(d)1})\\&\quad + B_2[(Ex_2 - \alpha Ex_1) + (Of_2 - \alpha Of_1)]\end{aligned}$$

$$+ B_2[(\hat{M}_1 + \hat{N}_1) - (\hat{M}_2 + \hat{N}_2)]\alpha F_{(d)1}$$
$$+ (B_2 - B_1)(I - \hat{M}_1 - \hat{N}_1)\alpha F_1 + (B_2 - B_1)\alpha(Ex_1 + Of_1) \quad (5.4)$$

Here, differential of two region Leontief inverse matrices $(B_2 - B_1)$ can be transformed and evolved as follows:

$$\begin{aligned} B_2 - B_1 &= B_2B_2^{-1}(B_2 - B_1)B_1^{-1}B_1 = B_2(I - B_2^{-1}B_1)B_1^{-1}B_1 = B_2(B_1^{-1} - B_2^{-1})B_1 \\ &= B_2[(I - \hat{M}_2 - \hat{N}_2)A_2 - (I - \hat{M}_1 - \hat{N}_1)A_1]B_1 \\ &= B_2[(I - \hat{M}_2 - \hat{N}_2)(A_2 - A_1) - (\hat{M}_1 - \hat{M}_2 + \hat{N}_1 - \hat{N}_2)A_1]B_1 \end{aligned} \quad (5.5)$$

so equation (5.4) is evolved more as follows:

$$\begin{aligned} \delta X &= B_2(I - \hat{M}_2 - \hat{N}_2)(F_{(d)2} - \alpha F_{(d)1}) + B_2[(Ex_2 - \alpha Ex_1) \\ &\quad + (Of_2 - \alpha Of_1)] + B_2[(\hat{M}_1 + \hat{N}_1) - (\hat{M}_2 + \hat{N}_2)]\alpha F_{(d)1} \\ &\quad + (B_2 - B_1)(I - \hat{M}_1 - \hat{N}_1)\alpha F_{(d)1} + (B_2 - B_1)\alpha(Ex_1 + Of_1) \\ &= B_2(I - \hat{M}_2 - \hat{N}_2)(F_{(d)2} - \alpha F_{(d)1}) + B_2[(Ex_2 - \alpha Ex_1) \\ &\quad + (Of_2 - \alpha Of_1)] + B_2[(\hat{M}_1 + \hat{N}_1) - (\hat{M}_2 + \hat{N}_2)]\alpha F_{(d)1} \\ &\quad + (B_2 - B_1)\alpha[(I - \hat{M}_1 - \hat{N}_1)F_{(d)1} + (Ex_1 + Of_1)] \\ &= B_2(I - \hat{M}_2 - \hat{N}_2)(F_{(d)2} - \alpha F_{(d)1}) + B_2[(Ex_2 - \alpha Ex_1) \\ &\quad + (Of_2 - \alpha Of_1)] + B_2[(\hat{M}_1 + \hat{N}_1) - (\hat{M}_2 + \hat{N}_2)]\alpha F_1 \\ &\quad + B_2[(I - \hat{M}_2 - \hat{N}_2)A_2 - (I - \hat{M}_1 - \hat{N}_1)A_1]B_1[\alpha(I - \hat{M}_1 - \hat{N}_1)F_{(d)1} \\ &\quad + (Ex_1 + Of_1)] = B_2(I - \hat{M}_2 - \hat{N}_2)(F_{(d)2} - \alpha F_{(d)1}) + B_2[(Ex_2 - \alpha Ex_1) \\ &\quad + (Of_2 - \alpha Of_1)] + B_2[(\hat{M}_1 + \hat{N}_1) - (\hat{M}_2 + \hat{N}_2)]\alpha F_{(d)1} + B_2 \\ &\quad \times [(I - \hat{M}_2 - \hat{N}_2)(A_2 - A_1)\alpha X_1 + B_2[(\hat{M}_1 + \hat{N}_1) - (\hat{M}_2 + \hat{N}_2)]A_1\alpha X_1 \\ &= B_2(I - \hat{M}_2 - \hat{N}_2)(F_{(d)2} - \alpha F_{(d)1}) + B_2[(Ex_2 - \alpha Ex_1) + (Of_2 - \alpha Of_1)] \\ &\quad + B_2[(\hat{M}_1 + \hat{N}_1) - (\hat{M}_2 + \hat{N}_2)]\alpha(F_{(d)1} + A_1X_1) \\ &\quad + B_2(I - \hat{M}_2 - \hat{N}_2)(A_2 - A_1)\alpha X_1 \\ &= B_2(I - \hat{M}_2 - \hat{N}_2)(F_{(d)2} - \alpha F_{(d)1}) + B_2(Ex_2 - \alpha Ex_1) + B_2(Of_2 - \alpha Of_1) \\ &\quad + B_2(\hat{M}_1 - \hat{M}_2)\alpha(F_{(d)1} + A_1X_1) + B_2(\hat{N}_1 - \hat{N}_2)\alpha(F_{(d)1} + A_1X_1) \\ &\quad + B_2(I - \hat{M}_2 - \hat{N}_2)(A_2 - A_1)\alpha X_1 \end{aligned} \quad (5.6)$$

In the similar way, equation (5.2′) also can be transformed:

$$\delta X = (B_2 - B_1)\alpha F_2 - B_1(F_2 - \alpha F_1) \tag{5.7}$$

From this transformation, we get:

$$\begin{aligned}\delta X = {} & B_1(I - \hat{M}_1 - \hat{N}_1)(F_{(d)2} - \alpha F_{(d)1}) + B_1(Ex_2 - \alpha Ex_1) + B_1(Of_2 - \alpha Of_1) \\ & + B_1(\hat{M}_1 - \hat{M}_2)\alpha(F_{(d)2} + A_2X_2) + B_1(\hat{N}_1 - \hat{N}_2)\alpha(F_{(d)2} + A_2X_2) \\ & + B_1(I - \hat{M}_1 - \hat{N}_1)(A_2 - A_1)\alpha X_1\end{aligned} \tag{5.8}$$

Let us make equation of (5.6) contrast with that of (5.8), those six pairs of corresponding component on the right-hand side of these two multinominal formulae do not necessarily coincide with one another because of the different weights to be applied. Here, we take the arithmetic mean of each pair for convenience's sake. Thus:

$$\begin{aligned}\delta A = {} & \{B_2[(I - \hat{M}_2 - \hat{N}_2)(A_2 - A_1)\alpha X_1] \\ & + B_1[(I - \hat{M}_1 - \hat{N}_1)(A_2 - A_1)X_2]\}/2\end{aligned} \tag{5.9}$$

$$\begin{aligned}\delta F_{(d)} = {} & \{B_2[(I - \hat{M}_2 - \hat{N}_2)(F_{(d)2} - \alpha F_{(d)1})] \\ & + B_1[(I - \hat{M}_1 - \hat{N}_1)(F_{(d)2} - \alpha F_{(d)1})]\}/2\end{aligned} \tag{5.10}$$

$$\delta Ex = \frac{B_2[(Ex_2 - \alpha Ex_1)] + B_1[(Ex_2 - \alpha Ex_1)]}{2} \tag{5.11}$$

$$\delta Of = \frac{B_2[(Of_2 - \alpha Of_1)] + B_1[(Of_2 - \alpha Of_1)]}{2} \tag{5.12}$$

$$\delta M = \frac{B_2(\hat{M}_1 - \hat{M}_2)\alpha(F_{(d)1} + A_1X_1) + B_1(\hat{M}_1 - \hat{M}_2)(F_{(d)2} + A_2X_2)}{2} \tag{5.13}$$

$$\delta N = \frac{B_2(\hat{N}_1 - \hat{N}_2)\alpha(F_{(d)1} + A_1X_1) + B_1(\hat{N}_1 - \hat{N}_2)(F_{(d)2} + A_2X_2)}{2} \tag{5.14}$$

are obtained, and all of them are $[n \times 1]$ column vectors.
Therefore:

$$\delta X = \delta A + \delta F_{(d)} + \delta Ex + \delta Of + \delta M + \delta N \tag{5.15}$$

In equation (5.15), these column vectors of $\delta A, \delta F_{(d)}, \delta Ex, \delta Of, \delta M$, and δN are the deviation factors of intermediate demand, intraregional final demand, export, domestic outflow, low dependency of imports, and low dependency of domestic inflow respectively. Thus, from the notation – negative (−) or positive (+) – of each factor, or those large and small, we obtain information on the factors that determine the level of each industrial sector's δX. And $F_{(d)}$ contains rural household consumption (C_r), urban household consumption (C_u), gross fixed capital formation (I_f), and changes in inventories (I_s) and so on.[6]

5.3 Findings

From the above extended methodological framework, the results of the DPG analysis of eight regions are indicated in Tables 5.1 to 5.8. The data shown in these tables are not substantially expressed ones, but are adjusted to express relative ones, which means the column sum of sectors whose δX are positive becomes +100 per cent and that of sectors whose δX are negative becomes −100 per cent. Thus, total column sum ($\sum_j \delta X_j$) is 0 per cent. In contrast, the column sums of each factor ($\sum_j \delta A_j$, $\sum_j \delta F_{(d)j}$, $\sum_j \delta Ex_j$, $\sum_j \delta Of_j$, $\sum_j \delta M_j$, $\sum_j \delta N_j$) cannot usually be 0 per cent, and each of these column sums are deviated more or less from 0 per cent for the direction to plus or minus. And when the data of each factor on arbitrary sectors indicates negative and their absolute values are higher (or indicates positive and their absolute values are higher), it is recognized that the corresponding factor enlarges (or reduces) its industrial sector at each region relative to the benchmark.

The following discussion of the results of all eight regions in this section will divide into two main parts depending on how large or small the δX of each sector is. The first part of these considers the balance of the factor of intermediate demand (δA) and the factor of intraregional final demand ($\delta F_{(d)}$) of the main sectors that seem to have comparative advantages, the second part considers the balance of foreign and domestic trade (δEx, δOf, δM, δN) of the main sectors. Although these eight tables are based on a 17-sector classification, we add more findings for each region by using the data calculated from 30-sector classification whenever the opportunity arises.

Northeast region

The balance of intermediate demand and intraregional final demands

According to the 17-sector classification, in the Northeast region, the δX of Mining, Metal products, Chemical products, and Machinery are substantially negative. With regard to the Mining sector, considering the 30-sector classification, only the Crude petroleum and Natural gas products sectors indicated $\delta X = -28.06$ per cent < 0 whereas

Table 5.1 The DPG results of Northeast region against benchmark

								Components of $\delta F_{(d)}$			
$\alpha = 1.283$	δX (%)	δEx (%)	δOf (%)	δM (%)	δN (%)	δA (%)	$\delta F_{(d)}$ (%)	δCr (%)	δCu (%)	δIf (%)	δIs (%)
Agriculture	7.11	1.02	6.20	−1.30	1.80	−1.05	0.43	12.03	−11.11	−1.03	0.70
Mining	−30.63	−2.45	−3.19	−4.10	−12.85	−8.87	0.84	1.01	−1.82	1.64	0.28
Food products	5.42	0.94	6.11	−1.06	2.28	1.55	−4.40	4.63	−9.41	−0.01	0.48
Textile and clothing	19.95	13.76	7.45	−1.87	0.97	3.02	−3.39	0.88	−5.09	0.11	0.78
Wooden products	1.06	1.00	1.15	−0.45	−0.10	−0.38	−0.15	0.16	−0.57	0.31	−0.01
Paper and printing	6.79	2.87	2.23	−0.88	0.13	2.92	−0.46	0.26	−0.77	0.16	−0.03
Chemical products	−15.86	0.96	11.42	−5.31	−12.98	−9.70	−0.25	2.93	−4.78	1.33	0.70
Non-metal mineral products	−8.47	0.66	8.90	−1.79	−6.73	−15.73	6.23	1.81	−0.99	5.04	0.76
Metal products	−17.56	4.26	19.95	−9.08	−17.42	−18.79	3.51	2.00	−2.31	4.20	0.10
Machinery	−10.77	3.12	8.63	−9.86	−5.47	−10.94	3.74	1.06	−1.41	3.87	0.46
Transport equipment	−2.38	−0.47	4.99	0.72	−4.44	−2.56	−0.62	0.60	−0.49	−0.42	−0.20
Electric products	12.20	6.64	6.39	−2.93	1.16	−0.60	1.54	0.72	−0.33	1.19	0.04
Other manufacturing products	5.23	2.82	3.45	−1.45	−1.38	1.63	0.15	0.78	−0.60	0.04	0.05
Electricity, gas, and water supply	2.90	0.89	3.20	−0.78	−1.46	2.10	−1.05	0.55	−1.94	0.38	0.07
Construction	10.11	0.16	0.22	−0.11	−0.08	2.74	7.18	0.08	−0.18	7.32	0.01
Trade and Transport	0.03	10.08	20.08	−4.43	−4.87	−10.83	−10.00	2.85	−15.16	2.09	0.83
Services	14.87	3.91	4.84	−2.04	−1.60	15.14	−5.37	3.33	−7.19	1.30	0.21
Total	0.00	50.17	112.01	−46.72	−63.05	−50.36	−2.05	35.68	−64.14	27.51	5.24

Table 5.2 The DPG results of North Municipalities against benchmark

								Components of $\delta F_{(d)}$			
$\alpha = 2.652$	δx (%)	δEx (%)	δOf (%)	δM (%)	δN (%)	δA (%)	$\delta F_{(d)}$ (%)	δCr (%)	δCu (%)	δIf (%)	δIs (%)
Agriculture	33.32	−0.07	2.53	2.80	2.77	5.61	19.67	14.78	3.74	0.96	0.08
Mining	10.46	−0.55	5.05	2.45	0.70	3.03	−0.22	0.55	−0.14	−0.74	0.04
Food products	9.52	−1.15	1.80	1.91	1.43	−1.08	6.63	6.59	−0.07	−0.07	0.06
Textile and clothing	12.88	1.06	2.76	3.75	0.15	3.16	2.01	1.61	0.38	−0.14	0.11
Wooden products	1.93	−0.78	0.53	0.37	0.25	1.65	−0.09	0.22	0.01	−0.35	0.00
Paper and printing	4.35	0.62	0.57	1.13	0.16	1.36	0.51	0.62	−0.08	−0.20	0.03
Chemical products	−1.35	0.47	−1.82	1.13	−3.69	−0.32	2.89	3.76	0.24	−1.51	0.05
Non-metal mineral products	10.61	0.08	1.66	1.62	2.72	5.91	−1.38	0.54	0.24	−2.26	0.02
Metal products	−12.40	−6.19	−1.63	8.45	−5.70	−2.87	−4.47	1.07	−0.73	−4.48	−0.48
Machinery	4.56	−0.94	1.18	6.61	−1.49	1.30	−2.10	0.29	−0.07	−2.39	0.03
Transport equipment	−10.01	−2.14	−3.54	4.59	−2.72	−3.58	−2.63	1.07	0.34	−4.18	0.07
Electric products	−23.96	−15.46	−7.77	14.37	−8.81	−3.52	−2.77	0.87	−0.95	−2.81	0.00
Other manufacturing products	3.56	0.55	0.88	1.00	1.27	−0.07	−0.07	0.33	−0.15	−0.27	−0.05
Electricity, gas, and water supply	4.06	−0.40	1.02	0.97	3.31	−0.77	−0.08	0.87	−0.54	−0.53	−0.01
Construction	−17.47	−0.21	0.12	0.49	−0.02	0.59	−18.44	0.36	−0.08	−18.88	0.00
Trade and transport	−3.47	−3.16	3.16	4.29	−1.07	−8.25	1.57	4.85	−0.51	−3.19	−0.04
Services	−26.57	−4.20	2.44	7.25	−0.46	−43.81	12.21	11.82	−2.76	−5.04	−0.03
Total	0.00	−32.45	8.93	63.18	−11.23	−41.66	13.25	50.20	−1.11	−46.06	−0.12

Table 5.3 The DPG results of North Coast region against benchmark

								Components of $\delta F_{(d)}$			
$\alpha = 0.877$	δX (%)	δEx (%)	δOf (%)	δM (%)	δN (%)	δA (%)	$\delta F_{(d)}$ (%)	δCr (%)	δCu (%)	δIf (%)	δIs (%)
Agriculture	−1.33	1.25	−6.91	−0.03	−1.76	−7.65	13.77	6.55	6.68	1.81	−1.30
Mining	−26.90	0.28	−12.37	−3.61	−6.42	−5.68	0.90	0.00	0.48	0.62	−0.22
Food products	−6.79	0.32	−6.65	−0.22	−1.06	−4.03	4.85	0.39	5.15	0.18	−0.90
Textile and clothing	23.67	40.64	−12.65	−8.01	−9.43	7.42	5.69	2.92	5.41	0.36	−3.05
Wooden products	6.17	1.74	0.05	−0.18	1.14	3.40	0.02	−0.27	0.18	0.27	−0.19
Paper and printing	−0.32	2.48	−1.98	−1.54	−0.49	0.64	0.58	0.02	0.59	0.15	−0.22
Chemical products	−13.59	7.29	−11.65	−9.68	−6.32	4.27	2.49	1.11	1.78	0.61	−1.06
Non-metal mineral products	−5.43	0.60	−4.47	−0.79	−1.50	1.02	−0.29	0.18	0.34	−0.28	−0.55
Metal products	−11.93	2.83	−11.33	−3.25	−2.56	0.43	1.95	0.13	0.52	1.40	−0.12
Machinery	−20.80	−0.28	−7.92	−6.18	−4.60	−7.56	5.74	−0.32	−0.09	6.65	−0.51
Transport equipment	13.04	1.89	0.38	−2.37	7.64	3.28	2.24	−0.49	0.34	2.56	−0.19
Electric products	24.36	16.90	4.90	−8.86	2.53	7.04	1.84	−0.04	0.43	1.44	−0.01
Other manufacturing products	5.16	7.54	−3.32	−3.79	1.10	2.26	1.36	0.28	0.05	1.31	−0.31
Electricity, gas, and water supply	2.70	2.68	−9.08	−2.37	0.52	8.38	2.56	0.11	2.12	0.55	−0.29
Construction	−4.80	0.46	−0.46	−0.38	−0.09	−2.35	−1.97	0.05	0.18	−2.20	−0.04
Trade and Transport	−3.89	10.05	−14.82	−5.37	−1.47	2.97	4.76	1.21	2.59	2.14	−1.28
Services	20.67	13.95	−12.27	−8.63	−2.82	18.66	11.77	2.67	9.38	−1.29	−1.16
Total	0.00	110.61	−110.55	−65.26	−25.58	32.51	58.27	14.50	36.14	16.27	−11.42

Table 5.4 The DPG results of East Coast region against benchmark

								Components of $\delta F_{(d)}$			
$\alpha = 0.540$	δX (%)	δEx (%)	δOf (%)	δM (%)	δN (%)	δA (%)	$\delta F_{(d)}$ (%)	δCr (%)	δCu (%)	δIf (%)	δIs (%)
Agriculture	27.20	−1.77	2.68	0.49	0.61	4.71	20.48	12.08	6.47	1.00	0.50
Mining	18.41	−1.05	6.58	0.91	9.63	1.40	0.94	0.26	0.25	0.19	0.08
Food products	10.76	−2.64	2.91	0.83	1.74	−0.80	8.72	4.20	3.70	0.08	0.35
Textile and clothing	−8.87	10.16	−2.05	−4.07	−9.68	−11.62	8.39	2.12	4.80	0.02	1.09
Wooden products	0.25	−0.86	−0.26	0.41	−0.76	0.24	1.46	0.28	0.64	0.34	0.09
Paper and printing	−1.91	0.89	0.26	0.18	−3.06	−1.67	1.49	0.33	0.38	−0.12	0.12
Chemical products	−36.65	−20.38	−5.24	1.93	−11.43	−9.04	7.50	3.01	2.25	0.37	0.66
Non-metal mineral products	8.14	−0.67	2.45	0.15	2.56	0.88	2.77	0.33	0.69	1.21	0.23
Metal products	−6.19	−10.23	5.91	3.20	3.75	−10.97	2.15	0.38	0.77	0.39	0.14
Machinery	−10.42	−5.86	−0.71	5.47	−3.10	−1.00	−5.22	0.37	0.36	−6.40	0.23
Transport equipment	−11.62	−5.88	−1.88	−0.17	−4.23	0.51	0.03	−0.36	−0.06	−0.01	0.27
Electric products	−19.94	0.14	−2.94	−6.08	−9.00	−4.32	2.26	0.26	1.00	0.42	0.05
Other manufacturing products	1.32	−0.47	0.64	0.82	−0.28	−0.23	0.85	0.29	0.42	−0.18	0.06
Electricity, gas, and water supply	0.78	−1.70	1.25	0.23	0.21	−0.77	1.57	0.51	0.42	0.09	0.08
Construction	6.00	0.03	0.08	0.11	−0.03	0.13	5.69	0.08	0.09	5.19	0.01
Trade and Transport	7.28	−2.85	2.62	0.29	−1.48	2.14	6.56	2.33	2.49	0.54	0.34
Services	15.47	1.39	1.25	1.22	−0.81	−2.53	14.95	1.11	1.70	0.41	0.23
Total	0.00	−41.77	13.55	5.92	−25.37	−32.93	80.60	27.57	26.38	3.56	4.54

Table 5.5 The DPG results of South Coast region against benchmark

								Components of $\delta F_{(d)}$			
$\alpha = 0.839$	δX (%)	δEx (%)	δOf (%)	δM (%)	δN (%)	δA (%)	$\delta F_{(d)}$ (%)	δCr (%)	δCu (%)	δIf (%)	δIs (%)
Agriculture	6.82	−6.45	2.04	5.49	5.45	−0.32	0.60	1.10	−1.07	0.01	0.58
Mining	14.49	−3.07	4.52	5.52	4.06	2.91	0.56	0.09	0.11	0.32	0.05
Food products	9.71	−2.79	1.62	3.53	0.75	1.09	5.50	1.56	3.49	0.05	0.42
Textile and clothing	−27.86	−36.28	−6.37	13.04	−2.30	1.49	2.55	0.61	1.27	0.08	0.59
Wooden products	−1.33	−2.85	0.44	1.10	2.43	−2.49	0.03	0.18	−0.25	0.07	0.04
Paper and printing	−7.09	−9.99	−1.06	5.49	−0.29	−1.27	0.04	−0.08	−0.14	0.13	0.14
Chemical products	22.37	−15.50	1.98	26.78	9.34	−1.68	1.45	0.50	0.36	0.30	0.32
Non-metal mineral products	8.35	−3.43	1.35	2.15	2.46	3.75	2.07	0.02	0.72	1.08	0.26
Metal products	17.60	−6.90	6.26	8.00	5.70	3.52	1.02	0.12	0.05	0.68	0.18
Machinery	12.65	−2.81	2.33	7.58	−1.09	3.43	3.20	0.08	0.10	2.90	0.13
Transport equipment	2.88	−1.93	0.59	1.80	−1.17	2.01	1.58	0.03	−0.09	1.46	0.19
Electric products	−27.05	−29.02	−9.02	17.32	−4.07	−0.55	−1.71	−0.20	−0.78	−0.75	0.04
Other manufacturing products	−7.22	−10.27	−0.73	4.71	0.53	−1.66	0.21	−0.19	−0.04	0.38	0.07
Electricity, gas, and water supply	−5.41	−4.44	1.16	3.84	−0.49	−6.22	0.73	0.08	0.21	0.36	0.10
Construction	3.05	−1.24	0.03	1.05	0.10	−1.17	4.28	0.05	0.07	4.15	0.02
Trade and Transport	−5.87	−22.22	0.83	10.88	1.04	−1.55	5.16	1.12	2.45	0.84	0.80
Services	−16.10	−21.15	0.60	12.54	1.64	−15.11	5.39	1.70	2.81	1.01	0.41
Total	0.00	−180.36	6.58	130.84	24.09	−13.82	32.66	6.78	9.26	13.06	4.34

Table 5.6 The DPG results of Central region against benchmark

								Components of $\delta F_{(d)}$			
$\alpha = 0.714$	δX (%)	δEx (%)	δOf (%)	δM (%)	δN (%)	δA (%)	$\delta F_{(d)}$ (%)	δCr (%)	δCu (%)	δIf (%)	δIs (%)
Agriculture	−22.31	2.49	−4.25	−2.65	−3.37	−1.57	−12.97	−10.81	−1.02	−0.46	−0.53
Mining	−5.59	4.36	−3.88	−4.39	0.73	−0.48	−1.91	−0.87	−0.18	−0.36	−0.37
Food products	−15.18	1.56	−3.84	−1.74	−2.73	−0.52	−7.91	−5.02	−2.35	−0.05	−0.36
Textile and clothing	22.64	25.19	1.62	−7.10	5.83	4.53	−7.42	−3.85	−2.57	−0.13	−0.70
Wooden products	−2.64	0.88	−0.65	−0.57	−0.88	−0.58	−0.84	−0.29	−0.17	−0.29	−0.04
Paper and printing	−0.56	2.05	−0.47	−1.50	0.27	−0.30	−0.62	−0.33	−0.04	−0.03	−0.08
Chemical products	−3.56	5.38	−2.07	−6.86	1.56	1.86	−3.44	−2.41	−0.31	−0.25	−0.22
Non-metal mineral products	−15.46	1.56	−3.89	−1.51	−2.53	−6.68	−2.42	−0.72	−0.64	−0.71	−0.24
Metal products	−4.55	2.98	−5.35	−3.64	0.21	2.85	−1.60	−0.63	−0.08	−0.76	−0.04
Machinery	−2.01	1.46	−1.03	−3.52	2.11	0.25	−1.27	−0.22	−0.02	−0.87	−0.11
Transport equipment	−0.55	0.86	−0.43	−1.26	0.96	−0.01	−0.67	−0.06	0.05	−0.53	−0.09
Electric products	63.43	34.99	13.30	−19.03	27.59	6.79	−0.22	−1.05	0.66	0.67	−0.18
Other manufacturing products	−0.83	6.52	−1.66	−4.67	−0.51	−0.05	−0.46	−0.54	−0.13	0.36	−0.01
Electricity, gas, and water supply	−3.44	1.24	−2.33	−1.16	−0.47	0.22	−0.94	−0.61	0.03	−0.15	−0.08
Construction	−1.77	0.26	−0.14	−0.25	−0.03	0.43	−2.04	−0.11	−0.01	−1.83	−0.01
Trade and Transport	−4.95	5.71	−3.95	−3.25	−0.96	1.49	−3.99	−2.33	−0.53	−0.46	−0.38
Services	−2.67	4.69	−2.13	−3.26	−0.34	4.71	−6.34	−2.83	0.03	−0.06	−0.19
Total	0.00	102.17	−21.14	−66.36	27.45	12.94	−55.06	−32.71	−7.27	−5.90	−3.62

Table 5.7 The DPG results of Northwest region against benchmark

								Components of $\delta F_{(d)}$			
$\alpha = 2.225$	δX (%)	δEx (%)	δOf (%)	δM (%)	δN (%)	δA (%)	$\delta F_{(d)}$ (%)	δCr (%)	δCu (%)	δIf (%)	δIs (%)
Agriculture	−26.44	4.08	−0.84	−1.48	2.35	−11.08	−19.47	−0.93	−14.07	−3.01	−0.77
Mining	−15.07	2.47	−6.29	−3.64	−2.25	−2.18	−3.18	−0.54	−0.85	−1.22	−0.14
Food products	4.98	1.72	1.57	−0.64	3.57	1.96	−3.20	−0.86	−1.45	−0.23	−0.22
Textile and clothing	17.88	8.42	4.88	−1.74	7.99	4.47	−6.14	−2.03	−2.51	−0.12	−1.35
Wooden products	2.98	0.91	0.87	−0.22	0.69	1.57	−0.84	−0.09	−0.29	−0.28	−0.09
Paper and printing	6.14	2.68	1.18	−0.71	2.48	1.06	−0.55	−0.02	−0.05	−0.14	0.04
Chemical products	8.28	6.71	1.09	−4.95	7.60	3.80	−5.98	−1.06	−2.18	−1.22	−0.77
Non-metal mineral products	4.17	1.77	1.62	−0.65	1.46	4.81	−4.85	0.20	−1.44	−3.20	−0.16
Metal products	7.86	3.30	−5.96	−1.08	4.89	9.72	−3.02	0.02	−0.74	−1.60	−0.46
Machinery	9.79	1.66	1.61	−1.08	4.97	1.66	0.97	−0.01	−0.11	1.29	−0.08
Transport equipment	7.77	1.03	1.55	−0.33	4.59	0.33	0.60	0.16	−0.06	0.69	−0.10
Electric products	11.67	8.36	2.20	−3.52	3.78	0.95	−0.08	−0.63	0.34	0.46	−0.03
Other manufacturing products	6.02	2.22	1.36	−0.68	2.26	1.73	−0.86	−0.04	0.01	−0.55	−0.04
Electricity, gas, and water supply	−1.04	1.79	0.16	−0.76	1.36	−1.55	−2.04	−0.18	−0.46	−0.69	−0.17
Construction	−16.96	0.43	−0.03	−0.27	0.33	0.46	−17.88	−0.13	−0.23	−17.12	−0.02
Trade and Transport	−12.82	9.80	−3.77	−2.87	10.05	−10.98	−15.04	−2.97	−5.82	−4.10	−0.63
Services	−15.21	7.96	−0.36	−3.23	5.20	3.94	−28.72	−4.23	−6.01	−2.07	−0.37
Total	0.00	65.31	0.84	−27.85	61.32	10.67	−110.29	−13.34	−35.93	−33.09	−5.38

Table 5.8 The DPG results of Southwest region against benchmark

								Components of $\delta F_{(d)}$			
$\alpha = 1.234$	δX (%)	δEx (%)	δOf (%)	δM (%)	δN (%)	δA (%)	$\delta F_{(d)}$ (%)	δCr (%)	δCu (%)	δIf (%)	δIs (%)
Agriculture	−58.69	6.38	4.66	−5.31	−4.92	−0.72	−58.78	−48.11	−7.85	−2.37	0.22
Mining	2.45	2.98	4.87	−2.91	−3.42	2.56	−1.63	−0.76	−0.26	−0.43	0.08
Food products	−17.57	3.16	2.26	−3.26	−3.60	1.72	−17.86	−12.11	−5.12	−0.21	0.14
Textile and clothing	25.07	11.48	6.44	−2.31	5.63	5.82	−1.99	−1.14	−0.84	−0.05	0.17
Wooden products	0.33	1.19	−0.22	−0.46	−0.91	1.36	−0.63	−0.43	−0.11	0.01	0.00
Paper and printing	2.30	3.26	1.38	−1.86	0.89	−0.70	−0.68	−0.30	0.02	−0.04	0.06
Chemical products	15.29	8.33	11.17	−8.25	3.55	5.51	−5.02	−3.34	−0.76	−0.41	0.09
Non-metal mineral products	6.03	1.81	2.20	−1.05	−0.57	5.77	−2.13	−0.68	−0.57	−0.72	0.06
Metal products	6.70	6.84	7.73	−6.50	−4.53	5.73	−2.58	−0.74	−0.25	−1.36	0.14
Machinery	8.60	2.04	3.23	−2.69	3.46	2.74	−0.18	−0.24	−0.08	0.25	0.01
Transport equipment	−3.67	2.37	1.94	−1.29	−0.95	−3.60	−2.14	0.18	−0.18	−1.63	−0.27
Electric products	13.88	9.43	4.97	−5.99	3.39	2.60	−0.52	−0.08	−0.14	−0.10	0.00
Other manufacturing products	3.69	3.35	2.22	−1.61	0.46	0.13	−0.87	−0.11	−0.18	−0.40	0.05
Electricity, gas, and water supply	3.37	1.74	2.53	−1.17	−0.27	1.82	−1.28	−0.65	−0.14	−0.19	0.02
Construction	−5.40	0.82	0.51	−0.61	0.02	−1.26	−4.88	−0.29	−0.07	−4.14	0.01
Trade and Transport	9.23	9.05	4.46	−3.65	0.39	3.71	−4.73	−3.40	0.44	−1.00	0.08
Services	−11.61	12.85	5.95	−7.14	0.66	−1.81	−22.12	−4.58	−1.85	−0.43	0.07
Total	0.00	87.08	66.31	−56.05	−0.72	31.39	−128.01	−76.79	−17.94	−13.21	0.92

all of the other sectors of Mining are $\delta X > 0$. Related to this, the Petroleum processing and Coking sector is $\delta X = -26.66\% < 0$. These petroleum-related sectors, thus, seem to be the largest and the second largest accumulative sectors in the Northeast region.

With regard to δA and $\delta F_{(d)}$, more sectors are $\delta A < 0$ and $\delta F_{(d)} > 0$ in heavy industries, such as Non-metal mineral products, Metal products, Machinery and Electric products. This means that those sectors supply their products to any industrial sectors as goods for intermediate input rather than supplying goods for final demand within the Northeast region. When we examine the 30-sector classification once more, the Petroleum processing and Coking sector is also notable $\delta A < 0$ (-11.99%; $\delta F_{(d)} = 0\%$). In light industries, by contrast, all sectors are $\delta F_{(d)} < 0$.

As for the relationship between mining sectors and its related processing sectors in the Northeast region, the relation between the sector of Crude petroleum and Natural gas products and the sector of Petroleum processing and Coking seems to be highly correlative. There also exist lesser correlation between other primary industries and the processing sectors.

Among the factors of intraregional final demand ($\delta F_{(d)}$) across all sectors, most sectors are mainly pulled by urban household consumption (δC_u), and the factors of rural household consumption (δC_r) and investments (δI_f, δI_s) are weak factors in the development of each sector.

The balance of foreign and domestic trade

In the aspect of trade, the Northeast region is not pulled by exports ($\sum_j \delta EX_j = 50.17\%$), and is also not pulled by domestic outflows ($\sum_j \delta Of_j = 112.01\%$) across all sectors. On the other hand, it is comparatively less dependent both on imports ($\sum_j \delta M_j = 46.72\%$) and on domestic inflows ($\sum_j \delta N_j = 63.05\%$).

When we turn to consider the patterns of comparative advantage sectors in each region according to whether or not they are pulled by exports and/or domestic outflows, and whether or not they are less dependent on imports and/or domestic inflows for reference, this will be considered in 16 different combinations, as shown in Table 5.9 later in this chapter.

With regard to the Northeast region, there are three types:

Type 1: Pulled both by domestic outflows and by exports, low dependency both on imports and domestic inflows: Mining.

Type 11: Pulled by export, low dependency on domestic inflows: Transport equipment.

Type 13: Neither pulled by domestic outflow nor by exports, low dependency both on imports and domestic inflows: Chemical products, Non-metal mineral products, Metal products, Machinery.

Table 5.9 The types of balance of foreign and domestic trade

	δOf	*δEx*	*δM*	*δN*	*Characteristics of each type*
Type 1	–	–	–	–	Pulled both by domestic outflows and by exports; Low dependency both on imports and on domestic inflows
Type 2	–	–	–	+	Pulled both by domestic outflows and by exports; Low dependency on imports
Type 3	–	–	+	–	Pulled both by domestic outflows and by exports; Low dependency on domestic inflows
Type 4	–	–	+	+	Pulled both by domestic outflows and by exports; Dependent both on imports and on domestic inflows
Type 5	–	+	–	–	Pulled by domestic outflows; Low dependency both on imports and on domestic inflows
Type 6	–	+	–	+	Pulled by domestic outflows; Low dependency on imports
Type 7	–	+	+	–	Pulled by domestic outflows; Low dependency on domestic inflows
Type 8	–	+	+	+	Pulled by domestic outflows; Dependent both on imports and domestic inflows
Type 9	+	–	–	–	Pulled by exports; Low dependency both on imports and on domestic inflows
Type 10	+	–	–	+	Pulled by exports; Low dependency on imports
Type 11	+	–	+	–	Pulled by exports; Low dependency on domestic inflows
Type 12	+	–	+	+	Pulled by exports; Dependent both on imports and on domestic inflows
Type 13	+	+	–	–	Neither pulled by domestic outflows nor by exports; Low dependency both on imports and on domestic inflows
Type 14	+	+	–	+	Neither pulled by domestic outflows nor by exports; Low dependency on imports
Type 15	+	+	+	–	Neither pulled by domestic outflows nor by exports; Low dependency on domestic inflows
Type 16	+	+	+	+	Neither pulled by domestic outflows nor by exports; Dependent both on imports and on domestic inflows

In the Mining sector, in considering the 30-sector classification, the sector of Crude petroleum and Natural gas products is typical of Type 1 ($\delta Of = -8.33\%$, $\delta Ex = -3.65\%$, $\delta M = -2.07\%$, $\delta N = -8.85\%$), and Non-ferrous mineral mining belongs to Type 13 (δOf = 1.89%, δEx = 0.57%, δM = −0.93%, δN = −3.34%). With regard to Chemical products, the sector of Petroleum processing and Coking belongs to Type 1 (δOf = −0.07%, δEx = −0.88%, δM = −2.98%, δN = −10.74%). Other sectors that are $\delta X < 0$, such as the sector of Maintenance and Repair of Machines and Equipment, that of gas production and supply, and that of Wholesale and Retail trade, all belong to Type 13.

Considering the Northeast region as a whole, heavy industries, and the sector of Crude petroleum and Natural gas and its related sectors, have comparative advantages. The main decisive factor behind this comparative advantage is the intermediate demand arising from most industrial sectors.

North Municipalities region

The balance of intermediate demand and intraregional final demands

In the North Municipalities region, δX of Electric products, Chemical products, Metal products, Transport equipment, Services, Construction, and Trade and Transport are all negative. Looking in more detail by using the 30-sector classification, with regard to heavy industries, δX of Electric and Telecommunication equipment (−25.56%), Metals smelting and processing (−12.61%), Transport equipment (−10.01%) are significantly negative. But, δX of Services (−26.57%) is the highest absolute value of any manufacturing sector. Although the accumulation of above-mentioned processing based heavy industries is also confirmed, almost all of the other manufacturing sectors' accumulation is not so inconspicuous.

Next, considering the δA of each sector, the most notable $\delta A < 0$ is Services (−43.81%), followed by the sector of Trade and Transport (−8.25%). These findings indicate the relative progress of tertiary industries as a post-industrializing characteristic of urban areas (Beijing and Tianjin) to supply their intermediate inputs to all other industries. In addition, according to the 30-sector classification, manufacturing sectors that are relatively notable $\delta A < 0$ are Metals smelting and processing (−5.36%), Transport equipment (−3.58%), and Electric and Telecommunication equipment (−4.07%).

As for the $\delta F_{(d)}$ of each sector, Wooden products, Non-metal mineral products, Metal products, Construction, and Mining are $\delta F_{(d)} < 0$.

Looking at each element of $\delta F_{(d)}$ across all sectors, gross fixed capital formation (I_f) is a more significant factor than household consumption in both the urban area and the rural area (C_u, C_r).

The balance of foreign and domestic trade

Across all sectors, the North Municipalities region is pulled by export ($\sum_j \delta Ex_j = -32.45\%$), but not pulled by domestic outflow ($\sum_j \delta Of_j = 8.93\%$). On the other hand, it is dependent on imports ($\sum_j \delta M_j = 63.18\%$), but not dependent on domestic inflows ($\sum_j \delta N_j = -11.23\%$). With regard to the comparative advantage sectors in the North Municipalities regions by 17-sector classification, there are only three types of combinations in the sphere of trade according to Table 5.9. These are:

Type 3: Pulled both by domestic outflows and exports, low dependency on domestic inflows: Metal products, Transport equipment, Electric products.

Type 7: Pulled by domestic outflows, low dependency on domestic inflows: Chemical products.

Type 11: Pulled by export, low dependency on domestic inflows. Construction, Trade and Transport, Services.

With regard to the 30-sector classification, the sector of Electric Telecommunication equipment is notably export- and domestic outflow-oriented ($\delta Ex = -15.99\%$, $\delta Of = -8.45\%$). Although Mining is not a comparatively advantage sector in the 17-sector classification, the only comparative advantageous sector of Crude petroleum and Natural gas products belongs to Type 11 ($\delta Of = 0.53\%$, $\delta Ex = -0.62\%$; $\delta M = 0.91\%$, $\delta N = -1.40\%$), and, related to this, the sector of Petroleum processing and Coking which belong to Chemical products is Type 3 ($\delta Of = -0.18\%$, $\delta Ex = -0.16\%$; $\delta M = 0.01\%$, $\delta N = -2.50\%$).

Considering the North Municipalities region in its entirety, Tertiary industries and Electric Telecommunication equipment are the comparatively advantageous sectors. The former is mainly pulled by intermediate demand, and the latter is mainly pulled by outflows.

North Coast region

The balance of intermediate demand and intraregional final demands

In the North Coast region, the sectors that are notable $\delta X < 0$ are Mining (–26.90%), Machinery (–20.80%), Chemical products

(−13.59%), Metal products (−11.93%), Construction (−4.80%), and Trade and Transport (−3.89%), and with a more detailed look using the 30-sector classification, they are notable in the Coal mining and processing (−13.12%), Chemicals (−10.51%), and Metal ore mining (−9.09%) sectors. Moreover, in contrast to the other coastal areas, δX of Agriculture is also negative (−1.33%).

Among those sectors which are $\delta X < 0$, $\delta A < 0$ are Agriculture (−7.65%), Machinery (−7.56%), Food products (−4.03%), and Construction (−2.35%). But, unlike the other coastal areas, $\sum_j \delta A_j$ denotes positive. This is by the fact there are relatively fewer manufacturing and tertiary industrial sectors that are $\delta A < 0$.

Next, in relation to intraregional final demand, with the exception of the Construction ($\delta F_{(d)} = -1.97\%$) and Non-metal mineral products ($\delta F_{(d)} = -0.29\%$) sectors, the rest of all 15 sectors are $\delta F_{(d)} > 0$.

The balance of foreign and domestic trade

Across all sectors, the North Coast region is not pulled by exports ($\sum_j \delta Ex_j = 110.61\%$), but is pulled by domestic outflows ($\sum_j \delta Of_j = -110.55\%$). On the other hand, it has a low dependency both on imports ($\sum_j \delta M_j = -65.26\%$) and on domestic inflows ($\sum_j \delta N_j = -25.58\%$).

According to Table 5.9, there are two types of domestic and foreign trade patterns of comparatively advantageous sectors in the North Coast region by the 17-sector classification, and those are:

Type 1: Pulled both by domestic outflows and by exports, low dependency both on imports and on domestic inflows: Machinery.

Type 5: Pulled by domestic outflows, low dependency both on imports and domestic inflows: Agriculture, Mining, Food products, Paper and printing, Chemical products, Non-metal mineral products, Metal products, Construction, Trade and Transport, Services.

In the Mining sectors, with a more detailed look using the 30-sector classification, Non-ferrous mineral minings belongs to Type 1 ($\delta Of = -1.16\%$, $\delta Ex = -0.05\%$, $\delta M = -0.26\%$, $\delta N = -0.90\%$), and the sector of Crude petroleum and Natural gas products is Type 2, that is pulled both by domestic outflows and by exports, low dependency on imports ($\delta Of = -2.01\%$, $\delta Ex = -0.14\%$, $\delta M = -1.08\%$; $\delta N = 0.21\%$).

Furthermore, considering the data of interregional transactions from the IO table of the North Coast region, it is recognized that all of the other sectors, with the exceptions of the sectors of Supply of Electricity,

Gas and Water, Transport equipment, and Electric and Telecommunication equipment, are pulled by domestic outflows, but the share of the domestic outflow to the neighbouring North Municipalities region is relatively low. Among those sectors which are pulled by domestic outflows, Crude petroleum and Natural gas products, Non-ferrous mineral mining, and Machinery equipment are also pulled by exports, but the pulling levels of exports do not exceed those of domestic outflows. Throughout all of the sectors, North Coast regions are less dependent on imports despite being located in the coastal region.

Considering the North Coast region in its entirety, where primary industries enjoy comparative advantage, the factor of intermediate demand is relatively weak, and with regard to the factor of external trade, most of the sectors are pulled by domestic outflows rather than by exports despite its location in the coastal region.

East Coast region

The balance of intermediate demand and intraregional final demands

In the East Coast region, the notable sectors with $\delta X < 0$ are Chemical products (−36.65%), Electric products (−19.94%), Transport Equipment (−11.62%), Machinery (−10.42%), Textile and Clothing (−8.87%), and Metal products (−6.19%). But tertiary industries including Services is unexpectedly $\delta X > 0$ despite its negative $\delta A < 0$ (−2.53%) of Services[7] and the existence of Shanghai Municipality where the GDP of the sector of Finance and Insurance, the progress of which is usually regarded as a yardstick of a highly industrialized system, is higher (68,503 million yuan) than in any other province.[8]

Among above-mentioned $\delta X < 0$ sectors, $\delta A < 0$ are Chemical products (−9.04%), Metal products (−10.97%), Textile and Clothing (−11.62%), Electric products (−4.32%), and Machinery (−1.00%).

By contrast to this, $\delta F_{(d)}$ and its components of all sectors except Machinery are positive.

The balance of foreign and domestic trade

Across all sectors, the East Coast region is pulled by exports ($\sum_j \delta Ex_j =$ −41.77%), but is not pulled by domestic outflows ($\sum_j \delta Of_j =$ 13.55%). On the other hand, it is dependent upon imports ($\sum_j \delta M_j =$ 5.92%), and low dependency on domestic inflow ($\sum_j \delta N_j =$ −25.37%).

Considering the manufacturing sectors, we can recognize the existence of the sectors that are pulled by domestic outflow at Textile and Wearing apparel, Wooden products, and Chemicals.

With regard to the patterns of balance of foreign and domestic trade shown in Table 5.9, comparative advantage sectors in the East Coast region are divided into the following five types:

Type 1: Pulled both by domestic outflows and by exports, low dependency both on imports and on domestic inflows: Transport equipment.
Type 3: Pulled both by domestic outflows and by exports, low dependency on domestic inflows: Chemical products, Machinery.
Type 5: Pulled by domestic outflows, low dependency both on imports and on domestic inflows: Textile and clothing, Electrical products.
Type 12: Pulled by exports, dependent both on imports and on domestic inflows: Metal products.
Type 15: Neither pulled by domestic outflows nor by exports, low dependency on domestic inflows: Paper and Printing.

As for Electrical products, we can consider this in more detail by considering the 30-sector classification, Electric equipment and Machinery belongs to Type 4 ($\delta Of = -1.40\%$, $\delta Ex = -1.55\%$, $\delta M = 0.17\%$, $\delta N = -5.04\%$). Besides, in the sector of Supply of Electricity, Gas, and Water which is $\delta X > 0$, the sector of Gas and Water production and supply which is $\delta X < 0$ belongs to Type 11 that is pulled by exports, has a low dependency on domestic inflows ($\delta Of = 0.07\%$, $\delta Ex = -0.20\%$, $\delta M = 0.02\%$, $\delta N = -0.24\%$).

Totally looking, in East Coast region most sectors are export-oriented, and among them, heavy industries are confirmed as notable comparative advantage sector.

South Coast region

The balance of intermediate demand and intraregional final demands

In the South Coast region, the sectors which are $\delta X < 0$ are Textile and Clothing (–27.86%), Electric products (–27.05%), Services (–16.10%), Other manufacturing products (–7.22%), Paper and Printing (–7.09%), Trade and Transport (–5.87%), and Supply of Electricity, Gas and Water (–5.41%). Looking in more detail by considering the 30-sector classification, $\delta X < 0$ are Clothing (–26.53%), Electric and Telecommunication Equipment (–18.31%), Electric Equipment and Machinery (–8.74%), and Transport and Warehousing (–5.60%). These findings mean that those sectors are especially accumulated in this region.

The sectors that are $\delta A > 0$ are recognized as Mining (2.91%) and Non-metal mineral products (3.75%), Metal products (3.52%), Machinery (3.43%), Transport equipment (2.01%), Textile and Clothing (1.49%), Food products (1.09%). In contract, those which are $\delta A < 0$ are Services (−15.11%), Electric products (−0.55%), Agriculture (−0.32%), Wooden products (−2.49%), Paper and Printing (−1.27%), Supply of Electricity, Gas and Water (−6.22%) and so on, those of which are all $\delta X < 0$, and among them the sector of Services is relatively significant. In heavy industries and mining, according to the 30-sector classification, denoted $\delta A < 0$ are Crude petroleum and Natural gas products (−0.09%), Petroleum processing and coking (−0.22%), Chemicals (−1.46%), Electric and Telecommunication equipment (−1.13%), Instruments, Meters, Cultural and Office machinery (−0.18%), and Other manufacturing products (−2.86%).

All of sectors whose $\delta F_{(d)}$ is positive, and as for each element of $\delta F_{(d)}$, also almost all of the sectors are positive, with the exception of Electrical products.

The balance of foreign and domestic trade

Across all sectors, the South Coast region is pulled by exports ($\sum_j \delta Ex_j = -180.36\%$), but not pulled by domestic outflows ($\sum_j \delta Of_j = 6.58\%$). On the other hand, it is dependent both on imports ($\sum_j \delta M_j = 130.84\%$) and on domestic inflows ($\sum_j \delta N_j = 24.09\%$). Thus, we can recognize the industrial character of the South Coast region as more linked with the world economy than any other coastal region on the sphere of trade. In the sectors of light industry and a part of heavy industry, there also exists the patterns of being pulled by domestic outflows. For reference, from Table 5.9, the classified patterns of comparative advantage sectors in the South Coast region by the 17-sector classification according to whether it is pulled by exports and/or domestic outflows or not, and whether it is less dependent on imports and/or domestic inflows or not are the following four types. Those are:

Type 3: Pulled both by domestic outflows and by exports, low dependency on domestic inflows: Textile and Clothing, Paper and Printing, Metal products, Electrical products.

Type 4: Pulled both by domestic outflows and by exports, dependent both on imports and on domestic inflows: Other manufacturing products.

Type 11: Pulled by exports, low dependency on domestic inflows: Supplies of Electricity, Gas and Water.

Type 12: Pulled by exports, dependent both on imports and on domestic inflows: Wooden products, Trade and Transport, Services.

Considering the sectors in more details by using the 30-sector classification, the sector of Transport and Warehousing belongs to Type 11 (δOf = 0.23%, δEx = −7.52%, δM = 5.44%, δN = −0.54%), the sector of Textile products belongs to Type 4 (δOf = −1.14%, δEx = −13.95%, δM = 9.06%, δN = 0.62%), among Electrical products, the sector of Electric equipment and Machinery belongs to Type 4 (δOf = −2.34%, δEx = −9.92%, δM = 4.30%, δN = 0.39%), and the sector of Instruments, Meters, Cultural and Office machinery belongs to Type 3 (δOf = −0.61%, δEx = −4.58%, δM = 1.40%, δN = −0.47%).

Considering the South Coast region in its entirety, all sectors are export-oriented. Among them, light industries and machinery products have a particularly strong comparative advantage.

Central region

The balance of intermediate demand and intraregional final demands

In the Central region, only two sectors are $\delta X > 0$: Textile and Clothing (22.64%) and Electrical products (63.43%). The other 15 sectors are all $\delta X < 0$. Among these, Agriculture is the most significant (δX = −22.31%), a sector that is mainly pulled by rural household consumption (δC_r = −10.81%). Examining the manufacturing sectors using the 30-sector classification, the tendency of $\delta X > 0$ is caused by those particular sectors whose degree of $\delta X > 0$ is much higher, e.g. Electric Telecommunications (42.22%), Clothing (23.91%), and Electric equipment and Machinery (21.21%).

According to 17-sector classification of the Central region, $\delta A < 0$ are Agriculture (−1.57%) and Mining (−0.48%), Food products (−0.52%), Wooden products (−0.58%), Paper and Printing (−0.30%), Non-metal mineral products (−6.68%), Transport equipment (−0.01%), and Other manufacturing products (−0.05%). From these findings, with the exception of Non-metal mineral products, all of the other sectors' absolute value of negative δA are very low. In contrast, all of the sectors are $\delta F_{(d)} < 0$. The exceptions which are $\delta F_{(d)} > 0$ by looking at 30-sector classification are Electrical equipment and Machinery (0.48%) and Instruments, Meters, Cultural and Office machinery (0.20%). Consider the relationship between primary industry and its processing, with the exception of the petroleum-related sector, the relationships of all other sectors is more or less confirmed.

The balance of foreign and domestic trade

Located in the middle of China and surrounded by other regions, it seems likely that there are greater opportunities for both domestic outflows and inflows in the Central region. And this region's industrial sectors are little affected by exports, and have a low dependency on imports. These are recognized across all sectors, that is, $\sum_j \delta Ex_j = 102.17\% > 0$, $\sum_j \delta Of_j = -21.14\% < 0$, $\sum_j \delta M_j = -66.36\% < 0$, and $\sum_j \delta N_j = 27.45\% > 0$.

With regard to the patterns of comparative advantage sectors in the Central region according to whether or not a sector is pulled by exports and/or domestic outflows, and whether or not it is less dependent on imports and/or domestic inflows, there are only two types: both are not pulled by foreign export but, rather, are pulled by domestic inflows. From Table 5.9, those are:

Type 5: Low dependency not only on imports but also on domestic inflows: Agriculture, Mining, Food products, Wooden Products, Non-metal mineral products, Metal products, Maintenance and repair of machine and equipment, Other manufacturing products, Scrap and waste, Supply of Electricity, Gas and Water, Construction, Trade and Transport, Services.

Type 6: Low dependency on imports: Paper and Printing, Chemical products, Metal products, Machinery, Transport equipment.

Furthermore, in relation to domestic outflows, though the δOf of heavy industries is negative, if we take a more detailed look at the 30-sector classification, the processing type of manufacturing heavy industries, such as Electric equipment and Machinery, Electric and Telecommunication equipment, Instruments and Meters were $\delta Of > 0$. In contrast, the material-processing type heavy industries all exhibited $\delta Of < 0$.

Considering the Central region, it has a clear comparative advantage in Agriculture and Food products. The decisive factor is this sector is that it is pulled by domestic outflows as a result of its location and is pulled by domestic final demand because of its population.

Northwest region

The balance of intermediate demand and intraregional final demands

In the Northwest region, the sectors which are $\delta X < 0$ are Agriculture (−26.44%), Construction (−16.96%), Services (−15.21%), Mining (−15.07%), Trade and Transport (−12.82%), and Supply of Electricity,

Gas and Water (−1.04%). With regard to heavy and light industries, when we use the 30-sector classification, the sector of Petroleum processing and coking is the only manufacturing sector which is $\delta X < 0$ (−10.91%). Vice versa, the most significant $\delta X > 0$ are Clothing (11.57%), Chemicals (19.19%), Machinery and equipment (9.79%), Transport equipment (7.77%), Metal products (7.59%), Electric and Telecommunications equipment (7.09%), and Paper and Printing (6.14%).

Those sectors which are $\delta A < 0$ are Agriculture (−11.08%), Trade and Transport (−10.98%), Mining (−2.18%), and Supply of Electricity, Gas and Water (−1.55%) based on the 17-sector classification; by contrast, $\delta F_{(d)}$ of all sectors, with the exception of Machinery and Electric products, are negative.

The most notable $\delta X < 0$ is Agriculture that is mainly pulled by urban household consumption ($\delta C_u = -14.07\%$) and demand for intermediate inputs ($\delta A = -11.08\%$). The sector of construction which is $\delta X = -16.96\%$ is mainly pulled by investment ($\delta I_f = -17.12\%$). Among the sector of Trade and Transport, $\delta X < 0$ of Transport and Warehousing are mainly pulled by δA. Services which also notably marked $\delta X < 0$ is mainly pulled by household consumption, which is different from the case in the North Municipalities region where the negative $\delta X < 0$ is pulled by δA.

With regard to the relationship between primary industries and their processing, the petroleum-related sector seems to be extremely correlated. Furthermore, though the δA of Agriculture is negative, correlations with Food products and Wooden products seem to be weak. In metal-related sectors there is a weak correlation. Though Coal mining and Electricity are correlated, but Coal and its material processes are not correlated without Coking.

The balance of foreign and domestic trade

Across all sectors, the Northwest region is not pulled by exports ($\sum_j \delta Ex_j = 65.31\%$), or by domestic outflows ($\sum_j \delta Of_j = 0.84\%$). On the other hand, it has a low dependency on imports ($\sum_j \delta M_j = -27.85\%$) and is dependent on domestic inflows ($\sum_j \delta N_j = 61.32\%$).

As for the patterns of comparative advantage sectors in Northwest from Table 5.9, there are three types:

Type 5: Pulled by domestic outflows, low dependency both on imports and domestic inflows: Mining.

Type 6: Pulled by domestic outflows, low dependency on imports: Agriculture, Construction, Trade and Transport, Services.

Type 14: Pulled neither by domestic outflows nor by exports, low dependency on imports: Supply of Electricity, Gas and Water.

Looking in more detail using the 30-sector classification, among Trade and Transport, the sector of Transport and Warehousing belongs to Type 6 ($\delta Of = -4.31\%$, $\delta Ex = 6.14\%$, $\delta M = -1.30\%$, $\delta N = 5.68\%$), and among Mining, the sector of Metal ore mining belongs to Type 8 that is pulled by domestic outflows, and dependent both on imports and on domestic inflows ($\delta Of = -1.83\%$, $\delta Ex = 0.43\%$, $\delta M = 0.11\%$, $\delta N = 0.23\%$). Besides, among Chemical products which is $\delta X > 0$ by the 17-sector classification, the sector of Petroleum processing and Coking which is $\delta X < 0$ belongs to Type 5 ($\delta Of = -4.38\%$, $\delta Ex = 1.43\%$, $\delta M = -2.00\%$, $\delta N = -1.46\%$).

Considering the Northwest region in its entirety, the comparatively advantaged sectors, especially Agriculture and Tertiary industries, their decisive factor is intraregional final demand rather than domestic outflows – with the exception of the petroleum-related sectors.

Southwest region

The balance of intermediate demand and intraregional final demands

In the Southwest region, the sectors which are $\delta X < 0$ are Agriculture (−58.69%), Food products (−17.57%), Services (−11.61%), Construction (−5.40%), and Transport equipment (−3.67%).

In addition, the Agriculture (−0.72%), Services (−1.81%), Paper and Printing (−0.70%), Transport equipment (−3.60%) and Construction (−1.26%) sectors are $\delta A < 0$, but these levels are relatively low. By contrast, all of 17 sectors are $\delta F_{(d)} < 0$, which are especially relatively pulled by rural household consumption (δC_r), and also recognized as pulled by investment (δI_f) whose level is not so high as the Northwest region.

With regard to the relationship between primary industry and its processing, the correlation between Agriculture and Food products seems to be good. By contrast, Petroleum- and/or Coal-related industry is not developed. In metal-related industries, Metal ore mining and Metals smelting and processing seem to have a weak correlation.

The balance of foreign and domestic trade

Across all sectors, the Southwest region is not pulled by exports ($\sum_j \delta Ex_j = 87.08\%$), or by domestic outflows ($\sum_j \delta Of_j = 66.31\%$). On the other hand, it has a low dependency both on imports ($\sum_j \delta M_j =$ -56.05%) and on domestic inflows ($\sum_j \delta N_j = -0.72\%$).

From Table 5.9, the patterns of comparative advantage sectors in Southwest by the 17-sector classification have the following two types of combinations:

Type 13: Neither pulled by domestic outflows nor by exports, low dependency on imports: Construction, Services.
Type 14: Pulled neither by domestic outflows nor by exports, low dependency both on imports and domestic inflows: Agriculture, Food products, Transport equipment.

Besides, although Mining and Metal products are $\delta X > 0$ in the 17-sector classification, there are sectors which are $\delta X < 0$ in the 30-sector classification. Among them, the sector Metal ore mining and the sector of Metals smelting and processing belong to Type 13, and the sector of Non-ferrous mineral mining is Type 5 – that is, pulled by domestic outflows, and with a low dependency both on imports and on domestic inflows ($\delta Of = -0.21\%$, $\delta Ex = 0.44\%$, $\delta M = -0.68\%$, $\delta N = -1.67\%$).

Additionally, while the sector of Agriculture which is substantially $\delta X < 0$ has a low dependency both on imports and on domestic inflows on the one hand, and is neither pulled by exports nor by domestic outflows, on the other, the sector of Food products is unexpectedly pulled neither by exports nor by domestic outflows, despite the existence of Yunnan province where the outflow of tobacco processing – a component of the sector of Food products – is extremely high.[9]

Considering the comparatively advantaged sectors in the Southwest region, especially Agriculture and its related food products, the decisive factor is not external outflows but residential household consumption.

5.4 Empirical remarks

Before concluding this chapter, we are going to give a brief summary of the above-mentioned results.

The first point to consider, in relation to intraregional demand, was: is each sector in each region more pulled by δA or $\delta F_{(d)}$? In general, the more developed the region is, the more complicated industrial structures it will exhibit and the larger its share of supplying intermediate inputs to various sectors. In this chapter, we regarded the average of eight regions IO data as the benchmark, and saw how far each industrial sector deviated from this benchmark. So, in the relatively industrialized and developed region, we can suppose the number of sectors which are $\delta A < 0$ would be more or $\sum_j \delta A_j < 0$, on the other hand in the relatively underdeveloped regions, we can suppose the number of sectors which are $\delta F_{(d)} < 0$ would be more or $\sum_j \delta F_{(d)_j} < 0$. Here, considering the case of China, we can examine whether or not the dichotomous image of the more progressed coastal region against the less developed inland region is an appropriate one.

So, δA and$\delta F_{(d)}$ across all sectors for the eight regions are compared in Table 5.10. From this table, the North Municipalities, East Coast, and South Coast regions are together $\sum_j \delta A_j < 0$ and $\sum_j \delta F_{(d)} > 0$. By contrast, the Central, Northwest, and Southwest regions are $\sum_j \delta A_j > 0$, and $\sum_j \delta F_{(d)} < 0$. And in the Northeast region both $\sum_j \delta A_j$ and $\sum_j \delta F_{(d)}$ is negative.

From these results and by the contrast of weight on intermediate demand or final demand, it may be almost recognized that the coastal region has more highly complex industrial structure than the inland region. But, such a recognition has the following problems.

First, if the North Municipalities, North Coast, East Coast, and South Coast regions are considered as a whole, then it cannot be asserted that there is a characteristic common to all high-level industrial structures. This can be seen from the fact that the North Coast's performance is different from that in other coastal regions. In the North Coast region, it was $\sum_j \delta A_j > 0$, so the factor of intermediate inputs is relatively weak, but is pulled by factors of final demand. Furthermore, the North Coast region has more comparative advantages in the primary industries sector than any other coastal region. Additionally, looking on external trade, though more sectors pulled by exports are mainly recognized in the coastal

Table 5.10 Contrast of δA and $\delta F_{(d)}$ across all sectors at each region

	$\sum_j \delta A_j$ (%)	$\sum_j \delta F_{(d)_j}$ (%)
Northeast	−50.36	−2.05
North Municipalities	−41.66	13.25
North Coast	32.51	58.27
Central Coast	−32.93	80.60
South Coast	−13.82	32.66
Central region	12.94	−55.06
Northwest	10.67	−110.29
Southwest	31.39	−128.01

region, in the North Coast, more sectors are pulled by domestic outflows than by exports. Considering the North Municipalities region, where the urban residential population is higher than any other region, the tendency towards post-industrialization is notably reconfirmed. Besides both $\delta A < 0$ and $\delta X < 0$ of the Services sector are much higher than in any other industrial sector. This finding is not shared by the with South Coast region, which has comparative advantages in both the Manufacturing and Services sectors, nor with the East Coast region, which has an unexpected result in the Services sector. We can conclude, that $\delta X < 0$ of Services in the inland region are mainly pulled by $\delta F_{(d)}$, and not by δA.

Secondly, if the Central, Northwest and Southwest regions are considered together as the inland region, they are common on $\sum_j \delta A_j > 0$ and/or the number of manufacturing sectors which are $\delta A < 0$ is relatively scarce. And among the elements of intraregional final demand ($\delta F_{(d)}$), gross fixed capital formation (δI_f) tends to pull their development, especially in the sector of Construction (and Agriculture) in this region. This seems to be recognized as the increase of demand for construction reflected by 'Western Area Development' Strategy. Still more, this region has more of a comparative advantage in primary industries than is the case for the coastal region (with the exception of the North Coast), but the level of development of processing sectors which make use of raw materials from those primary industries differs between sectors.

Lastly, the problem of positioning the Northeast region still remains: should the Northeast region be listed as part of the coastal region or as part of the inland region? Following our extended DPG analysis, the Northeast region seems to be different both from the coastal region and from the inland region. It had already formed industrial accumulation as a heavy industry base during the era of the planned economy. So, this phase will be reconfirmed at the level of $\delta A < 0$ at each sector of heavy industries. But, considering the $\delta F_{(d)}$, the sectors marked $\delta F_{(d)} < 0$ are light industries, the public sector (supply of Electricity, Gas and Water), tertiary industries, but as for heavy industries, this pattern is different from inland areas where all of $\delta F_{(d)}$ are denoted minus. Still more, among the components of $\delta F_{(d)}$, δI_f are denoted minus at Agriculture (−1.03%), Food products (−0.01%), Transport equipment (−0.42%), Other manufacturing (−0.26%), and the rest of all denoted plus. From this, we can guess the scarceness of pulling factor of investment to heavy industries in Northeast, and this performance is also different from the other region.

The second point is to consider whether or not the comparatively advantageous sectors in each region are export and/or domestic outflow oriented, and whether or not they are less dependent on imports and/or domestic inflows. The answer gained from analysis was not necessarily as clear. As we have already categorized each region in the former section, among these sectors there exists the pattern of δEx and/or $\delta Of > 0$. Still more, there exist the sectors that are at least dependent either on import or on domestic inflow. This suggests that in spite of the existence of a certain level of industrial accumulation, from the result of the high ratio of inflows to outflows, there occurs the possibility of inflows to satisfy intraregional demand despite the comparative advantage. Among them, particularly in the Northeast and Southwest regions, there exist more sectors that are $\delta X < 0$ and neither pulled by exports nor by domestic outflows on one hand, that exhibit a low dependency both on import and on domestic inflows on the other. These sectors have the low dependency of inflows, it suggests self-sufficient structure that are inflow and import-substitution industrialization.

5.5 Conclusion

In this chapter, as one of the Structural Decomposition Techniques that has been developed as research works using the IO model, DPG was used to analyse the factors on the interregional differentials of industrial structures in China. Through the quantitative comparison of DPG results of each region based on the common benchmark, the various combinations of differentials from the demand side of IO tables, such as the level of technological progress from the intermediate demand, the variation of intraregional final demand, and the level of openness with the outside region (either domestic or foreign), lead to interregional structural gaps between the eight regions. The findings we have obtained from the series of analysis would not only be useful for understanding the causes of inter- and intraregional linkage effects (either backward or forward) and spillover effects, but also would be suggesting politically for solving current regional problems which corresponds with 'Western Area Development' Strategy and so on.[10] As for the latter, for example, in order to determine selection of industrial sectors to develop for each region, and in order to promote the integration of the domestic market economy for sustainable growth across the country, similar analysis on more detail and classified sectors than 17 or 30 sectors of more than eight regions would be necessary if a similar types of interregional IO table were to be produced.

Notes

1. For the fundamental framework of structural decomposition techniques, see Rose and Casler (1996) and Dietzenbacher and Los (1998).
2. For the application of time-series DPG analysis into a cross-sectional analysis and its utility, see Fujikawa (1999, chapter 4). Based on this approach, Kanazawa (2003) uses regional IO tables to analyses interregional differences between industrial structures at the provincial level (Beijing, Tianjin, Jiangsu, Guangdong, Guangxi, Jiangxi, Ningxia, and Xinjiang) for China in 1997.
3. In the benchmark table, through the result of calculations, the data for the domestic outflows of all sectors becomes the same as those for domestic inflows.
4. The import coefficient of sector k (m_k) is expressed as $m_k = M_k / \sum_{l=1}^{n} x_{kl} + F_{(d)k}$, where M_k is that imports of sector k and x_{kl} is the total sum of intermediate demands from sector k to sector l. Similarly, domestic inflow coefficient of sector k (n_k) is expressed as $n_k = N_k / \sum_{l=1}^{n} x_{kl} + F_{(d)k}$, where N_k is the domestic inflow of sector.
5. In estimating the comparative advantage of sectors in other ways, the notion of location quotient (LQ) is also useful. The author has already calculated the LQ of each sector in each region this time, and has recognized the closer correspondence between δX and LQ. Here, by closer correspondence we mean that there exist several sectors that are not correspondent for a short while (in particular, the sectors of the Central region), whereas most sectors which are $\delta X < 0$ are LQ > 1.
6. Throughout this chapter, the factor of government consumption (δC_g) which belongs to $\delta F_{(d)}$ is not considered because the data on intermediate inputs of government consumption in each IO table are 0 all in all.
7. The data of LQ of services in East Coast calculated from the IO table is 0.887 (<1) whereas those in North Municipalities and South Coast are 2.112 (>1) and 1.130 (>1) respectively. Additionally, sector of services of 17 or 30-sector classification was the total of the sectors that are post and telecommunication, eating and drinking places, finance and insurance, real estate, social services, health services, education, scientific research, general technical services, and public administration and other sectors by 40-sector classification of national level IO table (see IDE–JETRO (2003), p. 13).
8. See National Bureau of Statistics of China (2001, p. 58).
9. As for the more remarkable comparative advantage of tobacco-processing sector of Southeast (in particular, Yunnan province) than any other region in 1993 and 1997, or than any other sector there, see Cheng (ed.) (2001, pp. 165, 264).
10. According to the Decision on Some Problems of Improving the Socialist Market Economic System which was adopted at the 3rd Plenum of the 16th Chinese Communist Party Central Committee in October 2003, in order to strengthen the balanced interregional development, the promotion of the past heavy industrial bases of the Northeast region is also indicated as well as 'Western Area Development'.

References

Cheng, X. (ed.) (2001) *Woguo Diqu Bijiaoyoushi Yanjiu (The Research of Regional Comparative Advantage in China)*, Beijing: China Planning Publishing House.

Dietzenbacher, E. and B. Los (1998) 'Structural Decomposition Techniques: Sense and Sensitivity', *Economic Systems Research*, 10, 307–23.

Fujikawa, K. (1999) *Guroobaru Keizai no Sangyorenkan Bunseki (Input–Output Analysis: Foudations and Extensions)*, Tokyo: Sobunsha.

Institute of Developing Economies–JETRO (2003) *Multi-regional Input–Output Model for China 2000*, Statistical Data Series no. 86, Chiba: Institute of Developing Economies–JETRO.

Kanazawa, T. (2003) 'Chugokuniokeru Chiikisangyokousei nikansuru Kousatsu – Chiiki Sangyorenkan DPG bunsekiwo Chuushinnishita Shoukyuukanhikaku' (The Consideration on Factors of Differences on Regional Industrial Structure: Inter-Provincial Comparison by Interregional DPG Analysis), in N. Okamoto (ed.), *Chugoku no Chiikikan Sangyokozo-Chiikikan Snagyorenkan Bunseki (II) (Inter-regional Industrial Structure in China – Interregional Input–Output Analysis)*, Asian Input – Output Series no. 63, Chiba: Institute of Developing Economies–JETRO, chapter 5.

National Bureau of Statistics of China (2001) *Chinese Statistical Yearbook 2001*, Beijing: China Statistics Press.

Rose, A.Z. and S. Casler (1996) 'Input–Output Structural Decomposition Analysis: A Critical Appraisal', *Economic Systems Research*, 8, 33–62.

6 Spatial Linkages of the Chinese Economy

Wenqing Pan and Qiyun Liu

6.1 Introduction

Covering a vast territory, the Chinese economy shows considerable diversity across different regions. Following the central Chinese government's implementation of its 'economic reform and open door' policy, the South Coast and East Coast regions of China have experienced more development than the central and western regions. In 2002, the eastern, central and western regions of China showed per capita GDP of 13,335 yuan, 6,978 yuan and 5,388 yuan, respectively. By contrast, Shanghai's per capita GDP is the highest in China, at 33,285 yuan – 10 times the level of the lowest-income region in China, Guizhou. The disparities between the regional economies of China are not only illustrated by the different levels of economic development, but are also reflected in differences in natural resources, industrial structure, human resources, and so on. With regard to natural resource distribution, coal, oil, natural gas, metal ore and agricultural resources are mainly distributed throughout the central and western regions of China, while the resources of the sea are obviously concentrated in the coastal areas, which are also dominated by a number of manufacturing industries. This has produced a particular spatial linkage in the Chinese economy: coal, oil, natural gas, metal ore and agricultural resources flow from the central and western regions to the coastal region, while manufactured products flow from the coastal region to the central and western regions. This will focus on the linkage between the regions in China at the beginning of the twenty-first century, and will use an input–output analysis to carry this out.

Walter Isard (1951) is regarded as the forerunner of operational regional science, having advanced an interregional input–output (IRIO) model. At the time he was writing, one of the most common assumptions of economics was that a nation's economic activity took place without any reference to spatial aspects. Yet different activities occur at different locations, and a specific activity in one region will usually affect another region's economy, meaning that there must be interactions between locations. Thus, it was clear that an explicitly regional approach was called for. Isard paid attention to two aspects in his study of spatial economics – the structure of activities within each region and the nature of the connections that link the regions. Isard captured these two aspects of the regional view in his IRIO model, in which intraregional structures appear in on-diagonal blocks and interregional connections are captured in off-diagonal blocks of a spatially explicit technical coefficients matrix.

Since Isard's pioneering publication there has been much work on the theory and empirical studies of spatial economy. This has included measures of the interdependence of input–output matrices, linkage indices and so on. The most widely used measures have been backward linkages and forward linkages.

Backward linkages focus primarily on the dependence of one sector on those other sectors which provide intermediate inputs in the form of materials. There are two kinds of backward linkages: the direct backward linkage and the total backward linkage. Direct backward linkage, which is the summation over all sectors of one column of the input coefficient matrix, captures the total value of intermediate inputs by one sector in producing one unit of its output. By contrast, total backward linkage, which is the summation over all sectors of one column of the Leontief inverse, captures the output of all sectors that would increase as a result of a one-unit increase in the final demand in one sector. The total backward linkages are measured using the traditional Leontief input–output model, which is essentially a demand-driven input–output model.

In contrast to backward linkages, the main focus of forward linkages is on the effect of the changes of other sectors' output values, induced by the change of the output value of one sector as a supplier. As mentioned in relation to backward linkages, forward linkages also consist of both a direct forward linkage and a total forward linkage. Direct forward linkage, which is calculated as a row sums of the output coefficient matrix, measures the percentage of one sector's gross output that is sold to all sectors as intermediate inputs. In contrast to the measures of total backward linkage, the measure of total forward linkage have been discussed for some considerable time. Originally, total forward linkage was calculated as a row sums of the Leontief inverse. Their interpretation is the additional value of output in one sector as induced by one unit of additional final demand in each sector. Where backward linkages are viewed as measuring a sector's dependence upon inputs from other sectors, forward linkage is clearly opposite in its nature. It is obvious that the model used is still the traditional demand-driven input–output model, and that the matrix used is still the Leontief inverse. In order to resolve the problem of the ambiguity of these measures, people began to use input (or supply) multipliers within the 'supply-driven' input–output model. These multipliers are obtained as row sums of the Ghosh inverse. Based on the output (or allocation) coefficient matrix, Ghosh (1958) advanced an input–output model, which is symmetrical to Leotief's input–output model. The Ghosh input–output model connects the change of the value-added to the change in gross output, and it is termed a supply-driven input–output model.

For a long time, however, this interpretation was questioned since it was believed that the supply-driven input–output model was implausible. Oosterhaven (1988) questions the plausibility of the supply-driven input–output model in a most convincing way. His major point of critique can be best explained by the following simple example. Suppose that the value added (or the input of, say, labour) in one sector is increased by one unit, then the supply-driven input–output model will show the increase of the output in every sector. Hence, in any other sector, the production is increased without any increase in the value-added terms (such as labour and capital). However, Dietzenbacher (1997) showed that this implausibility vanishes once the supply-driven input–output model is interpreted as a price model. Interpreted in this way the multipliers, which are row sums of the Ghosh inverse, then reflect the effect of an increase of one dollar in the primary cost (e.g. labour costs, or depreciation of fixed assets) of one industry on the total value of gross production. If forward linkages are viewed as measuring a sector's dependence upon other sectors as buyers of its output, these multipliers are forward in nature. They measure how much the output value of all sectors increases when there is an initial increase in the primary costs of one sector.

In China, the input–output technique was employed to analyse the reality of the Chinese economy from the beginning of the 1960s onwards, and flourished in the 1980s and in the 1990s. However, there is little research on the spatial linkage of the Chinese economy which employs input–output technology. The main problem with using the method is that there was no interregional input–output table of China before this date. Furthermore, some domestic researchers continue to use outdated methods. For example, many researchers still use the Leontief inverse to measure the forward linkages. Qiyun Liu (1993) became the first Chinese economist to advance a supply-driven input–output model for studying the Chinese economy. Liu also produced a set of analysis methods which was in reverse to what was used in the traditional demand-driven input–output model. In 1992, Liu made the first call for the use of the output coefficient matrix and the Ghosh inverse to measure the forward linkages, and advanced the weighted measures of backward and forward linkages in China in 2001.

It should be mentioned that backward linkages were originally measured from the output multiplier. Recently, this has been extended to measuring variable such as the value-added multiplier, the import multiplier, and the labour-income multiplier. Similarly, forward linkages have been measured by extending the multipliers from output multiplier to final output multipliers, such as the consumption multiplier, the investment multiplier, the export multiplier, and so on. (Dietzenbacher 2002).

6.2 Methodology

In this section, we will concentrate on the measurement of China's regional spatial linkages. The data sets used are the 2000 China Multiregional Input–Output (CMRIO) data bases, which were compiled by the Institution of Developing Economies–JETRO and the State Information Centre of China (Institute of Developing Economies 2003).

According to Isard's two-region (one region/rest of the country) IRIO model, inter-industry transactions include intraregional and interregional transactions:

$$\mathbf{Z} = \begin{bmatrix} \mathbf{Z}^{LL} & \mathbf{Z}^{LM} \\ \mathbf{Z}^{ML} & \mathbf{Z}^{MM} \end{bmatrix} \quad \text{where } \mathbf{Z}^{LM} = \left(z_{ij}^{LM}\right)$$

Superscripts L and M denote two regions respectively. In the same way, final demand is given as:

$$\mathbf{Y} = \begin{bmatrix} \mathbf{Y}^{LL} & \mathbf{Y}^{LM} \\ \mathbf{Y}^{ML} & \mathbf{Y}^{MM} \end{bmatrix} \quad \text{where } \mathbf{Y}^{LM} = \left(y_j^{LM}\right)$$

Primary input vector and gross output vector are given respectively as:

$$\mathbf{V} = [\mathbf{V}^{L} \quad \mathbf{V}^{M}] \quad \text{where } \mathbf{V}^{L} = (v_i^{L})$$

$$\mathbf{X} = \begin{bmatrix} \mathbf{X}^{L} \\ \mathbf{X}^{M} \end{bmatrix} \quad \text{where } \mathbf{X}^{L} = \left(x_j^{L}\right)$$

Denote direct purchase coefficient matrix A (also called input coefficient matrix) and Leontief inverse L as follows:[1]

$$\mathbf{A} = \begin{bmatrix} \mathbf{A}^{LL} & \mathbf{A}^{LM} \\ \mathbf{A}^{ML} & \mathbf{A}^{MM} \end{bmatrix} = \mathbf{Z}(\hat{\mathbf{X}})^{-1} \quad \text{where } \mathbf{A}^{LM} = \left(a_{ij}^{LM}\right)$$

$$\mathbf{L} = (\mathbf{I} - \mathbf{A})^{-1} = \begin{bmatrix} \mathbf{L}^{LL} & \mathbf{L}^{LM} \\ \mathbf{L}^{ML} & \mathbf{L}^{MM} \end{bmatrix} \quad \text{where } \mathbf{L}^{LM} = \left(l_{ij}^{LM}\right) = \left(\frac{\partial x_i^L}{\partial y_j^M}\right)$$

Similarly, the direct output coefficient matrix H (or called allocation coefficient matrix) and Ghosh inverse G can be denoted as:[2]

$$\mathbf{H} = \begin{bmatrix} \mathbf{H}^{LL} & \mathbf{H}^{LM} \\ \mathbf{H}^{ML} & \mathbf{H}^{MM} \end{bmatrix} = (\hat{\mathbf{X}})^{-1}\mathbf{Z} \quad \text{where } \mathbf{H}^{LM} = \left(h_{ij}^{LM}\right)$$

$$\mathbf{G} = (\mathbf{I} - \mathbf{H})^{-1} = \begin{bmatrix} \mathbf{G}^{LL} & \mathbf{G}^{LM} \\ \mathbf{G}^{ML} & \mathbf{G}^{MM} \end{bmatrix} \quad \text{where } \mathbf{G}^{LM} = \left(g_{ij}^{LM}\right) = \left(\frac{\partial x_j^M}{\partial v_i^L}\right)$$

Direct backward linkages

In the context of the two-region IRIO model, the direct backward linkage of sector j in region L will now contain an intraregional component, B_j^{LL}, and an interregional component, B_j^{LM}, where:

$$B_j^{LL} = \sum_i \left(z_{ij}^{LL}/x_j^L\right) = \sum_i a_{ij}^{LL}$$

$$B_j^{ML} = \sum_i \left(z_{ij}^{ML}/x_j^L\right) = \sum_i a_{ij}^{ML}$$

These represent, respectively, the dependence of sector j in region L on Inter-industry suppliers located within that region and outside of the region.

It is obvious that the interregional direct backward linkages can be defined as:

$$B^{ML} = \sum_j B_j^{ML} = \sum_j \sum_i \left(z_{ij}^{ML}/x_j^L\right) = \sum_j \sum_i a_{ij}^{ML}$$

In words, B^{ML} captures the total value of direct intermediate inputs coming from region M when each sector produces one unit output simultaneously in region L, measuring the dependence of region L as a purchaser on region M as an intermediate inputs supplier. The larger this measure is, the more dependent is region L on region M's intermediate inputs.

Since each sector in region L has a different output in any specific year, we can define weighted interregional direct backward linkage as follows:

$$B^{ML} = \sum_j \alpha_j^L B_j^{ML} = \sum_j \sum_i \alpha_j^L a_{ij}^{ML}$$

Here, $\alpha_j^L = x_j^L / \sum_j x_j^L$ denotes the proportion of sector j's output in total region L output. In words, B^{ML} captures the total value of direct intermediate inputs coming from region M in producing one unit of average output in region L in the specific year. Thus, the weighted direct spatial backward linkage is given a much more explicit meaning.

Similarly, the weighted intraregional direct backward linkage can be defined as:

$$B^{LL} = \sum_j \alpha_j^L B_j^{LL} = \sum_j \sum_i \alpha_j^L a_{ij}^{LL}$$

Finally, we have found it useful to convert the measures to percentages, and define the relative interregional direct backward linkage as:

$$B^L = \frac{B^{ML}}{(B^{LL} + B^{ML})}$$

Of course, direct backward linkages can be extended to the measurement of the dependence on intraregional primary inputs. For example, we can define the weighted backward linkage for the primary input category k as follows:

$$N_k^L = \sum_j \alpha_j^L N_{kj}^L = \sum_j \alpha_j^L \left(v_{kj}^L / x_j^L\right)$$

where $N_{kj}^L = v_{kj}^L / x_j^L$, called the primary input coefficient, captures the direct dependence of sector j on primary input k in region L.

Total backward linkages

Similar to direct backward linkages, for the two-region IRIO model, the total backward linkage of sector j in region L also contain an intraregional component, $\bar{B}_j^{LL}$, and an interregional component, $\bar{B}_j^{LM}$, where:

$$\bar{B}_j^{LL} = \sum_i l_{ij}^{LL}$$

$$\bar{B}_j^{ML} = \sum_i l_{ij}^{ML}$$

It is obvious that the interregional total backward linkage for region L can be defined as:

$$\bar{B}^{ML} = \sum_j \bar{B}_j^{ML} = \sum_j \sum_i l_{ij}^{ML}$$

Here, l_{ij}^{ML} denotes the element of the Leontief inverse, which is obtained as:

$$\mathbf{L} = [\mathbf{I} - (\mathbf{I} - \hat{\mathbf{M}})\mathbf{A}]^{-1}$$

Where $\hat{\mathbf{M}}$ denotes the diagonal matrix with the ratio of imports to total domestic demand as the diagonal element. In words $\bar{B}^{ML}$, capturing the increase of the output required in region M when each sector increases by one unit on final demand in region L, measures the dependence of region L as a purchaser on region M as a supplier.

Similarly, we can define the weighted interregional total backward linkage as follows:

$$\bar{B}^{ML} = \sum_j \beta_j^L \bar{B}_j^{ML} = \sum_j \sum_i \beta_j^L l_{ij}^{ML}$$

Here, $\beta_j^L = f_j^L / \sum_j f_j^L$ denotes the proportion of sector j's final demand in total final demand in region L. In words, $\bar{B}^{ML}$ measures the increase of the output required in region M induced by a one unit increase of average final demand in region L in the specific year. It is obvious that the weighted measures have a much more explicit meaning than the unweighted measures.

The relative interregional total backward linkage can also be defined as:

$$\bar{B}^L = \bar{B}^{ML} / (\bar{B}^{LL} + \bar{B}^{ML})$$

Here, $\bar{B}^{LL} = \sum_j \beta_j^L \bar{B}_j^{LL} = \sum_j \sum_i \beta_j^L l_{ij}^{LL}$, called the weighted intraregional total backward linkage, measures the increase of the output required in region L induced by a one unit increase of average final demand in that region in the specific year.

In the same way, we can measure the dependence of region L on the primary input k within and outside of that region as follows:

$$\bar{N}_k^{LL} = \sum_j \sum_i N_{Ki}^L \left(\beta_j^L l_{ij}^{LL}\right)$$

$$\bar{N}_k^{ML} = \sum_j \sum_i N_{Ki}^M \left(\beta_j^L l_{ij}^{ML}\right)$$

Direct forward linkages

Similar to direct backward linkage, in the context of a two-region IRIO model, the direct forward linkage of sector i in region M will now contain an intraregional component, F_i^{MM}, and an interregional component, F_i^{ML}, where:

$$F_i^{MM} = \sum_j \left(z_{ij}^{MM}/x_i^M\right) = \sum_j h_{ij}^{MM}$$

$$F_i^{ML} = \sum_j \left(z_{ij}^{ML}/x_i^M\right) = \sum_j h_{ij}^{ML}$$

These represent, respectively, the dependence of sector i in region M on inter-industry purchasers located both within that region and outside that region.

It is also obvious that the interregional direct forward linkage can be defined as:

$$F^{ML} = \sum_i F_i^{ML} = \sum_i \sum_j \left(z_{ij}^{ML}/x_i^M\right) = \sum_i \sum_j h_{ij}^{ML}$$

In words, F^{ML}, denoting the proportion of direct intermediate input from region M to region L in total region M output, measures the direct dependence of region M as a supplier on region L as a purchaser.

The weighted interregional direct forward linkage of region M can be defined as:

$$F^{ML} = \sum_i \alpha_i^M F_i^{ML} = \sum_i \sum_j \alpha_i^M h_{ij}^{ML}$$

Here, $\alpha_i^M = x_i^M / \sum_i x_i^M$ denotes the proportion of sector i's output in region M in total region M output. In words, F^{ML} measures the intermediate inputs from region M to region L when region M averagely produces one unit output in the specific year.

Similarly, we can also define the weighted intraregional direct forward linkage of region M as:

$$F^{MM} = \sum_i \alpha_i^M F_i^{MM} = \sum_i \sum_j \alpha_i^M h_{ij}^{MM}$$

and define the relative interregional direct forward linkage as:

$$F^M = F^{ML}/(F^{MM} + F^{ML})$$

Just like backward linkages, direct forward linkages can also be extended to measuring the dependence of one region on intraregional final demand. For example, we can define the weighted direct forward linkage for final demand category k as follows:

$$M_k^M = \sum_i \alpha_i^M M_{ik}^M = \sum_i \alpha_i^M \left(y_{ik}^M / x_i^M\right)$$

Here, $M_{ik}^M = y_{ik}^M / x_i^M$, denotes the direct final output coefficient.

Total forward linkages

Parallel to total backward linkages, in the two-region IRIO model, total forward linkages of sector i in region M also contain an intraregional component, $\bar{F}_i^{MM}$, and an interregional component, $\bar{F}_i^{ML}$, where:

$$\bar{F}_i^{MM} = \sum_j g_{ij}^{MM}$$

$$\bar{F}_i^{ML} = \sum_j g_{ij}^{ML}$$

It is obvious that interregional total forward linkage for region M can be defined as:

$$\bar{F}^{ML} = \sum_i \bar{F}_i^{ML} = \sum_i \sum_j g_{ij}^{ML}$$

Here, g_{ij}^{ML} denotes the element of the Ghosh inverse. In words, $\bar{F}^{ML}$, capturing the increase of the output value in region L when each sector increase one unit primary input cost in region M, measures the dependence of region M as a supplier on region L as a purchaser.

Similarly, we can define the weighted interregional total forward linkage as follows:

$$\bar{F}^{ML} = \sum_i \gamma_i^M \bar{F}_i^{ML} = \sum_i \sum_j \gamma_i^M g_{ij}^{ML}$$

Here, $\gamma_i^M = v_i^M / \sum_i v_i^M$ denotes the proportion of sector i's primary input in total primary input in region M. In words, $\bar{F}^{ML}$ measures the increase of the output value in region L induced by one unit increase of the average primary input cost in region M in the specific year.

The relative interregional total forward linkage can also be defined as:

$$\bar{F}^M = \bar{F}^{ML} / (\bar{F}^{MM} + \bar{F}^{ML})$$

Here, $\bar{F}^{MM} = \sum_i \gamma_i^M \bar{F}_i^{MM} = \sum_i \sum_j \gamma_i^M g_{ij}^{MM}$, called the weighted intraregional total forward linkage, measures the increase of the output required in region M induced by one unit increase of average primary input cost in that region in the specific year.

In the same way, we can measure the dependence of region M on the final demand k (k can denote consumption, investment or exports) within the region and outside of the region as follows:

$$\bar{M}_k^{MM} = \sum_i \sum_j M_{jk}^M (\gamma_i^M g_{ij}^{MM})$$

$$\bar{M}_k^{ML} = \sum_i \sum_j M_{jk}^L (\gamma_i^M g_{ij}^{ML})$$

6.3 Empirical results

Our empirical study is based on the 2000 CMRIO (Institute of Developing Economies 2003). The model defines eight regions as follows: Northeast (Heilongjiang, Jilin, Liaoning), North Municipalities (Beijing, Tianjin), North Coast (Hebei, Shandong), East Coast (Jiangsu, Shanghai, Zhejiang), South Coast (Fujian, Guangdong, Hainan), Central (Shanxi, Henan, Anhui, Hubei, Hunan, Jiangxi), Northwest (Inner Mongolia, Shannxi, Ninxia, Gansu, Qinghai, Xinjiang) and Southwest (Sichuan, Chongqing, Yunnan, Guizhou, Guangxi, Tibet). The sector classifications were 3 sectors, 8 sectors, 17 sectors and 30 sectors respectively.

The measured direct and total backward linkages based on three sectors (see Appendix Tables 6.A.1 and 6.A.2) and 17 sectors (see Tables 6.1 and 6.2). The two results are very close. In the text that follows in this section, we focus primarily on the empirical results obtained from the 17-sector input–output model.

Table 6.1 Direct backward linkages for eight regions

	Northeast	*North Municipalities*	*North Coast*	*East Coast*	*South Coast*	*Central*	*Northwest*	*Southwest*
Weighted direct backward linkages								
$B^{ML} + B^{LL}$	0.6480	0.6645	0.6417	0.7022	0.6664	0.6212	0.5828	0.5804
B^{LL}	0.5670	0.5686	0.5604	0.5875	0.5485	0.5362	0.4542	0.4980
B^{ML}	0.0811	0.0958	0.0813	0.1148	0.1179	0.0851	0.1287	0.0824
Relative interregional direct backward linkage (%)								
$B^{ML}/(B^{ML} + B^{LL})$	12.51	14.42	12.67	16.34	17.69	13.69	22.08	14.20

Table 6.2 Total backward linkages for eight regions

	Northeast	North Municipalities	North Coast	East Coast	South Coast	Central	Northwest	Southwest
Weighted total backward linkages								
$\bar{B}^{ML} + \bar{B}^{LL}$	2.6407	2.4558	2.5387	2.6777	2.2832	2.5105	2.3508	2.2996
$\bar{B}^{LL}$	2.2170	1.9565	2.1674	2.1553	1.8144	2.1337	1.8069	1.9458
$\bar{B}^{ML}$	0.4237	0.4993	0.3713	0.5223	0.4688	0.3767	0.5439	0.3538
Relative interregional total backward linkage (%)								
$\bar{B}^{ML}/(\bar{B}^{ML} + \bar{B}^{LL})$	16.05	20.33	14.63	19.51	20.53	15.01	23.14	15.38

Backward linkage of China's eight regions

Direct backward linkages

The results for direct backward linkages are reported in Table 6.1. Generally speaking, those regions with higher incomes appear to have larger direct backward linkages than those with lower incomes. For example, the absolute value of the direct backward linkage for East Coast is the largest, at 0.70. This is followed by the South Coast, with 0.67 as the weighted direct backward linkage. The downward ranking of the other regions is as follows: North Municipalities, Northeast, North Coast, Central, Northwest and Southwest.

The Central region still has the largest intraregional weighted direct backward linkage, 0.59. It is followed by the rest of the regions in the following order: North Municipalities, Northeast, North Coast, South Coast, Central, Southwest and Northwest. It is clear from this that the South Coast region is relatively independent of the other regions.

The order of the interregional weighted direct backward linkage values is different. Here, the Northwest region takes the top position, with 0.13 as its value. The remaining region are ordered as follows: South Coast, East Coast, North Municipalities, Central, Southwest, North Cost and Northeast. The lower down the ranking a region appears, the more independent it is of other regions.

With regard to the measure of the proportion of interregional direct backward linkage in total (intra- plus interregional) direct backward linkage, namely relative interregional direct backward linkage, the Northwest region records the highest value and the Northeast region records the lowest value. This shows that a higher percentage of the inter-industry inputs in the Northwest region came from outside the region and a lower percentage in the Northeast region came from outside the region.

Total backward linkages

Direct backward linkages measure the direct dependence of one region on the other regions. Total backward linkages, capturing the effect of a change in final demand in one region on output within the region and outside of the region, measure the dependence of one region both on this region and on other regions.

For total backward linkage values, namely output multipliers, Table 6.2 shows a slightly different order from that observed for direct backward linkage values. The East Coast region has the largest total backward linkage value, followed in order by the Northeast, North Coast, Central,

North Municipalities, Northwest, Southwest and South Coast regions. The South Coast region shows less backward linkage, reflecting the point that the increase of the final demand in this region has less effect on each regions output of China, and also indicating that this region is more dependent on foreign economies.

Regarding intraregional total backward linkages, the Northeast region has the highest value, reflecting the fact that this region is more dependent on its own economy than on other regions. The other regions are ordered as follows: North Coast, East Coast, Central, North Municipalities, Southwest, South Coast and Northwest.

For the interregional total backward linkages, the Northwest region has the largest value, showing that this region is more dependent on other regions. In other words, the increase of final demand in the Northwest region induces the output in other regions. The order of the rest of the regions is as follows: East Coast, North Municipalities, South Coast, Northeast, Central, North Coast and Southwest.

For the relative interregional total backward linkage, reflecting interregional effects, Northwest is still at the top of the order. This means the Northwest region has a larger relative effect on other regions' output than have other regions. The order of the rest of the regions is: South Coast, North Municipalities, East Coast, Northeast, Southwest, Central and North Coast.

Generally speaking, the dependence of the Northwest region on the other seven regions is by far the largest, followed by, the South Coast, East Coast and North Municipalities regions. By contrast, the Northeast, North Coast, Central and Southwest are comparatively less dependent on other regions.

Regional backward linkages on primary inputs

Table 6.3 shows that the regions with the highest income are less dependent on primary inputs than those regions with low incomes. For example, the dependence on primary inputs of the Southwest region is by far the largest. When there is a one unit increase of final demand in Southwest, there will be a 0.95 unit increase of primary inputs of all eight regions. The dependence on primary inputs of the South Coast region is by far the smallest, with only 0.81 of the backward linkage value on primary inputs.

On the other hand, from the point of view of regional dependence on outside total primary inputs, Table 6.3 shows that those regions with the highest incomes have a higher percentage of interregional total backward linkage values than do regions with low incomes, reflecting the relatively higher interregional effect on those regions with high incomes.

Table 6.3 Total backward linkages on primary inputs

	Northeast	*North Municipalities*	*North Coast*	*East Coast*	*South Coast*	*Central*	*Northwest*	*Southwest*
Weighted total backward linkage								
$\bar{N}^{ML} + \bar{N}^{LL}$	0.9150	0.8321	0.9343	0.8640	0.8075	0.9475	0.9443	0.9545
$\bar{N}^{LL}$	0.7712	0.6571	0.8065	0.6843	0.6504	0.8227	0.7619	0.8372
$\bar{N}^{ML}$	0.1438	0.1750	0.1278	0.1796	0.1571	0.1248	0.1825	0.1173
Relative interregional total backward linkage (%)								
$\bar{N}^{ML}/(\bar{N}^{ML} + \bar{N}^{LL})$	15.7	21.0	13.7	20.8	19.5	13.2	19.3	12.3

For example, the proportion of the interregional backward linkage on primary inputs in the total (intra- plus interregional) backward linkage on primary inputs is 21 per cent for North Municipalities, and 20.8 per cent and 19.5 per cent for East Coast and South Coast, respectively. By contrast, for the relatively undeveloped regions such as the Southwest and Central, the percentage is only 12.3 per cent and 13.2 per cent respectively. Northwest is the only exception to this pattern, with a figure of 19.3 per cent proportion. The major reason for this is that the Northwest region's dependence on outside products is by far the largest.

Forward linkages for China's eight regions

Direct forward linkages

Table 6.4 shows that those regions with higher incomes have much larger direct forward linkage values than those with lower incomes. For example, the relative weighted forward linkage values were 0.66, 0.71 and 0.67 for the North Municipalities, North Coast and East Coast regions respectively, whereas the values were 0.62 for the Northeast, and only 0.56 for both the Northwest and Southwest regions.

From the point of view of interregional forward linkages, the bottom panel of Table 6.4 shows that the Central region has the largest proportion of the interregional forward linkage in the total (intra- plus interregional) backward linkage. The other regions of China are ranked as follows: North Coast, Northwest, South Coast, North Municipalities, East Coast, Southwest and Northeast. It should be mentioned that the Central region, which is located advantageously in terms of transportation, usually depends to a considerable extent on outside regions.

Total forward linkages

Direct forward linkages measure the degree to which one region as a supplier depends directly on itself and other regions, whereas total forward linkages measure how the increase of primary inputs in one region affects the output both within and outside this region.

Table 6.5 shows that the North Coast, East Coast, Central and North Municipalities regions have larger total forward linkage values. For example, a one unit increase of the primary input cost in the North Coast region will induce a 3.24 unit increase of the output value in the whole country. The Northwest, Southwest and Northeast regions, where the economies are undeveloped, have smaller total forward linkage values. For example, the value of total forward linkage is only 2.32 for the Northwest region. It should be mentioned that the South Coast is

Table 6.4 Direct forward linkages for eight regions

	Northeast	North Municipalities	North Coast	East Coast	South Coast	Central	Northwest	Southwest
Weighted direct forward linkages								
$F^{ML} + F^{MM}$	0.6212	0.6552	0.7063	0.6686	0.6345	0.6769	0.5599	0.5599
F^{MM}	0.5670	0.5686	0.5604	0.5875	0.5485	0.5362	0.4542	0.4980
F^{ML}	0.0542	0.0866	0.1459	0.0811	0.0859	0.1407	0.1057	0.0620
Relative interregional direct forward linkage (%)								
$F^{ML}/(F^{ML} + F^{MM})$	8.73	13.21	20.66	12.14	13.55	20.79	18.88	11.06

Table 6.5 Total forward linkages for eight regions

	Northeast	North Municipalities	North Coast	East Coast	South Coast	Central	Northwest	Southwest
Weighted total forward linkages (17 sectors)								
$\bar{F}^{ML} + \bar{F}^{MM}$	2.7109	2.9014	3.2366	2.978	2.7542	2.9769	2.4579	2.3236
$\bar{F}^{MM}$	2.3072	2.3379	2.3093	2.4747	2.2535	2.1774	1.8636	1.9902
$\bar{F}^{ML}$	0.4037	0.5635	0.9273	0.5034	0.5007	0.7994	0.5944	0.3335
Relative interregional total forward linkage (%)								
$\bar{F}^{ML}/(\bar{F}^{ML} + \bar{F}^{MM})$	14.9	19.4	28.7	16.9	18.2	26.9	24.2	14.4

the most developed region, but its total backward linkage value is below the average level of the whole country. The major reason for this may be the high ratio of exports in this region. In fact, the ratio of exports to total output is 23.9 per cent for the South Coast, whereas the average ratio for the whole of China is only 8.3 per cent.

Considering the proportion of interregional total forward linkage in total (intra- plus interregional) forward linkage for one region, namely relative interregional total forward linkage, the North Coast region is still at the top of the order, indicating that among the increase of the output of China induced by the increase of primary inputs cost in North Coast, the percentage of the other regions' output increase is 28.7 per cent. The order of the rest of the regions is as follows: Central, Northwest, North Municipalities, South Coast, East Coast, Northeast and Southwest.

Total forward linkages on final demand

Table 6.6 gives the values of the regional total forward linkages on final demand (called the final demand multiplier). It shows that the increase in primary input costs in the Central and the North Coast regions will induce an increase of final demand value across the whole country. For example, if the primary input cost increases by one dollar in the Central region, there will be a 1.23 dollar increase in final demand value in the whole country. By contrast, the increase in primary input costs in North Municipalities and Northeast regions have less effect on the increase of final demand value across the country. For example, the value of the total forward linkage on final demand is only 0.91 for the North Municipalities region.

The bottom panel of Table 6.6 shows that the North Coast has a relatively high percentage of interregional forward linkages – 27.7 per cent. The percentage contributions of interregional forward linkages range from 18.0 per cent to 21.2 per cent for the North Municipalities, East Coast, South Coast, Central and Northwest regions. The Northeast and Southwest regions have by far the smallest percentage. For example, the percentage for the Southwest region is only 11.6 per cent.

Table 6.7 gives the results of regional total forward linkages on exports (called the export multiplier). It shows that the increase of primary input cost in the South Coast and East Coast regions induce a greater increase of the export values of the whole country than in the case for other regions. By contrast, the undeveloped regions, such as Northwest and Southwest, have very little effect on the export values of China.

On the other hand, the Central, Northwest and Southwest regions have a far higher percentage contribution of interregional total forward

Table 6.6 Total forward linkages on final demand

	Northeast	North Municipalities	North Coast	East Coast	South Coast	Central	Northwest	Southwest
Weighted total forward linkages								
$\bar{M}_f^{ML} + \bar{M}_f^{MM}$	0.9302	0.9093	1.1194	0.9328	0.9561	1.2359	0.9773	0.9955
$\bar{M}_f^{MM}$	0.8035	0.7199	0.8097	0.7533	0.7836	0.9741	0.7795	0.8799
$\bar{M}_f^{ML}$	0.1267	0.1894	0.3097	0.1795	0.1725	0.2618	0.1978	0.1155
Relative interregional total forward linkage (%)								
$\bar{M}_f^{ML}/(\bar{M}_f^{ML} + \bar{M}_f^{MM})$	13.6	20.8	27.7	19.2	18	21.2	20.2	11.6

Table 6.7 Total forward linkages on exports

	Northeast	*North Municipalities*	*North Coast*	*East Coast*	*South Coast*	*Central*	*Northwest*	*Southwest*
Weighted total forward linkages								
$\bar{M}_e^{ML} + \bar{M}_e^{MM}$	0.1471	0.2981	0.1909	0.3078	0.5542	0.1305	0.0950	0.0781
$\bar{M}_e^{MM}$	0.1123	0.2462	0.1031	0.2527	0.5205	0.0423	0.0476	0.0358
$\bar{M}_e^{ML}$	0.0348	0.0520	0.0877	0.0551	0.0337	0.0883	0.0474	0.0424
Relative interregional total forward linkage (%)								
$\bar{M}_e^{ML}/(\bar{M}_e^{ML} + \bar{M}_e^{MM})$	23.7	17.4	46	17.9	6.1	67.6	49.9	54.2

linkages on exports, with values of 67.6, 49.9 and 54.2 per cent respectively. But the East Coast and South Coast regions have little percentage contribution of interregional linkages. The main reason may be that these two regions focus on exporting domestic products.

6.4 Conclusion

In this chapter, by means of an input–output technique, we have measured the spatial linkages of the Chinese economy in 2000. From these analyses, we can draw the following conclusions: For backward (direct, total) and forward (direct, total) linkages, Figure 6.1 gives the two-way tables that display the relative value of the proportion of interregional linkages in total (inter- plus intraregional) linkages for each region. In Figure 6.1, 'low' refers to a score less than the average score, and 'high' to a score more than the average score. Then, generally speaking, one might characterize regions in the following way in terms of their 'connection' with the rest of the Chinese economy, depending upon where their pair of relative linkage values placed them in such a table:

I: Generally independent;
II: Dependent on interregional demand;
III: Generally dependent;
IV: Dependent on interregional supply.

Comparing the direct and total spatial linkages in Figure 6.1, we can see that these measures provide virtually identical classifications, with the exception of North Municipalities which is in quadrant I in the direct linkage table and in quadrant II in the total linkage table. Figure 6.1 also shows the following basic features of spatial linkages in China in 2000: the Northeast and Southwest regions have the smallest connection to the

		Direct backward linkage	
		Low	High
Direct forward linkage	Low	1\2\8 (I)	4\5 (II)
	High	3\6 (IV)	7 (III)

		Total backward linkage	
		Low	High
Total forward linkage	Low	1\8 (I)	2\4\5 (II)
	High	3\6 (IV)	7 (III)

Figure 6.1 China: regional direct and total relative linkages, 2000

Final demand multiplier		Primary input multiplier: Low		Primary input multiplier: High	
	Low	1\8	(I)	5	(II)
	High	3\6	(IV)	2\4\7	(III)

Figure 6.2 China: regional relative linkages on final demand and on primary input, 2000

outside regions, whereas the Northwest region has the largest one. The East Coast, South Coast and North Municipalities regions have larger backward linkage values but smaller forward linkage values, meaning that these three regions depend much more on other regions as purchasers than they do as suppliers. By contrast, the North Coast and Central regions have higher forward linkage values but lower backward linkage values, meaning that these two regions depend much more on other regions as suppliers than they do as purchasers.

In addition, we also arrange each region's final demand multiplier (forward linkage) and primary input multiplier (backward linkage) into a two-way table (Figure 6.2). This shows that the Northeast and Southwest regions are less dependent on other regions in terms of both the looking backward primary input multipliers and the looking forward final demand multipliers, again reflecting the lower level of connection to other regions. In contrast, the North Municipalities, East Coast and Northwest regions have a greater dependence on other regions in terms of both primary input multipliers and final demand multipliers. The South Coast region depends to a considerable extent on the primary input of other regions, whereas both the North Coast and Central regions depend more on the final demand of other regions.

Finally, the Central, Northwest and Southwest regions have much greater effects on the external exports value when the three region's primary input costs increase, whereas the East Coast and the South Coast have a smaller effect.

From these results, we can draw the following conclusions:

First, along with the implementation of the Western Area Development policy, the Northwest region has been developing the greatest spatial linkages to other regions in China. Thus, expending consumption and investment in the Northwest region, cannot only strengthen the development of the Northwest region, but will also enhance the development of other regions' economies.

Secondly, mainly because of the limitations of its transport infrastructure, the Southwest region is much more independent. The Northeast region is in a similar position, yet, this is mainly because of the slow rate of reform of its economic structure and the difficulty of overcoming large and heavy state-owned enterprises. It can be said therefore that the Southwest and Northeast regions are still in the process of developing their economies. Therefore, while the Southwest region should enhance its infrastructure construction, especially in the area of transport, in order to improve its spatial linkage, the Northeast region should abandon its outdated traditional economic structures, speed up the pace of economic reforms and simultaneously develop economic ties with other regions.

Thirdly, the North Coast and Central regions depend more on other regions in terms of forward linkages. Thus, the development of other regions can benefit the economy of these two regions since they will be suppliers of intermediate goods and primary products.

Finally, as the most developed regions in China, the North Municipalities, the East Coast and the South Coast regions are likely to become the growth engine driving forward the national economy of China.

Appendix

Table 6.A.1 Direct backward linkages for eight regions, 2000

	Northeast	*North Municipalities*	*North Coast*	*East Coast*	*South Coast*	*Central*	*Northwest*	*Southwest*
Weighted direct backward linkage (3 sectors)								
$B^{ML} + B^{LL}$	0.6480	0.6645	0.6417	0.7022	0.6664	0.6212	0.5828	0.5804
B^{LL}	0.5670	0.5686	0.5604	0.5875	0.5485	0.5362	0.4542	0.4980
B^{ML}	0.0811	0.0958	0.0813	0.1148	0.1179	0.0851	0.1287	0.0824
Relative interregional direct backward linkage (3 sectors)								
$B^{ML}/(B^{ML} + B^{LL})$	12.51	14.42	12.67	16.34	17.69	13.69	22.08	14.20

Table 6.A.2 Total backward linkages for eight regions, 2000

	Northeast	North Municipalities	North Coast	East Coast	South Coast	Central	Northwest	Southwest
Weighted total backward linkages (3 sectors)								
$\bar{B}^{ML} + \bar{B}^{LL}$	2.6504	2.4371	2.5754	2.6970	2.3043	2.5452	2.3625	2.3261
$\bar{B}^{LL}$	2.2253	1.9641	2.1851	2.1704	1.8128	2.1415	1.8067	1.9541
$\bar{B}^{ML}$	0.4251	0.4731	0.3902	0.5266	0.4915	0.4038	0.5558	0.3720
Relative interregional total backward linkage (3 sectors)								
$\bar{B}^{ML}/(\bar{B}^{ML} + \bar{B}^{LL})$	16.04	19.41	15.15	19.52	21.33	15.86	23.52	15.99

Notes

1. Strictly, the direct purchase coefficient matrix is a part of the input coefficient matrix which also includes the direct primary input coefficient.
2. Strictly, the direct allocation coefficient matrix is a part of the output coefficient matrix, which also includes the direct final-output coefficient.

References

Beyers, W.B. (1976) 'Empirical Identification of Key Sectors: Some Further Evidence', *Environment and Planning A*, 8, 231–6.

Blair, P.D. and R.E. Miller (1990) 'Spatial Linkages in the US Economy', in M. Chatterrji and R.E. Kuenne (eds), *Dynamics and Conflict in Regional Structural Change*, London: Macmillan, pp. 156–79.

Dietzenbacher, E. (1997) 'In Vindication of the Ghosh Model: A Reinterpretation as a Price Model', *Journal of Regional Science*, 37, 629–51.

Dietzenbacher, E. (2002) 'Interregional Multipliers: Looking Backward, Looking Forward', *Regional Studies*, 36(2), 125–36.

Ghosh, A. (1958) 'Input–Output Approach in an Allocation System', *Economica*, 25, 58–64.

Institute of Developing Economies–JETRO (2003) *Multi-regional Input–Output Model for China 2000*, Statistical Data Series No. 86, Chiba: Institute of Developing Economies–JETRO.

Isard, W. (1951) 'Interregional and Regional Input–Output Analysis: A Model of Space Economy', *Review of Economics and Statistics*, 33, 318–28.

Jones, L.P. (1976) 'The Measurement of Hirschmanian Linkages', *Quarterly Journal of Economics*, 90, 323–33.

Liu, Q. (1992) 'Touru Chanchu Moxing Jiegou Fenxi de Mofanhua Wenti' (On the Standardization of Input–Output Model Structure Analysis), in Q. Li (eds), *Dangdai Zhongguo Touru Chanchu Yingyong yu Fazhan (Application and Development of Input–Output Analysis in China)*, Beijing: China Statistics Press, pp. 211–22.

Liu, Q. (1993) *Jingji Xitong Cuihua Fangfa he Moxing (Planning Method and Models for Economic System)*, Beijing: China Statistics Press.

Liu, Q. (2002) 'Shichang Jingji wei Touru Chanchu Moxing Yingyong Tuokai Gengguang Kongjian' (Analysis of Input–Output Coefficient Structure), in X. Xu and Q. Liu (eds), *Zhongguo Touru Chanchu Lilun yu Shijian 2001 (Input–Output Theory and Practice in China 2001)*, Beijing: China Statistics Press, pp. 11–13.

Oosterhaven, J. (1988) 'On the Plausibility of the Supply-driven Input–Output Model', *Journal of Regional Science*, 28(2), 203–17.

Shao, G. and R.E. Miller (1990) 'Demand-side and Supply-side Commodity–Industry Multiregional Input–Output Models and Spatial Linkages in the U.S. Regional Economy', *Economic Systems Research*, 2(3), 385–405.

7

Agglomeration, Intraregional and Interregional Linkages in China

Nobuhiro Okamoto

7.1 Introduction

Today, one of the most important developments in economics is the consideration of its spatial aspects and the revival of new economic geography. This aspect of economics allows us to explain how regional inequalities develop and how they change the siting of production facilities.

Fujita, Krugman and Venables (1999, chapter 15) explained the spread of development from a core industrialized economy to a peripheral undeveloped economy in the following terms:

> We imagine a world economy in which some one region has initially managed to get a self-reinforcing advantage in manufacturing, an advantage that allows it to pay higher wages than other countries. Over time, however, the world's demand for manufactures rises. This increases the level of activity in the manufacturing region, reinforcing the agglomeration and also increasing wages. As this process continues, the wage gap between regions may become too large to be sustainable. It is then profitable for individual firms to set up manufacturing in a second region, which begins to develop self-reinforcing advantages of its own and thus has a surge in wages. Then at a later date, third region goes through the same process, and so on. (Fujita, Krugman and Venables 1999, pp. 263–4)

They recognize that the movement of a manufacturing sector depends upon the factor of wages and linkages among sectors. The wages are given, the linkages among sectors will be important for the movement of industry from the agglomerated region to other regions. Those sectors with few linkages will move rapidly from the region because it is not necessary for them to supply intermediate goods to sectors in this region. In Fujita, Krugman and Venables (1999, p. 274), upstream industry (those with large forward linkages and few backward linkages) move quickly and downstream industry (those with few forward linkages and many backward linkages) move more slowly. Or the sector with few backward and forward linkage move first and, then, the sector with large forward and backward linkage move later.

In this chapter, we will apply this idea to the regional development of China. We measure the linkages in industrial regions such as the East Coast and South Coast in China, and consider the relation between linkage and agglomeration. Linkage is a very important feature of form of agglomeration. We make a particular effort to identify the intraregional and interregional linkage of the sector in the agglomerated region and consider the possibility of change of the agglomeration sites.

The rest of this chapter is organized as follows. In section 7.2, we consider the concept of agglomeration and linkage, and the relationship between them. Section 7.3 presents the changes of production base or agglomeration of industry in China over space and time, and section 7.4 will show the model and the empirical results. Finally we have a summary and conclusion.

7.2 Agglomeration and linkage

In this chapter, we will make frequent use of the terms 'agglomeration' and 'linkage'. 'Agglomeration' is defined as a cumulative process of the geographical concentration of industry. This leads us to consider the following question: why should industrial activity or economic activity be concentrated in a specific location? According to Marshall (1920), externalities are crucial in the formation of economic agglomerations. He identifies three sources of externalities: thick markets for specialized skills of labour; forward and backward linkages of intermediate inputs associated with large local markets; and knowledge spillover. Although the mechanism for the formation of economic agglomeration is a kind of black box, spatial economists have tried to identify its mechanism based on the increasing returns, transportation costs and market demand (Krugman 1991; Fujita, Krugman and Venables 1999; Fujita and Thisse 2002).

Once economic agglomeration has occurred, economies of scale occur and this calls for further agglomeration. This agglomeration yields advantage in a particular location, and this advantage in turn explain its forms of agglomeration – this idea is a vital concept in understanding the spatial unevenness of industry and regional development.

The idea that agglomeration is a self-organizing process, as mentioned above, is very similar to the concept of 'circular and cumulative causation' advanced by Myrdal (1957).

'Linkage' is the same concept as used by Hirschman (1958). That is, backward linkage means that 'every nonprimary economic activity, will induce attempts to supply through domestic production the inputs needed in that activity' (Hirschman 1958, p. 100) or the increase of demand for intermediate goods when the industry produces the final goods. Forward linkage means that 'every activity ... will induce attempts to utilize its outputs as inputs in some new activities' (Hirschman 1958, p. 100) or the increase of supply of intermediate goods when the industry produces new or additional goods. For example, the establishment of an automobile industry in one region induces a demand for iron for the car bodies and engines and many kind of glass as inputs through backward linkage, and it induces the supply of car bodies from the iron industry, engines from the machinery industry and glass for car use from the glass industry as outputs through forward linkage. Thus Hirschman (1958, pp. 116–17) remarked:

> Forward linkage could never occur in pure form. It must always be accompanied by backward linkage, which is the result of the 'pressure of demand'. In other words, the existence or anticipation of demand is a condition for forward linkage effects to manifest themselves.
>
> While forward linkage cannot therefore be regarded as an independent inducement mechanism, it acts as an important and powerful reinforcement to backward linkage.

However, linkage analysis should be considered in terms of both backward and forward linkages since forward linkage is the reverse of backward linkage, though Hirschman regards backward linkage as more important.

In investigating the mechanism of agglomeration, we usually consider a world where increasing returns and transport costs works, but forward and backward linkages are both important because they can create a circular lock-in effect of agglomeration, 'That is, other things being the same, producers want to locate close to their suppliers and to their customers which means that they want to locate close to each other' (Fujita,

Krugman and Venables 1999, p. 345). Thus, linkage itself can be regarded as a force of concentration of industry.

A region where large manufacturing sectors are concentrated can provide a greater variety of intermediate goods, implying lower costs of purchasing the intermediate goods for the production of final goods. This is forward linkage. Conversely, a large final goods sector in manufacturing provides a large local market for intermediate goods, which is backward linkage. The result of these linkages can lead to a process of agglomeration that concentrates manufacturing or particular industries in the region:

> Producers want to choose locations that have good access to large markets and to supplies of goods that they or their workers require. However, a place that for whatever reasons already has a concentration of producers tends to offer a large market and a good supply of inputs and consumer goods. These two advantages correspond precisely to the backward linkages and forward linkages of development theory. Because of these linkages, a spatial concentration of production, once established, may tend to persist, and a small difference in the initial economic size of two otherwise equivalent locations may grow over time. (Fujita, Krugman and Venables 1999, p. 5)

From this argument, we can draw the hypothesis that the place where industries are concentrated leads to the formation of complicated and strong linkages among other industries located in the core region. The linkage structure or the degree of linkage will form the agglomeration in the core region.

7.3 Spatial economy in China

As mentioned in the introduction to this chapter, regional development can be regarded as the movement of the place of industrial agglomeration. Once one region begins the development by historical accident or the advantage of initial conditions (resource endowment, climate, access to international markets, and so on), the agglomeration of industry occurs by its externality and leads to the self-reinforcing concentration of industry in that region.[1] However, more concentration eventually brings diseconomies of agglomeration (an increase in wages, pollution in the city, and so on) in that region. Then some industry moves to the place where labour costs and land is cheaper. But what kinds of sector or industry move first? Fujita, Krugman and Venables (1999) suggest that industry with high levels of labour and few linkages to other sectors move first. If an industry located in the core developed region has strong linkages to other industries in that region, it seems that it will be less likely to move from that place.

Regional development

In recent years, there have been a number of studies of regional development in China and on the economic disparities between Chinese regions. Among the earliest contributions in this field are Tsui (1991) and Lyons (1991), which measures the disparity in the regional economy, and Tsui (1993) and Lee (2000) decomposed the regional disparity into inter-provincial, intra-provincial and urban–rural disparities. Ying (1999) and Akita, Yue and Kawamura (1999) used the Theil index to examine the contents of regional disparities. From the viewpoint of new economic growth theory, Jian, Sachs and Warner (1996), Raiser (1998) and Yao and Zhang (2001) attempt to identify the mechanism of convergence and divergence of regional disparities. However, to date the literature in this field is inconclusive.

Figure 7.1 shows the changes of regional disparity and industrial disparity during two decades in China by utilizing the coefficient of variation (CV) for per capita GDP of the provinces and the Gini coefficient

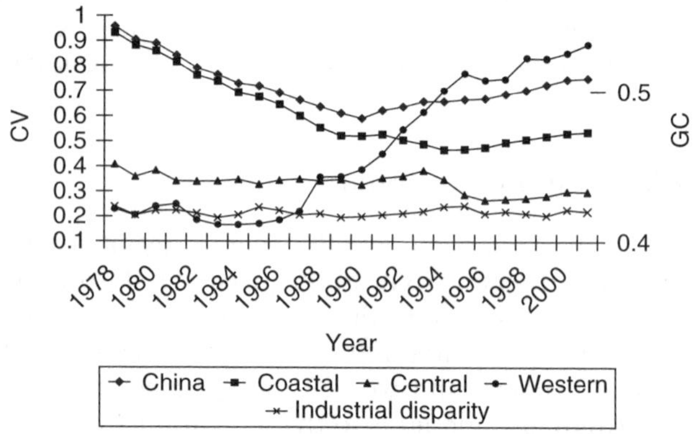

Figure 7.1 Regional and industrial disparity

Notes: Coastal includes the North Municipalities North Coast, East Coast and South Coast regions. Central includes the Northeast and Central regions. The other region is the Western region.

Sources: National Bureau of Statistics (1999), *Comprehensive Statistical Data* and *Materials on 50 years of New China*; China Statistical Press, *China Statistical Yearbook*, various years. The figure for the Gini coefficient of industrial disparity is from Kimura (2003, Table 9.1).

(GC) for gross industrial output value. Industrial disparity here presents inequality of industrial development among regions.[2]

First, the disparities between provinces reduced in the 1980s and rose gradually in the 1990s. The coastal region shows almost the same trend as the whole of China, while the central and western regions remain stable. Yet the disparity within the coastal region is not as wide as that for the whole of China in the 1990s and this implies a widening disparity between the coastal and interior regions. On the other hand, industrial disparity has been increasing during the period under examination.

Table 7.1 presents the growth of real GDP of Chinese provinces during the period 1978–98. The South Coast region, Guangdong and Fujian achieved rapid growth during this period with the spread of the market economy in China while Liaoning, Beijing and Shanghai, which were

Table 7.1 Ratio of provincial to national per capita GDP

	1978	*1998*	*Change in ratio*	*Rank*
Fujian	0.72	1.62	0.90	1
Zhejiang	0.87	1.76	0.89	2
Guangdong	0.97	1.74	0.77	3
Shandong	0.83	1.27	0.44	4
Jiangsu	1.13	1.57	0.44	5
Hebei	0.96	1.02	0.06	11
Guangxi	0.59	0.64	0.05	12
Liaoning	1.79	1.46	−0.33	23
Beijing	3.40	2.89	−0.51	26
Tianjin	3.06	2.32	−0.74	27
Shanghai	6.59	4.42	−2.17	28
Henan	0.61	0.74	0.13	7
Hubei	0.88	0.99	0.11	8
Anhui	0.64	0.72	0.08	10
Hunan	0.75	0.77	0.02	14
Jiangxi	0.73	0.70	−0.03	15
Inner Mongolia	0.84	0.79	−0.05	16
Jilin	1.01	0.93	−0.08	17
Shaanxi	0.77	0.60	−0.17	19
Shanxi	0.96	0.79	−0.17	20
Heilongjiang	1.49	1.18	−0.31	21
Xinjiang	0.83	0.97	0.14	6
Yunnan	0.60	0.68	0.08	9
Sichuan	0.67	0.69	0.02	13
Guizhou	0.46	0.37	−0.09	18
Ningxia	0.98	0.67	−0.31	22
Gansu	0.92	0.54	−0.38	24
Qinghai	1.13	0.68	−0.45	25

Source: Golley (2002, Table 1).

regarded as developed regions under the planned economy regime which prevailed before 1978, have fallen back in comparison. Naughton (2002) also revealed it from rank order of provincial GDP per capita.

Following economic reforms and the open door policy, the South Coast region and the East Coast region has been developing as a result of the introduction of foreign direct investment (FDI) and the market mechanism into the region. Once this industrial agglomeration starts, it leads to a narrowing of the gap between this region and the north region, like Northeast (i.e. Liaoning, Jilin and Heilongjiang heavy industrial areas). This leads to a reduction of the regional disparity between the coastal region and the rest of China. During the 1990s, the rapid growth of the South Coast and East Coast regions continued. Thus, regional disparity in the 1990s is widening while the rest of China has been left behind as a result of the biased development strategy. Once again, before the introduction of economic reforms and the open door policy, the central government was well aware of the historical tendency towards regional disparity in China. When the Communist Party assumed control of the whole of China in the year 1949, production capacity was highly concentrated in the coastal region. The central government made efforts to relocate industry to the interior during its First Five-Year Plan and the construction of the Third Front. The policy at the time focused on the development of heavy and defence-related state-owned industries. In 1978, the Northeast and interior regions were characterized by low levels of light industry and were dominated by heavy-state-owned industry. The economic reforms and open door policy, adopted from 1978, led to the development of the South Coast region. The lack of heavy and state-owned industries in this area resulted in the emergence of light, textile and processing industries, which were much more in line with both regional and national comparative advantage. Furthermore, the advantage of location (near both Hong Kong and Macau), could introduce FDI in light industry,[3] being associated with the increase of labour costs in Hong Kong. The light and processing industry concentrated in that region and also in Guangdong and Fujian have experienced rapid growth. At the end of the 1980s the government policy bias was formalized in a 'Coastal Development Strategy'. Preferential policies were extended from SEZs to other Open Coastal Cities and Economic and Technological Development Zones. As a result, industrial disparity has increased sharply from 1988 and industrial agglomeration in the coastal region could be observed from the end of the 1980s. The East Coast region, like Jiangsu, Shanghai and Zhejiang, also benefited from these preferential policies. Township and village enterprises became a leading sector of development in that region, Shanghai opened Pudong New Area in 1990 and a variety of FDI flowed into this area. With the rapid reform of state-owned enterprises, a variety of businesses have led the development of this region, and major industries started concentrating in East Coast region in the 1990s. This inequality of industrial agglomeration among regions leads to uneven regional development across China.

Industrial agglomeration in China

Many studies about regional development in China have focused on the spatial concentration of industries. After the introduction of economic reforms and the open door policy, a lot of FDI has come into the coastal region because of its easy access to international markets.

Kato (2003, pp. 81–4) calculated the locational Gini coefficients, developed by Krugman (1991), by using employment data from 29 manufacturing sectors in 1988, 1991, 1997 and 2000. He found that the sectors which have been concentrating for this period are: food manufacturing; textiles; clothing; leather and furs; cultural, education and sports articles; paper manufacturing; metal products; machinery; electric equipment and machinery; electronic and telecommunications equipment; and instruments, meters and other measuring equipment. Golley (2002, Table 2) also shows locational Gini coefficients for manufacturing sectors[4] in 1985, 89, 94 and 1997. From this result, we can see that the sectors which experienced increasing degrees of localization are: food, beverages and tobacco; clothing; leather and furs; paper manufacturing; plastic manufactures; medical and pharmaceutical; metal products; machinery; electric equipment; and electronic and telecommunication equipment. Kimura (2003) presents the Gini coefficient as an industrial disparity index for machinery sectors in 1994 and 2000, then suggests that all of machinery sectors, like metal products; ordinary machinery; special equipment; transport equipment, electric machinery; electronic and telecommunication equipment; and metres and other measuring equipment, is concentrating geographically.

Since both the selected industry and the reference year was different, the results obtained are not directly comparable. However, we can conclude that machinery sectors, especially electric machinery, and electric and telecommunication equipment are now highly agglomerated in China and that industrial agglomeration is occurring at many sectors and at the provincial level. It remains to be seen where that agglomeration is taking place.

Table 7.2 shows the production share of high-ranking provinces by sector for the year 2000. If we assume that the sector in which top four

Table 7.2 Production share of high-ranking provinces by sector, 2000

	Share of top 4 provinces	*First (%)*	*Second (%)*	*Third (%)*	*Fourth (%)*
Coal mining	54.0	Shaanxi (20.3)	Shandong (15.4)	Henan (12.9)	Hebei (5.4)
Crude petroleum and natural gas	57.3	Heilongjiang (20.9)	Tianjin (16.2)	Shandong (11.5)	Liaoning (8.7)
Metal mining	62.8	Hebei (34.2)	Hubei (12.1)	Liaoning (8.3)	Shandong (8.2)
Food processing	43.9	Guangdong (15.0)	Shandong (13.0)	Hebei (8.3)	Henan (7.6)
Beverage	41.3	Guangdong (11.5)	Zhejiang (11.1)	Shandong (9.9)	Jiangsu (8.8)
Tobacco	40.2	Yunnan (17.0)	Guizhou (8.5)	Henan (7.7)	Hubei (7.0)
Textile	67.8	Jiangsu (23.3)	Zhejiang (22.9)	Shandong (11.9)	Guangdong (9.7)
Paper products	56.7	Guangdong (16.8)	Shandong (14.8)	Jiangsu (12.6)	Zhejiang (12.5)
Petroleum processing	44.7	Liaoning (12.6)	Jiangsu (11.9)	Guangdong (11.1)	Shanghai (9.1)
Chemical	47.1	Jiangsu (17.1)	Guandong (11.7)	Shandong (9.4)	Zhejiang (8.9)
Medicine and pharmacy	38.8	Zhejiang (11.7)	Guangdong (9.8)	Shanghai (9.0)	Hebei (8.3)
Chemical fibre	66.1	Zhejiang (26.8)	Jiangsu (21.4)	Shandong (11.2)	Fujian (6.7)
Non-metallic ore processing	46.4	Guangdong (14.8)	Shandong (13.1)	Jiangsu (11.2)	Henan (7.3)
Metal ore processing	44.3	Shanghai (12.5)	Jiangsu (12.2)	Hebei (10.5)	Liaoning (9.1)
Metal products	61.1	Guangdong (24.7)	Jiangsu (15.3)	Zhejiang (12.2)	Shanghai (8.9)
Machinery	56.6	Jiangsu (19.1)	Shandong (14.4)	Zhejiang (13.5)	Shanghai (9.6)
Transport machinery	42.3	Shanghai (14.6)	Jilin (10.9)	Guangdong (8.5)	Hubei (8.3)
Electric machinery	64.2	Guangdong (27.4)	Jiangsu (12.4)	Zhejiang (12.2)	Shandong (12.2)
Electric and telecommunication equipment	65.5	Guangdong (34.5)	Shanhai (12.9)	Beijing (10.0)	Jiangsu (8.1)
Meters and other measuring equipment	70.6	Guangdong (39.5)	Jiangsu (12.1)	Shanghai (9.5)	Zhejiang (9.5)
Electricity, steam and hot water	35.9	Jiangsu (11.4)	Shandong (8.4)	Guangdong (8.3)	Hubei (7.8)

Note: Provinces highlighted indicate the Coastal region.

Source: *2001 China Industry Economy Statistical Yearbook*.

provinces' production share exceeds 60 per cent is regarded as an instance of agglomeration, then we can observe that metal mining, textiles, chemical fibres, metal products, electric machinery, electronic and telecommunication equipment and meters and other measuring equipment are all agglomerated sectors.

If we analyse the results by sector, we can see that the mining sector of coal, crude petroleum and metal is agglomerated in the northern parts of China, especially Shaanxi (coal mining), Heilongjiang (crude petroleum) and Hebei (metal mining). The food, beverages and tobacco sector exhibits less agglomeration while textile and paper products are likely to be agglomerated. Guangdong, Jiangsu and Zhejiang have concentrations of light industry, while the tobacco industry is concentrated to some extent in Yunnan and Guizhou. In Jiangsu, Shanghai, Zhejiang and Guangdong agglomeration is occurring in the chemical fibre sector. The metal and non-metal processing sector is dispersed over the nation; however, the machinery sector, and in particular electric equipment and electronic and telecommunication equipment, is highly agglomerated while such patterns are not so evident in respect of machinery and transport equipment. In China, light and heavy industry, for example, food, beverage, chemical, metallurgy, machinery sector, etc., was decentralized over the nation during the era of the planned economy. Under Mao's Third Front Development, regions were encouraged to be self-reliant, and each region established all kinds of industries. However, textile and electric industry has been developing as an export industry, so these industries have been concentrated in the coastal region. It has to be mentioned that electric machinery and related equipment industry is highly agglomerated in Guangdong, and that Jiangsu and Zhejiang also have high production shares in most sectors. In summary, the South Coast and East Coast regions remain locations where a high degree of industrial agglomeration is taking place.

7.4 Analysis of the regional agglomeration and linkage structure

Methodology

As we mentioned, in this chapter agglomeration is viewed as the geographic concentration of economic activity. In the place where economic activity is concentrated, industries, or units of economic activity, purchase intermediate goods in this area and also sell intermediate goods to other industries in the same area, and then these industries reap the economic benefits of location. This advantage leads to the formation of linkages between the industries. Linkage is viewed as the relation between the industries, since the industries are closely tied together such that changes in activities of one industry affect other industries' activities. In this regard, it is likely that linkages between the sectors will be strong in those sites where industry is agglomerated.

In order to clarify the linkage structure in the region where industrial agglomeration has occurred, the Multi-regional Input–Output Model for China (CMRIO) (Institute of Developing Economies 2003) will be utilized. As mentioned before, CMRIO divides the country into eight regions: North East, North Municipalities, North Coast, East Coast, South Coast, Central, Northwest and Southwest. If we use most detail sector classification for this analysis, there are 30 sectors and eight regions in our model. Since there are 240 sectors (30 sectors times eight regions), we will focus on machinery industries in our analysis because: (1) machinery industries has been concentrated in the East Coast and the South Coast regions; (2) machinery industries seems to be main beneficiaries of advantage of agglomeration; (3) machinery industries would play an important role in the development of manufacturing sector.

Before we proceed to the methodology for studying linkages in the agglomerated region, we will investigate some of the literature on linkage analysis. There are several ways in which linkages may actually be measured. The traditional method is the column sum of input coefficients for backward linkage and the row sum of output coefficients for forward linkage (Chenery and Watanabe 1958), and the column sum of the Leontief inverse for backward linkage and the row sum for forward linkages (Rasmussen 1956). However, the measurement of forward linkages has been widely discussed, and in particular the row sum of the Leontief inverse, used as a forward linkage measure, has been continuously criticized. Jones (1976) and Beyers (1976) suggested that the row sum of the Ghosh inverse (Ghosh 1958) might be used as the forward linkage. Following recent discussion on the interpretation of the Ghosh model (Oosterhaven 1988; Dietzenbacher 1997), it is currently felt by some that the row sum of the Ghosh inverse might be regarded as an appropriate forward linkage measure (see, for example, Miller 1998; Dietzenbacher 2002).

However, the linkage measure, discussed above, can be used to answer the interesting question of how much an industry was linked to ALL other sectors in the national economy or regional economy and in other regions in the context of an interregional input–output model. However, it does not answer the question of which industries are most closely tied together. Simpson and Tsukui (1965) suggest employing a triangularization of the input–output matrix, which shows the hierarchical structure of industry. Ozaki (1980) proposed a Unit structure, in which the relation of intermediate transactions between sectors might be presented in terms of the increase of one unit of production of final goods. Defourny and Torbecke (1984) suggest a structural path analysis, clarifying the influence path between the sectors. Finally, a qualitative input–output analysis, which identifies the strong ties between sectors, was proposed by Holub, Schnabl and Tappeiner (1985) and Schnabl (2001).

It is very important to investigate both the degree and the structure of industrial linkage at the same time. Even though industry has a small linkage index, if it has a complex structure, then it is not straightforward to relocate the industry. Similarly, it appears that industry can easily relocate when its linkage is big, but the linkage structure is comparatively simple. Therefore we have to consider both the degree and the structure of industrial linkage in the region.

If we consider the agglomeration, size of production and transaction, then the focus should be on the absolute size of the transaction. It seems to be larger than that in non-industrial agglomeration area. Firstly, the linkage will be defined directly on the regional and interregional intermediate transaction matrices.

Here, let the intermediate transaction matrix of CMRIO Z, intraregional and interregional transaction sub-matrices be composed as follows:

$$Z = \begin{bmatrix} Z^{11} & Z^{12} & \cdots & Z^{18} \\ Z^{21} & Z^{22} & \cdots & Z^{28} \\ \vdots & \vdots & \ddots & \vdots \\ Z^{81} & Z^{82} & \cdots & Z^{88} \end{bmatrix}$$

Z^{RS}: Transaction matrix of region R to region S (R,S $= 1, 2, \ldots, 8$)

The intermediate transaction shows the volume of transactions between sectors and regions. It is natural that this volume will be larger in the area where the industries are concentrated. But not all of the transactions might be important in terms of the absolute volume. Thus, relative large transactions and linkages should be determined based on the volume of transaction. The selection of large transactions and linkages will be as follows:

$$z_{ij}^{rs} > \alpha$$

where z_{ij}^{rs} is the intermediate sales from sector i in region r to sector j in region s.

This methodology is very similar to the cluster analysis conducted by Oosterhaven, Eding and Stelder (2001). However, the linkage structure selected in the above methodology shows us the absolute volume of intermediate transaction and sales direction. It is not the linkage structure from the viewpoint of the technological relationship between sectors. The technological relationship is shown in the input–output coefficient matrix, indicating the amount of inputs per unit of production and the amount of outputs per unit of production. Usually the input–output coefficient gives the additional amount of input or outputs from a sector that is required for one additional unit of gross output in another sector – this is also termed direct backward or forward linkage. However, these measures do not contain the indirect effects of linkage. If one unit of production increases, the increase of intermediate inputs requires additional inputs to meet this additional increase of production; this process will continue until the amount of final demand increase is satisfied. These effects are included in inverse matrix,[5] thus, we use the Leontief inverse matrix for backward linkage and the Ghosh inverse matrix for forward linkage. In addition, we have one further advantage, since the linkage measure can also be extended to spatial context since we use the interregional input–output model.[6]

The direct and indirect linkage structure is also determined using the same method as the absolute volume of intermediate transaction. Therefore:

$$b_{ij}^{rs} > \beta \text{ for backward linkage}$$

$$g_{ij}^{rs} > \theta \text{ for forward linkage}$$

Here, $b_{ij}^{rs} = \{B - I\}$ and $g_{ij}^{rs} = \{G - I\}$. B denotes the Leontief inverse, G the Ghosh inverse and I the unit matrix. Inverse matrix is regarded as a multiplier, to be measured for its response to an economic stimulus in the case of an increase of one unit towards final demand. One unit increase of final demand induces the one unit production on this sector. Associated with this increase in output is an own sector increase in output. This initial effect of stimulating the economy is shown in the unit matrix of

Table 7.3 Selection of important transactions

	Number of cells
Absolutely larger than average	4,715
Absolutely 10× larger than average	1,042
Absolutely 100× larger than average	84
Absolutely 200× larger than average	32

Total number = 57,600.

inverse calculation. Thus, in order to get rid of this initial effect from this stimulus process, the unit matrix is deducted from the inverse matrix, which presents the direct and indirect linkages between the sectors.[7]

In our view, the first linkage presents the absolute volume of transactions between sectors and the second linkage is more important as it directly considers at the strength, direction (forward and backward) and direct and indirect effects of the linkages, not taking into account the size of the sectors.

The choice of filter value α, β and θ is arbitrary. To determine which linkages are significant enough to be considered, the filter value should be selected carefully. The filter value will be set as low as possible, subject to the requirement that the information may still be summarized. In this study, a 240-sector matrix will be used as units in observation. Table 7.3 shows the changes in the number of selected transactions. The choice of filter value is based on the average transaction amount – that is, $\alpha = i'(B - I)i/n^2$, where n is the number of sectors, and i is a unit vector of the appropriate size (i.e. a summation vector of $1, 1, 1, \ldots 1$). Out of a total of 57,600 (240 × 240), about 53,000 cells are smaller than the average cell and only about 4,700 cells are larger than the average cell. Furthermore, only about 1,000 cells are 10 times larger than average. Hence, there are many small cells and relatively few large cells that are really important. In this essay, we consider the filter value to be 10 times average.

Empirical results

Basic features of the regions studied

Some basic statistics on the regions studied are shown in Table 7.4. The share in national total for each items are also shown in the table. Since the Central region includes many provinces, the amount and share of population, GDP and employment seems bigger; however, the per capita GDP is not high and it is said that the central region is not so well

Table 7.4 Basic statistics about the regions studied, 2001

		Northeast (%)	North Municipalities (%)	North Coast (%)	East Coast (%)	South Coast (%)	Central (%)	Northwest (%)	South West (%)	China
Area	(1000 km^2)	789 (8)	29 (0)	345 (4)	211 (2)	333 (3)	1,028 (11)	4,267 (44)	2,603 (27)	9,605
Population	(million)	1,070 (8)	239 (2)	1,574 (12)	1,358 (11)	1,202 (9)	3,591 (28)	1,157 (9)	2,487 (20)	12,678
Employment	(million)	452 (7)	104 (2)	805 (13)	703 (11)	598 (9)	1,814 (29)	519 (8)	1,310 (21)	6,305
Per capita GDP	(yuan)	1,002	1,963	954	1,562	1,285	600	566	470	843
GDP	(billion yuan)	1,072 (10)	469 (4)	1,502 (14)	2,121 (20)	1,545 (14)	2,153 (20)	655 (6)	1,170 (11)	10,686
Primary	(billion yuan)	136 (9)	17 (1)	227 (15)	186 (12)	186 (12)	418 (27)	123 (8)	260 (17)	1,554
Secondary	(billion yuan)	532 (11)	194 (4)	742 (15)	1,072 (22)	736 (15)	967 (20)	225 (5)	461 (9)	4,929
Tertiary	(billion yuan)	394 (10)	258 (6)	532 (13)	863 (21)	623 (15)	768 (19)	249 (6)	449 (11)	4,137
Fixed capital investment	(billion yuan)	309 (9)	222 (6)	470 (13)	766 (21)	487 (13)	639 (18)	283 (8)	433 (12)	3,609
Export	(billion US$)	14.5 (5)	16.8 (6)	21.9 (8)	80.5 (30)	111.3 (42)	11.2 (4)	4.0 (2)	5.9 (2)	266
Import	(billion US$)	14.2 (6)	29.1 (12)	16.2 (7)	71.6 (29)	94.8 (39)	8.0 (3)	5.0 (2)	4.8 (2)	244
Foreign direct investment	(billion US$)	3.2 (7)	3.9 (8)	4.2 (9)	13.4 (29)	16.3 (35)	3.4 (7)	0.6 (1)	1.3 (3)	46

Source: 2002 China Statistical Yearbook.

developed, even though both statistics show big figures. In contrast, the North Municipalities region shows the highest per capita GDP in China because this is an urban economy with a fairly small population and GDP. The East Coast and South Coast regions are the growth centres, recording the two highest GDPs per capita, foreign trade and foreign direct investment. On the other hand, the western part of China is a regional economic problem area, because regardless of the vast area of the Northwest region and the large population in the Southwest region, economic development is relatively slow. From these basic statistics, we can see that the coastal region is the developed area with the agglomeration of economic activity, and that the interior region is the underdeveloped part of China.

Linkage structure of absolute transaction

As we have seen, the South Coast and the East Coast are reinforcing the agglomeration of industry and have developed very rapidly in recent years. Guangdong, Jiangsu and Zhejiang have the most diverse industrial sectors. This unevenness of industrial agglomeration determined the economic development of the region in China. Because of this, the South Coast and East Coast will be the subjects of this linkage analysis in order to identify the contents of the agglomeration in this region.

The number of selected transaction cells of our CMRIO is shown in Table 7.5. This illustrates the concentration of important transactions among both sectors and regions. The highest numbers of intraregional transactions is recorded for the East Coast, the second most for the Central region and the third for the South Coast. Since the Central region includes many relatively large provinces, the most important transactions among sectors within regions take place in both the East Coast and the South Coast. With regard to interregional transactions, Central supplies intermediate goods mainly to the North Coast, East Coast and South Coast, while the East Coast demands intermediate goods primarily from the North Coast, the South Coast and the Central regions. As a result, interregional transactions seems to be occurring mainly between the East Coast and Central regions and between the East Coast and South Coast regions. The East Coast is the growth point where industrial and interregional transaction is concentrated, and the South Coast is also the area with the highest levels of intermediate transactions within the region.

Figure 7.2, which shows the results of our linkage analysis, shows the absolute size as well as the direction of the intermediate sales for machinery sectors in East Coast and South Coast.

Table 7.5 Number of selected transactions between regions

	Northeast	*North Municipalities*	*North Coast*	*East Coast*	*South Coast*	*Central*	*Northwest*	*Southwest*	*Total Supply*	*Supply to ROC*
Northeast	110	0	1	1	0	0	0	0	112	2
North Municipalities	0	51	0	0	0	0	0	0	51	0
North Coast	1	1	138	14	1	4	1	0	160	22
Central Coast	1	0	1	185	13	6	0	1	207	22
South Coast	0	0	0	9	148	0	0	1	158	10
Central	0	0	4	18	11	174	0	0	207	33
Northwest	0	0	1	1	0	3	49	0	54	5
Southwest	0	0	0	1	1	0	0	91	93	2
Total demand	112	52	145	229	174	187	50	93		
Demand from ROC	2	1	7	44	26	13	1	2		

Note: ROC is the rest of China.

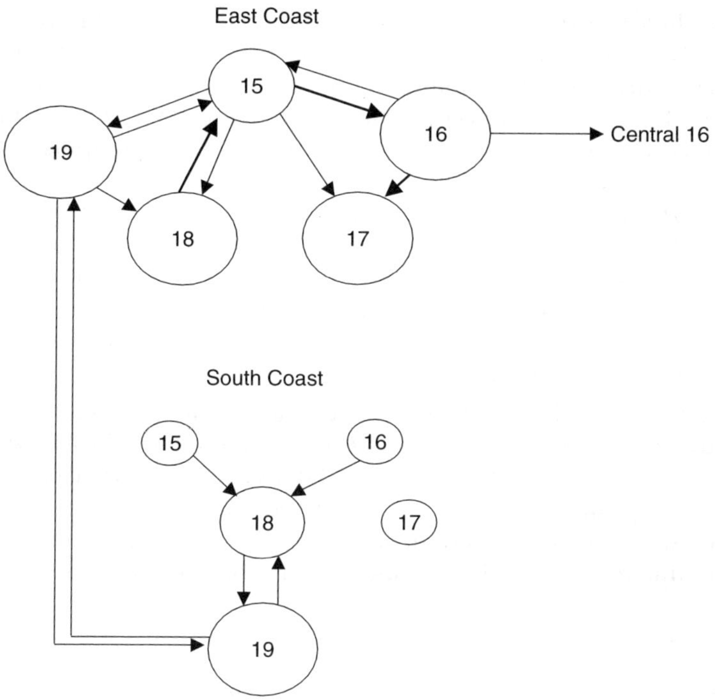

Figure 7.2 Linkages structure of machinery sectors (absolute transactions) in the East Coast and the South Coast regions

Notes

Small size circle displays the amount of transactions with the size between 10 times average and 50 times average.

Medium-sized circle for the amount being between 50 times and 100 times average.

Large-sized circle for the amount being larger than 100 times average.

In the East Coast region, metal products (15) sell intermediate goods to all other machinery sectors, while machinery sector (16), electric equipment (18) and electronic and telecommunication equipment (19) also sell goods to the metal products sector (15). The machinery sector (16) supplies intermediate goods to the transportation equipment sector (17), and the electronic and telecommunication equipment sector (19) provides electronic parts to the electrical equipment sector (18). With regard to the interregional transactions, machinery sector (16) sells to the same sector in the Central region, and the electronic and telecommunication sector (19) in the East Coast region has a relatively large transaction with the same sector (19) in the South Coast region.

The linkage structure in the South Coast is noticeably different from that observed in the East Coast. The largest transaction in this region is electronic and telecommunication equipment (19) itself and this forms the dominant linkage structure in this region: that is, metal products (15) and machinery sector (16) go to electric equipment (18), then the intermediate transaction occurred between electric equipment (18) and electronic and telecommunication equipment (19). With regard to interregional transactions, electronic and telecommunication equipment (19) provides the intermediate goods to the same sector in both the East Coast and South Coast regions.

Forward and backward linkage structure

The structure of the direct and indirect linkage both forward and backward is also removed from the inverse matrix according to the filter value, which is 10 times the average. Figure 7.3 shows the forward and backward linkage structure in both the East Coast and the South Coast regions.

The structure of backward linkages is noticeably different to the forward linkage structure. In the East Coast region, machinery sector (16)

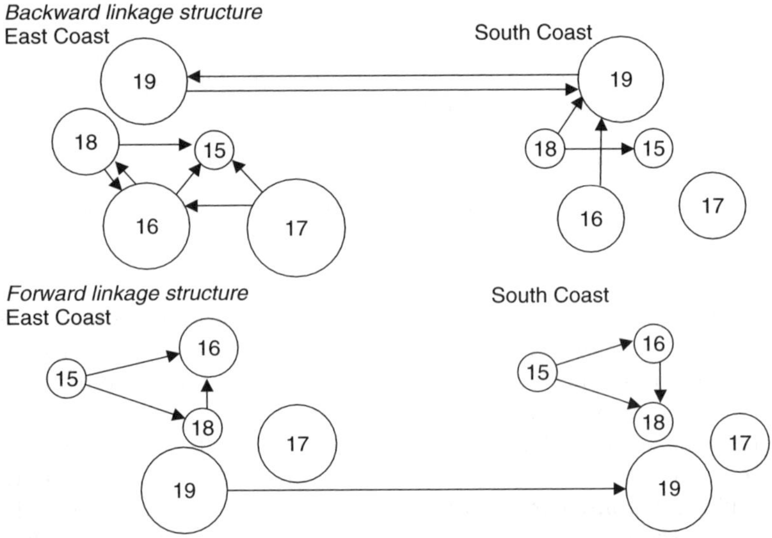

Figure 7.3 Backward and forward linkages structure in the East Coast and South Coast regions

Notes: Size of circle represents the value of the intra-sectoral linkage, the smallest with smaller than 20 times average, the second smallest is between 20 and 30 times average, the second largest between 30 and 40 times average and the largest with larger than 50 times average.

is linked to both metal products (15) and electric equipment (18), transport equipment (17) stimulates the production of the metal products (15) and machinery sectors (16), and electric equipment (18) goes to the metal products (15) and machinery (16) sectors. Electronic and telecommunication equipment (19) has a strong self-linkage and interregional linkage with the same sector (19) in the South Coast. In the structure of the South Coast, machinery sector (16) and electric equipment (18) promote the production increase of electronic and telecommunication equipment (19), and then this sector is linked with the same sector in East Coast through interregional transactions. However, the forward linkage structure in both the East Coast and South Coast regions is relatively similar, except that the linkage direction between machinery sector (16) and electric equipment (18), electric equipment (18) in South Coast is a downstream sector compared to that sector in the East Coast region. And the electronic and telecommunication equipment sector (19) has only one-way linkage in terms of forward direction. It seems to us that the machinery sector (16) exists for the sake of providing intermediate goods to the electric equipment sector (19) in the South Coast region. And the electronic and telecommunication equipment sector (19) in the East Coast region seems to be the upstream position so that it supplies the intermediate goods to this sector in the South Coast region.

Intraregional and interregional linkages

The linkage measure used is based on the Leontief inverse and the Ghosh inverse. These are calculated from the interregional model, so we had to break down intraregional and interregional linkage so that we could distinguish the strength of linkage within the region from the strength of linkage with the outside region.

Therefore, we define it as follows:

Intraregional linkage:

$$\sum_i b_{ij}^{rr} - 1 \text{ for backward and } \sum_j g_{ij}^{rr} - 1 \text{ for forward}$$

Interregional linkage:

$$\sum_r \sum_i b_{ij}^{rs} - \left(\sum_i b_{ij}^{rr} - 1 \right) \text{ for backward and}$$

$$\sum_s \sum_j g_{ij}^{rs} - \left(\sum_j g_{ij}^{rr} - 1 \right) \text{ for forward}$$

A way of presenting results on both forward and backward linkages is to normalize by dividing by the average of a particular measure over all sectors, for example, if this index of backward linkage, divided by the average of all sectors, is larger than one, this sector is considered to be more dependent than the average regional sector on inputs from sectors within the region. Similarly, if it is smaller than one, then this sector is considered to be less dependent on the regional inputs. Forward linkage measure could be similarly normalized. The normalized measure of both forward and backward linkages is presented in Figure 7.4. Those sectors that appear in the upper right of the figure can then be regarded as relatively most important in the regional economy since they are above average on both forward and backward linkage measures. But we have to be careful that the measure in intraregional linkage means the dependency on the *regional* economy while that in interregional linkage shows the relative dependency on the *outside* economy.

Figure 7.4 shows us the intraregional forward and backward linkages, normalized by the average of all of the sectors in each region. As a whole, in intraregional and interregional linkage, the backward linkage of all of machinery industry in both regions is larger than the average for each region, and the forward linkage is smaller than the regional average. It can be said that the machinery industry stimulates production in other

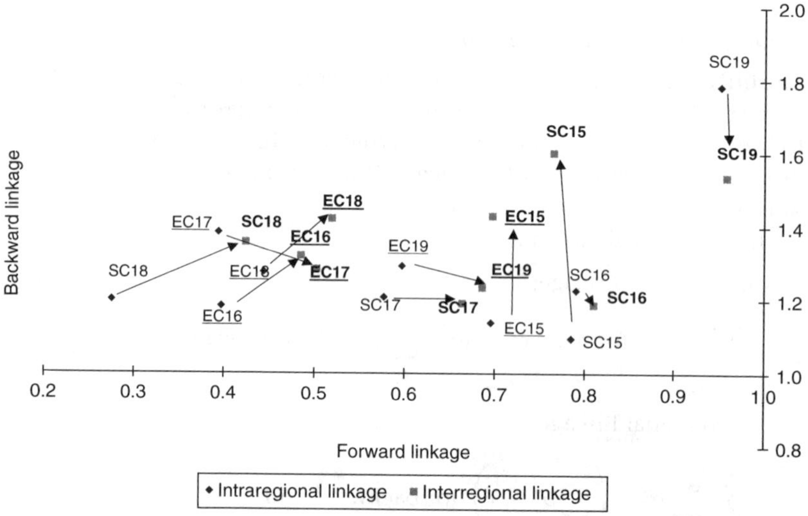

Figure 7.4 Intraregional and interregional linkages in the East Coast and South Coast regions

industries both inside and outside the region when final demand is generated, so this industry is a sector that supplies relatively more final goods than the intermediate goods to other sectors in the region. The electronic and telecommunications in the sector South Coast region (SC19) is the highest both backward and forward linkage and intraregional backward linkage of this sector is higher than the interregional one; this implies that locating in the South Coast region might be preferable for this sector. On the other hand, metal products in both regions (SC15, CC15) provide higher interregional than intraregional backward linkages with the stable forward linkages, and with the small changes of backward linkage, interregional forward linkage in transport equipment in South Coast (SC17) is higher than intraregional one, and also, for machinery sector in East Coast (EC16), electric equipment in both region (EC18, SC18), both interregional forward and backward linkage is larger than intraregional linkage. Needless to say, this intraregional linkage does not include the initial linkage effect and it is normalized by the intraregional linkage average in the region. From our results, we cannot say that most sectors – except SC19 – can easily be moved to other regions, but the intermediate demand from these industries spreads to other regions, like spillover effects, since these industries locate in a developed region.

7.5 Concluding remarks

In this final section, we summarize the discussion and empirical results through this analysis.

With the development of the degree of openness, the South Coast region has started economic growth by introducing FDI into the region. The South Coast region was regarded as an underdeveloped region during the era of the planned economy, then its rapid growth leads to a narrowing of the gap of interregional inequality between the South Coast and the North Coast region, which seemed to be a relatively developed region. In 1990, Shanghai established the Pudong New Area and opened its domestic market; this led to the development of FDI and domestic industry through the reform of enterprises. This development in a part of the coastal region led to a new inequality of development in China in the 1990s.

In focusing on industrial agglomeration, this uneven regional development could be reinterpreted as a change of production sites from the South Coast to the East Coast. The rapid growth in Guangdong and Fujian has been brought about by light and processing industries, and the agglomeration of process and assembling industry in electronics has been particularly remarkable. Although Shanghai and its peripheral region has had a lot of state-owned enterprises and various kind of sectors,[8] established during the era of the planned economy, they have been developing by reforming old management systems and old production technology through market competition with foreign enterprises. In other words, the East Coast has experienced rapid growth of its industrial base, which was established during the planned economy.

This chapter attempted to understand the context of an agglomeration sector by explaining the degree and structure of linkage among machinery sectors. From our analysis, the following conclusions can be drawn:

(1) Though the linkage structure in the South Coast region is relatively simpler than that in the East Coast region, the electronic and telecommunication sector is a core of linkage in the region, and, furthermore, the intraregional linkage of this sector is quite strong within the region. Thus, it is not possible for this sector to move to other places. However, this sector might be a growth engine to stimulate the development of other regions since the spillover effect on other regions is larger in terms of interregional linkage.

(2) The East Coast region has advantages for development since it includes several sectors which were established during the planned economy period. On this advantage, linkage structure among machinery industries has been forming meaningfully in terms of direction, volume and technical relation. So this region might be the major beneficiary of economies of agglomeration, as Marshall (1920) mentioned. The lock-in effect in this place seems to be working strongly. Therefore, the East Coast region would continue to enjoy these external economies of agglomeration.

To the present day, it is not obvious that agglomeration sites will move to other places as envisaged by Fujita, Krugman and Venables (1999) in their examination of machinery industries, yet there would be spillover effects from the East Coast and South Coast regions to the Central region in China. Perhaps even more important, is the recognition that the machinery industries are agglomerating in a relatively complicated structure in the East Coast region and the electronic industry is a core growth sector with strong intraregional linkages in the South Coast region.

In the end, we have to remark that there are a lot of areas which should be considered by future research. Because of data limitation, only one interregional input–output model was used in this chapter. Linkage analysis, undertaken in this chapter, needs to be extended to cover a longer time period in order to trace more accurately the dynamic pattern of agglomeration and the dispersal of machinery industries. Beyond machinery industries, a similar analysis could be applied to other sectors in order to cover the whole idea of industrial agglomeration.

Notes

1. Therefore, uneven spatial development is explained as the unevenness of the spatial agglomeration of production or economic activity.
2. For more detail, see Kimura (2003).
3. Most of the FDI flowed into the Special Economic Zones (SEZ), and three of the four SEZs were established in Guangdong province.
4. The Gross Value of Industrial Output is used.
5. This is a direct and indirect backward linkage. Forward linkage is interpreted in a similar manner.
6. Spatial linkage measures had been developed by Shao and Miller (1990) and Blair and Miller (1990).
7. See West and Jensen (1980) for the initial effect, both direct and indirect. Basically we follow their definition. Furthermore, the intraregional multiplier in these inverses for forward and backward linkages contains the interregional feedback effect (Miller 1966), which is the effect to be stimulated through interregional linkage, from the repercussion occurring in the original location. This seems to be an effect that is obtained from the location of industry in that place. Thus, we do not consider interregional feedback effects here.
8. The policy of establishing township and village enterprises had also brought about the development of Jiangsu and Zhejiang in the 1980s.

References

Akita, T., K. Kawamura and B. Xie (1999) 'The Regional Economic Development of Northeast China an Interregional Input–Output Analysis', *The Journal of Econometric Study of Northeast Asia*, 1(1), 53–78.

Akita, T., N. Yue and K. Kawamura (1999) 'Inter-Provincial Income Inequality in China, 1985–1997: an Inequality Decomposition Analysis', *The Journal of Econometric Study of Northeast Asia*, 1(2), 55–71.

Beyers, W.B. (1976) 'Empirical Identification of Key Sectors: Some Further Evidence', *Environment and Planning A*, 8, 231–6.

Blair, P.D. and R.E. Miller (1990) 'Spatial Linkages in the US Economy', in M. Chatterji and R.E. Kuenne (eds), *Dynamics and Conflict in Regional Structural Change*, London: Macmillan, pp. 156–79.

Chenery, H.B. and T. Watanabe (1958) 'International Comparisons of the Structure of Production', *Econometrica*, 26, 487–521.

Defourny, J. and E. Torbecke (1984) 'Structural Path Analysis and Multiplier Decomposition Within a Social Accounting Matrix Framework', *The Economic Journal*, 94, 111–36.

Dietzenbacher, E. (1997) 'In Vindication of the Ghosh Model: A Reinterpretation as a Price Model', *Journal of Regional Science*, 37, 629–51.

Dietzenbacher, E. (2002) 'Interregional Multipliers: Looking Backward, Looking Forward', *Regional Studies*, 36(2), 125–36.

Fujita, M., P. Krugman and A.J. Venables (1999) *The Spatial Economy: Cities, Regions, and International Trade*, Cambridge, MA: The MIT Press.

Fujita, M. and J.C. Thisse (2002) *Economics of Agglomeration*, Cambridge, UK: Cambridge University Press.

Ghosh, A. (1958) 'Input–Output Approach in an Allocation System', *Economica*, 25, 58–64.

Golley, J. (2002) 'Regional Patterns of Industrial Development during China's Economic Transition', *Economic of Transition*, 10(3), 761–801.

Hirschman, A. (1958) *The Strategy of Economic Development*, New Haven: Yale University Press.

Holub, H.W., H. Schnabl and G. Tappeiner (1985) 'Qualitative Input–Output Analysis with Variable Filter', reprinted in H.D. Kurz, E. Dietzenbacher and C. Lager (eds) (1998) *Input–Output Analysis: Volume III*, The International Library of Critical Writings in Economics, 141(2), 282–300.

Institute of Developing Economies–JETRO (2003) *Multi-Regional Input–Output Model for China 2000*, Statistical Data Series no. 86, Chiba: Institute of Developing Economies–JETRO.

Jian, T.L., J. Sachs and A. Warner (1996) 'Trends in Regional Inequality in China', *National Bureau of Economic Research Working Paper:* 5412.

Jones, L.P. (1976) 'The Measurement of Hirschmanian Linkages', *Quarterly Journal of Economics*, 90, 323–33.

Kato, H. (2003) *Chikino Hatten: Sevies Gendai Chugoku Keizai 6 (Regional Development: Sevies Contemporary Chinese Economy 6)*, Nagoya: Nagoya University Press.

Kimura, K. (2003) 'China's Regional Industrial Disparity From the Viewpoint of Industrial Agglomeration', in M. Kagami and M. Tsuji (eds), *Industrial Agglomeration: Facts and Lessons for Developing Countries*, Chiba: Institute of Developing Economies–JETRO.

Krugman, P. (1991) *Geography and Trade*, Cambridge, MA: The MIT Press.

Lee, J. (2000) 'Changes in the Source of China's Regional Inequality', *China Economic Review*, 11(3), 232–45.

Lyons, T. (1991) 'Interprovincial Disparities in China: Output and Consumption, 1952–1987', *Economic Development and Cultural Change*, 39, 471–506.

Marshall, A. (1920) *Principles of Economics*, London: Macmillan Press.

Miller, R.E. (1966) 'Interregional Feedback Effects in Input–Output Models: Some Preliminary Results', *Papers of Regional Science Association*, 17, 105–25.

Miller, R.E. (1998) 'Regional and Interregional Input–Output Analysis', chapter 3 in W. Isard, I.J. Azis, M.P. Drennan, R.E. Miller, S. Saltzman and E. Thorbecke (eds), *Methods of Interregional and Regional Analysis*, Aldershot: Ashgate, pp. 41–134.

Myrdal, G. (1957) *Economic Theory and Underdeveloped Regions*, London: Gerald Duckworth.

Naughton, B. (2002) 'Provincial Economic Growth in China: Causes and Consequences of Regional Differentiation', in M.F. Renard (eds), *China and its*

Regions: Economic Growth and Reform in Chinese Provinces, Massachusetts: Edward Elgar, pp. 57–86.

Oosterhaven, J. (1988) 'On the Plausibility of the Supply-driven Input–Output Model', *Journal of Regional Science*, 28, 203–17.

Oosterhaven, J., G.J. Eding and D. Stelder (2001) 'Clusters, Linkages and Interregional Spillovers: Methodology and Policy Implications for the Two Dutch Mainports and the Rural North', *Regional Studies*, 35(9), 809–22.

Ozaki, I. (1980) 'Keizai Hatten no Kozo Bunseki (3)' (Structural Analysis on Economic Development (3)), *Mita Gakkai Zasshi* (Mita Journal of Economics), 73(5), 66–94.

Raiser, M. (1998) 'Subsidizing Inequality: Economic Reforms, Fiscal Transfers and Convergence Across Chinese Provinces', *Journal of Development Studies*, 34(3), 1–26.

Rasmussen, P.N. (1956) *Studies in Intersectoral Relations*, Amsterdam: North-Holland.

Schnabl, H. (2001) 'Structural Development of Germany, Japan and the USA, 1980–1990: A Qualitative Analysis Using Minimal Flow Analysis', in M.L. Lahr and E. Dietzenbacher (eds), *Input–Output Analysis: Frontiers and Extensions*, New York: Palgrave, pp. 245–69.

Shao, G. and R.E. Miller (1990) 'Demand-side and Supply-side Commodity–industry Multiregional Input–Output Models and Spatial Linkages in the US Regional Economy', *Economic Systems Research*, 2(3), 385–405.

Simpson, D. and J. Tsukui (1965) 'The Fundamental Structure of Input–Output Tables, an International Comparison', *Review of Economics and Statistics*, XLVIII(4), 434–46.

Tsui, K.Y. (1991) 'China's Regional Inequality, 1952–1985', *Journal of Comparative Economics*, 15, 1–21.

Tsui, K.Y. (1993) 'Decomposition of China's Regional Inequalities', *Journal of Comparative Economics*, 17, 600–27.

West, G.R. and R.C. Jensen (1980) 'Some Reflections on Input–Output Multipliers', *Annals of Regional Science*, 14(2), 77–89.

Yao, S. and Z.Y. Zhang (2001) 'Regional Growth in China Under Economic Reforms', *Journal of Development Studies*, 38(2), 167–86.

Ying, L.G. (1999) 'China's Changing Regional Disparities During the Reform Period', *Economic Geography*, 75(1), 59–70.

8

The Magnitude of Interregional Input–Output Spillover Effects in China and its Implications for China's Uneven Regional Growth

*Shiro Hioki**

8.1 Introduction

China has experienced rapid economic expansion since the central government began to introduce economic reforms in 1978. However, the fruits of this growth have not been shared equally by regions. The coastal regions[1] have absorbed most of the FDI to Mainland China and have achieved export-oriented industrialization rapidly, partly because they enjoyed favourable geographical and historical conditions during the initial stages of the development, partly because they also enjoyed preferential regional development policies during the 1980s. By contrast, the inland region has experienced a relatively slow rate of growth. From the standpoints of social and political stability, the Chinese government became concerned with the growing regional disparities and launched new regional development policies which have given preferential treatment to inland regions since the middle of the 1990s (Hu, Wang and Kang 1995; Onishi 2001).

Widening regional disparities have led to a considerable degree of academic interest both in China and abroad. To date, a large number of studies have investigated the problem. Among these, some researchers have paid full attention to the interactions between the 'core' and the

* I would like to express my appreciation to Nobuhiro Okamoto and Satoshi Inomata of the Institute of Developing Economies for the entire translation of this chapter, except for sections 8.1 and 8.2. I remain solely responsible for any errors and omissions in this chapter.

'periphery' during the process of widening regional disparities (Chen 1998; Ying 2000; Brun Combes and Renard 2002). Using a variety of methods, these studies measured the spillover effects from the coastal region to the inland regions. Such attempts are essential when we attempt to evaluate the validity of China's past regional development policies in terms of regional disparities.

The object of this chapter is to briefly analyse the magnitude and the structure of interregional input–output spillover effects[2] from China's coastal regions to its inland regions, using our interregional table. It will be seen from this chapter that the spillover effects are one of the main factors constituting the trickle-down effects in the classic literature of development economics. I will then try to interpret the results and draw some conclusions that will be useful in trying to understand China's regional disparities and to evaluate China's past and present regional policies. Even though the spillover effects through input–output linkages are only one aspect of the trickle-down effects, and this drawback may somewhat limit the validity of this research, the analysis should address some additional and complementary issues that previous researches have not offered.

Section 8.2 takes a brief look at previous studies on China's regional disparities and explains some theoretical backgrounds that this chapter is based on. Section 8.3 measures the output induced by final demand and the simple output multiplier. In the concluding section, I interpret the results and draw some implications.

8.2 Background to the study

A review of previous studies on China's regional disparities

Let us begin by giving an overview of the previous studies on China's regional disparities. To date, a large number of academic works have been devoted to this subject. For the sake of convenience, I will divide them into three groups as follows: (1) those which measure the tendency of China's regional disparities using descriptive statistics; (2) those which examine the tendency towards convergence in regional growth; (3) those which identify the factors or mechanisms generating regional disparities.

As Nakagane (1996) indicated, regional disparities can be measured in various ways using different indices and/or different kinds of data. Different results can be derived from the different ways of measurement, but there are some facts that many of the studies commonly confirmed. They are: (1) that the overall inter-provincial income disparities decreased during the 1980s and have begun to increase since the beginning of the 1990s; and (2) that the interregional income disparities (i.e. the between-set disparities such as the coastal–inland disparities) have been increasing continuously during the reform period (Chen 1996; Ying 1999); (3) Compared with the inter-provincial and interregional disparities, the intra-provincial disparities explains a more substantial part of the overall inter-county (or inter-prefecture) income disparities (Tsui 1993; Akita 2001); and (4) a substantial part of the disparities is explained by the rural–urban gap (Tsui 1993; World Bank 1997; Kanbur and Zhuang 1999).

Considering recent growth theory, a large number of studies have examined whether or not China's provincial per capita income has exhibited a tendency towards convergence. Most of them have concluded that conditional convergence could be observed in the regional growth which occurred during the reform period (Chen and Fleisher 1996; Jian, Sachs and Warner 1996; Wei et al. 1997; Chen and Feng 2000; Demurger 2001; Yao and Zhang 2001; Brun, Combes and Renard 2002; Cai et al. 2002). However, we should note the fact that coastal and inland regions have been forming 'groups' respectively, within which provincial income exhibits a tendency towards convergence, but between which there is a widening income inequality (Chen and Fleisher 1996; Yao and Zhang 2001; Zhang, Liu and Yao 2001).

Previous studies have reported a variety of factors which have affected regional growth and generated regional inequalities. These include: (1) initial conditions as regards the geographical, locational and environmental aspects of regions (Nakagane 1996; Bao et al. 2002); (2) the level of infrastructure development (Demurger 2001); (3) the level of physical and human capital accumulation (Chen and Fleisher 1996); (4) the level of liberalization or privatization (Chen and Feng 2000); (5) the level of openness to international mashets (Kato 1997); (6) policy or institutional factors such as a set of preferential policies favouring coastal region (Kato 1997), weakening fiscal re-distributional ability during the market reform (Wang and Hu 1999), urban-biased fiscal and monetary policies (Yang 2002), and remaining restrictions on the interregional labour mobility (Cai et al. 2002); and (7) agglomeration factors (Fujita and Hu 2001; Chen 2002; Kimura 2003).

One major drawback of neoclassical growth theory, on which most of the convergence literature listed above was based, is that the theory is unlikely to explain the *widening* regional inequalities that have occurred during the market reforms. It may provide an explanation of *decreasing*, but not of *increasing* regional inequalities, which China has been suffering from recently (Fujita and Hu 2001). One possible way to elucidate the mechanism of increasing disparities is to introduce the notion of the agglomeration economy into the model. To date, only two studies have employed models in which agglomeration has played a key role. Golley (2002) employed the circular or cumulative causation theory (Myrdal 1957) to explain the gap in provincial industrial development during the reform period. Alternative theory useful to understand China's experience is the economics of agglomeration. Fujita and Hu (2001) argued that the agglomeration of industries in the coastal regions would generate the growing coastal–inland regional disparities under some conditions which are characteristic of those to be found in China (i.e., the absence of interregional labour migration and the existence of agricultural surplus labour in the coastal regions).

Settings of this study

Following Golley (2002), in this study I employ the inverted-U hypothesis in order to analyse China's regional disparities. Myrdal (1957), Hirschman (1958), and especially Williamson (1965), argued that the relation between regional disparities and economic growth should take an inverted-U shape – that is, regional disparities increase during the early stages of growth, then stabilize and finally begins to fall during the mature period of growth. Once favourable factors such as good geographical conditions, good resource endowments or 'historical accidents' enable a region to grow more rapidly than other regions, the high growth rates of the region tend to sustain or fortify themselves because of the positive externalities of the agglomeration process. The high-growth region (hereafter termed the 'north') will flourish, absorbing the productive factors from the relatively stagnant regions (hereafter the 'south') surrounding the north. The economic expansion of the north may generate two kinds of effects on the south. One is the effect favouring economic growth in the south (the spread effects discussed by Myrdal or the trickle-down effects discussed by Hirschman, hereafter 'trickle-down effects'). The expansion of the northern economy may generate an increase in northern purchases and investments in the south. The technological diffusion from the north may become the driving force behind southern economic progress. The second effect is that producing negative influences on southern growth (the backwash effects by Myrdal or the polarization effects by Hirschman, hereafter the polarization effects). The south may lose their most productive labour or their entrepreneurs through selective migration. Capital may flow from the south to the north because the growing north has many investment opportunities of which return to capital tends to be higher and more certain. Such adverse flows of capital may deprive the south of potential for growth. Free trade may have destructive effects on southern infant industries because they cannot match the productivity levels of northern industries. The inverted-U shape is explained as a result of the interactions between the trickle-down effects and the polarization effects during the period of national economic growth. In general, northern economic growth, in its early stages, may generate more polarization effects than trickle-down effects on the south because most of the factors of production in the south tend to be absorbed by the northern economy. Therefore, regional differentials may increase during the early stage of economic growth. However, further expansion of the northern economy tends to bring about increasing negative externalities (i.e., higher congestion costs, rent, etc.) and this will gear up for the reallocation of the northern economic activities to the south. Therefore, along with maturing economic growth, the trickle-down effects will gradually overcome the polarization effects. Furthermore, central governments will also increase public investments to the south because of growing political concerns for egalitarianism. All of these changes will finally lead to a decrease in regional inequalities. This is a summary of the inverted-U curve story.

I chose the inverted-U hypothesis as the framework of this study because it pays full attention to trickle-down effects, which were seen as of considerable importance in China's past policy debates. In order fully to appreciate this point, we should briefly review China's regional development policies during the post-Mao period.

One of the main goals of Maoist regional development strategy was to promote egalitarianism between the regions. From the time of the first five-year plan (1953–7), the Chinese government had allocated vast amounts of investment to the interior regions. This tendency reached its peak during the Construction of the Third Front (*Sanxian jianshe*), which aimed to construct heavy industrial bases, mainly in the southwestern and northwestern regions. Even though such redistributive policies favouring the inland region were implemented, regional income inequalities continued to widen during this period. The failure of the Maoist strategy to seek regional equity at the expense of efficiency might lead to the policy shift in the post-Mao China (Yang 1990).

Regional development strategy has been transformed drastically since the beginning of the economic reforms under Deng. The most important goal of regional development strategy was changed from equality or a balance between regions to the pursuit of efficiency and high levels of growth. A certain degree of increase in regional disparity was tolerated.

The theoretical backbone behind this policy transformation is the 'Step Ladder Theory' or 'Gradient Theory' (*Tidu lilun*). According to this theory, China is usually divided into three regions: the eastern, the central, and the western regions. Because the eastern region is far superior to the other regions in terms of infrastructure, physical and human capital, and geographical location, it is in the best position to accelerate its economic growth. Concentrating scarce investment resources in the eastern region is believed to generate much quicker aggregate growth than spreading the resources across many regions. Therefore, it is necessary to allow the eastern region to take off first. After the take-off of the eastern region, the other inland regions should be allowed to take off step by step, using the trickle-down effects from adjacent developed regions (Yang 1990; Fan 1995; Wang and Hu 1999). In essence, the 'Step Ladder' theory can be regarded as a Chinese version of the uneven development strategy proposed by Hirschman.

Against this theoretical background, China's regional policies after 1978 have drastically changed in order to be coastally-oriented. Four Special Economic Zones (SEZs) were established first in the southeastern part of China at the beginning of the economic reform era. Later on regions such as the Pearl River Delta were designated as Coastal Economic Development Zones (CEDZs) and 14 coastal cities were opened to foreign investment. In these coastal open cities, Economic and Technology Development Zones (ETDZs) were established to absorb the high-technology and management skills of foreign firms. It was only during the 1990s that the inland cities were finally opened to foreign investment. In addition, the coastal regions enjoyed a wide range of preferential policies. Guangdong and Fujian were allowed to enjoy various privileges (e.g. greater discretion for regional governments to attract foreign investment, adopting a favourable fiscal contracting system and so on) by central government. The SEZs, CEDZs, and ETDZs have been granted various preferential treatments such as tax reduction for firms located in these regions (Yang 1990; Ohashi 2003). The share of public investment allocated to the coastal regions by central government has also increased since the reforms (Kato 1997). An incremental opening-up policy in which the inland region lagged far behind the coastal region and preferential policies favouring the coastal region are regarded as major reasons generating widening regional disparities during the reform period.

From the above statement, we can appreciate that the anticipated existence of trickle-down effects from the coastal region to the inland region played an important role in the arguments justifying the coastally oriented regional development policies during the early phase of the reforms. The question now arises: how strong have the trickle-down effects actually been? Seeking an answer to this question is essential to understanding China's past regional development policies in terms of regional disparities. And answering the question will also be helpful in trying to understand some of the implications of China's current regional development policies.

As important as the question is, there have been some previous studies tackling it. Chen (1998) was the first to measure the interregional spillover effects induced by the demands of coastal regions. Using different statistical methods, both Ying (2000) and Brun, Combes and Renard (2002) have also tested the existence of spillover effects[3] from coastal regions to inland regions.

The purpose of this study is to briefly analyse the magnitude and the structure of the interregional spillover effects from coastal regions to inland regions in China, using our interregional input–output table. In this chapter, the input–output spillover effects are regarded as one of the main factors contributing to the trickle-down effects in the inverted-U hypothesis. Other aspects, such as effects like capital dispersion across the country, and technological diffusion, are outside our present concerns. Therefore the trickle-down effects are not analysed fully and this may be one drawback of the study. But we can identify the volume of the trickle-down effects through interregional trade activity using input–output analysis, which previous studies have not considered. This will also provide some insights into the demand-side determinants of China's regional growth.

In the next section, I calculate some basic indicators to analyse the spillover effects. The data source used for this analysis is IDE-JETRO (2003)[4]. The time period of the analysis is 1997. In the following analysis, China will be divided into three regions: eastern, central and western regions. The eastern region comprises four sub-regions: the North Coast, the North Municipalities, the East Coast, and the South Coast. The central region is composed of two sub-regions, namely the Central and Northeast regions. Finally, the western region is also composed of two sub-regions, the Southwest and Northwest regions. The basic statistical index of each region is listed in Table 8.1.

8.3 Empirical results

For the purposes of measuring spillover effects, I calculate the output induced by each region's final demand (hereafter, the impact of final demand on output) and the simple output multipliers. The impact of

Table 8.1 Main statistical indexes of each region, 1997

	Northeast	*North Coast*	*North Municipalities*	*East Coast*	*South Coast*	*Central*	*Northwest*	*Southwest*
GDP (100 million yuan)	7,738	3,045	10,604	14,679	10,726	16,388	4,644	9,002
Primary industry	17	5	18	12	16	25	25	28
Secondary industry	49	45	48	52	47	45	41	40
Tertiary industry	34	50	33	36	37	31	35	32
Export (10 thousand dollars)	1,285,998	1,101,460	1,435,541	3,994,614	8,775,621	901,981	269,317	505,132
Population (10 thousand people)	10,428	2,117	15,335	12,876	10,975	34,981	11,133	24,052
Area (square km)	787,200	28,105	3,444,700	210,746	333,300	1,027,300	4,275,600	2,507,400
Per capita GDP (yuan)	7,420	14,389	6,915	11,400	9,773	4,685	4,172	3,743
Population desity (person/square km)	132	753	445	611	329	341	26	96

Source: National Bureau of Statistics (1999) *Comprehensive Statistical Data and Materials on 50 years of New China*, China Statistical Press.

final demand on output is to measure a repercussion effect, in which the magnitude and the structure of final demand in each region are taken into account. We can calculate it for a given set of F and E in equation (1). The simple output multiplier of a sector is derived by column summation of the sector in the Leontief inverse matrix. This shows the level of impact on production induced by one unit increase in final demand (Miller and Blair, 1985):

$$X = \left[I - \left(I - \hat{M}\right)A\right]^{-1}\left[\left(I - \hat{M}\right)F + E\right] \tag{8.1}$$

where X denotes total output, I denotes the unit matrix, $\hat{M}$ the diagonal matrix of import ratios, A the technical coefficient matrix, F the final demand and E the exports.

The measurement of impact of final demand on output[5]

Table 8.2 gives a summary of the measured impact of final demand on output. From the table, we can find that, averaged across the eight districts, 76.9 per cent of the total impact is domestically absorbed and 23.1 per cent goes to the other regions. That is, on average, almost three-quarters of the total impact induced by a region's final demand stays within the region and less than a quarter spills over to other regions, a finding which seems to show the immaturity of interregional linkages in China.

Table 8.3 shows the level of spillover effects from coastal regions to inland regions. Eighty-eight per cent of the impact of the final demand of coastal regions stays within the coastal regions, while only 12.0 per cent leaks to inland regions (of which 9.1 per cent goes to the central region and 2.9 per cent to the western region). This result is perhaps in line with what we might expect considering the country's scale and regional location. However, the spillover effect from the coastal regions to the inland regions, is still surprisingly small.

In contrast, let us consider the spillover effects from coastal regions from the point of view of the inland regions. Although the spillover effects are small in terms of interregional linkage, they may nevertheless have a considerable impact on the scale of an inland region's economic activities. To see this, the share of total output induced by each region's final demand is shown in Table 8.4. From this, we discover that the share of the output induced by the coastal final demands in each region's total output is as follows: 9.1 per cent in the Northeast, 20.5 per cent in the Central, 12.0 per cent in the Northwest and 10.3 per cent in

Table 8.2 Impact of final demand in a region on the output of each region (unit: %)

Final demand / *Output*	*Northeast*	*North Municipalities*	*North Coast*	*East Coast*	*South Coast*	*Central*	*Northwest*	*Southwest*
Northeast	78.4	2.1	2.3	1.4	0.9	1.1	2.2	0.8
North Municipalities	1.1	74.9	1.4	0.7	0.7	0.7	1.5	0.5
North Coast	6.6	10.0	80.7	6.9	4.4	6.7	7.8	4.1
East Coast	4.9	3.2	6.1	76.8	7.1	6.6	6.0	4.5
South Coast	2.0	1.3	1.5	3.1	74.6	2.6	3.0	3.9
Central	5.0	6.0	5.8	8.7	8.1	78.9	9.5	7.0
Northwest	1.2	1.8	1.4	1.1	0.9	1.7	66.9	1.7
Southwest	0.9	0.7	0.8	1.4	3.2	1.7	3.1	77.6
Total (%)	100.0	100.0	100.0	100.0	100.0	100.0	100.0	100.0
Total (10 million yuan)	20,993.6	9,164.1	26,332.7	46,435.8	36,922.1	40,011.5	12,764.0	22,093.1

Source: Calculated from Institute of Developing Economies–JETRO (2003).

Table 8.3 Impact of final demand in coastal regions on the output of each region (unit: 10 million yuan, and percentage)

To Coastal Regions	104,533.7	88.0
to North Municipalities	7,826.1	6.6
to North Coast	27,002.0	22.7
to East Coast	40,191.5	33.8
to South Coast	29,514.0	24.8
To Central Regions	10,868.2	9.1
to Northeast	1,740.9	1.5
to Central	9,127.3	7.7
To Western Regions	3,452.9	2.9
to Northwest	1,348.0	1.1
to Southwest	2,104.9	1.8
Total	118,854.7	100.0

Source: As Table 8.1.

the Southwest respectively. This result indicates that coastal regions have considerable impacts on the production activity of the central region,[6] while other inland regions experience only a limited impact from coastal regions.

These impact analyses show that the spillover effect from coastal regions to inland regions, and especially to the western region, is of limited importance at present. Of course, we cannot draw any specific conclusions from this result without a careful comparison with the experiences of other countries. But from this result, we may get the impression that the spillover effects are not large enough to convince us that the growth of coastal regions should assure the sustainable development of inland regions (especially that of the western region).

The measurement of the output multiplier

Table 8.5 shows the output multiplier of each region (an average of 17 sectors). From the table, we can draw the following conclusions:

(1) The share of an interregional output multiplier from the coastal regions to the inland region in terms of an overall multiplier is 10.4 per cent (an average of four coastal regions) and that to the western region is 2.6 per cent. The magnitude of interregional output multiplier to the western region is 0.065 on average (which means that 65 RMB of production is induced in the western region by 1,000

Table 8.4 Impact of the final demand in each region on the output of a region (unit: %)

Final demand / *Output*	*Northeast*	*North Municipalities*	*North Coast*	*East Coast*	*South Coast*	*Central*	*Northwest*	*Southwest*	*Total*	*Total (10 million yuan)*
Northeast	86.3	1.0	3.1	3.3	1.7	2.2	1.4	0.9	100.0	19,083.9
North Municipalities	2.7	79.5	4.2	4.0	3.0	3.1	2.3	1.2	100.0	8,631.1
North Coast	4.2	2.8	64.5	9.7	5.0	8.1	3.0	2.7	100.0	32,959.8
East Coast	2.2	0.6	3.5	78.1	5.8	5.8	1.7	2.2	100.0	45,631.8
South Coast	1.3	0.4	1.3	4.5	85.6	3.2	1.2	2.7	100.0	32,195.2
Central	2.3	1.2	3.4	9.1	6.7	71.0	2.7	3.5	100.0	44,504.7
Northwest	2.2	1.5	3.2	4.4	3.0	6.2	76.3	3.3	100.0	11,187.7
Southwest	0.9	0.3	1.0	3.1	5.7	3.4	1.9	83.5	100.0	20,522.6

Source: As Table 8.1.

Table 8.5 Output multiplier of each region

Region	*Total*[a]	*Inside Region*[b]	*Outside Region*[c]	*Coast*[d]	*Inland*[e]	*Central Region*[f]	*Central*[g]	*Northeast*[h]	*Western Region*[I]	*Northwest*[j]	*Southwest*[k]
Northeast	2.693	2.233	0.460	0.307	0.153	0.107	0.107	—	0.046	0.027	0.019
North	2.373	1.900	0.473	0.268	0.205	0.156	0.117	0.039	0.049	0.036	0.013
Municipalities											
North Coast	2.682	2.252	0.430	0.187	0.243	0.190	0.129	0.061	0.053	0.036	0.018
East Coast	2.694	2.115	0.578	0.260	0.319	0.256	0.221	0.035	0.062	0.028	0.035
South Coast	2.359	1.814	0.545	0.256	0.289	0.195	0.175	0.020	0.093	0.020	0.073
Central	2.688	2.220	0.468	0.355	0.113	0.026	—	0.026	0.087	0.049	0.038
Northwest	2.444	1.821	0.624	0.339	0.285	0.225	0.181	0.044	0.059	—	0.059
Southwest	2.552	2.100	0.453	0.258	0.194	0.157	0.140	0.018	0.037	0.037	—

Note: The figure is the average of 17 sectors in each region. a = b + c, c = d + e, e = f + I, f = g + h, I = j + k.

Source: As Table 8.1.

RMB of additional final demand in the coastal regions), indicating that spillover effects to the western region is rather limited,

(2) The overall output multiplier of the East Coast is the largest, and an interregional output multiplier to the inland regions (especially that to the central region) is also the largest. These findings mean that the East Coast plays an important role in the development of inland regions in terms of spillover effects,

(3) The North Municipalities and the North Coast regions also have a large overall output multiplier, yet their interregional output multiplier to inland region is not very impressive. Rather, the North Coast region has a large intraregional output multiplier and thus shows a tendency to absorb its spillover effects internally,

(4) The region South Coast has the smallest overall output multiplier of all of the coastal regions. Considering the presence of industrial agglomeration in the Pearl River Delta, this might appear to be a rather surprising result. It is explained by the fact that relatively large amounts of imports are induced by the processing trade prevailing in the region. The multiplier of the South Coast naturally gets smaller than those of other regions if we remove the effect of imports when we compute them. What is important about the South Coast is that it has the second largest interregional output multiplier, behind the East Coast region. Furthermore if we consider its interregional effect in relation to the western region, then the figure becomes even larger than that of the East Coast region. Especially, almost 80 per cent (0.073) of the interregional output multiplier from the South Coast to the western region goes to the Southwest, indicating the presence of a relatively large spillover effect from the South Coast to the Southwest.

Considering these findings about the spillover effects to inland regions, we can conclude that among coastal regions, the East Coast and the South Coast play the role of 'Growth Poles'.[7] This conclusion ties in with the results of Chen (1998) and Ying (2000), both of whom found that Guangdong had a fairly strong spillover effect to the surrounding regions. They identified Guangdong as a 'growth pole' or 'core' and this corresponds to our identification of the South Coast as a growth pole. However, our conclusion differs from Ying (2000) in some important aspects: (1) we identified two growth poles, the East Coast and the South Coast regions, while Ying identified only one core (Guangdong); (2) Ying insisted that Guangdong had a polarization effect on its surrounding hinterland in the central region (i.e., Hunan and Jiangxi). The former difference may be explained by the fact that Ying analyzed the

1978–94 period, during which the high growth rates recorded in the Yangtze River Delta, especially Shanghai, had just taken place, while the later difference, however, is left to further investigation.

The Central region has the third largest output multiplier, behind the East Coast and the Northeast region. The overall output multiplier and interregional output multiplier to inland regions of Northeast are larger than Central, yet most of the interregional effect to inland regions goes to the Central region. In contrast, the Central has some characteristics which are listed below: (1) It has a relatively large interregional output multiplier to coastal regions; (2) among the interregional output multiplier to all inland regions, that to the western region is relatively high (for example, the one to the Northwest is the highest of all of the eight regions). Central, along with the South Coast region, plays an important role in terms of the spillover effects to the western region.

Next, let us turn to a sectorial comparison of the interregional output multipliers. Table 8.6 shows the top five sectors in terms of the magnitude of the interregional output multiplier to inland regions. These include Metal Products, Wooden Products, Non-metal Mineral Products, Machinery sectors (Machinery and Equipment, Electric Machinery and Transportation Equipment), Construction and Electricity, Gas and Water Supply.[8] This indicates the possibility that an increase in the export demands for the machinery sectors in the coastal regions could spread spillover effects to the inland regions. However, it should be pointed out that the range of the effects is rather limited. For example, among interregional output multipliers to inland regions the one to the Central region generally earns a large magnitude, with 57.1 per cent (average of sectors) for the North Municipalities, 53.0 per cent for the North Coast region, 69.4 per cent for the East Coast region and 32.4 per cent for the South Coast. In contrast, the multipliers to the western region was relatively low, except for 32.4 per cent for the South Coast.

Finally, those sectors which have the largest interregional output multiplier from the Central region to other inland regions are: metal products, machinery, transport equipment, electric machinery and chemical products (see Table 8.7). Comparing with the interregional output multiplier from the coastal regions, the machinery industry exhibits a relatively large effect. This indicates that spillover effects from the Central region play a key role in developing machinery industries in the western region.

Table 8.6 Top five sectors with the largest interregional output multiplier from coastal regions to inland regions

North Municipalities		*North Coast*		*East Coast*		*South Coast*	
Sector	*Multiplier*	*Sector*	*Multiplier*	*Sector*	*Multiplier*	*Sector*	*Multiplier*
Metal	0.333	Metal	0.367	Metal	0.550	Metal	0.512
Construction	0.297	Wooden products	0.315	Electricity, gas, water	0.428	Construction	0.383
Food	0.296	Electric machinery	0.308	Machinery	0.407	Wooden products	0.380
Non-metal mineral products	0.267	Construction	0.298	Construction	0.399	Electricity, gas, water	0.357
Wooden products	0.261	Transport equipment	0.292	Transport equipment	0.392	Non-metal mineral products	0.335
Average of all sectors	0.205	Average of all sectors	0.243	Average of all sectors	0.319	Average of all sectors	0.289

Source: As Table 8.1.

Table 8.7 Top five sectors with the largest interregional output multiplier from Central to other inland regions

Sector	*Multiplier*
Metal	0.193
Machinery	0.182
Transport equipment	0.180
Electric machinery	0.176
Chemical products	0.145
Average of all sectors	0.113

Source: As Table 8.1.

8.4 Conclusion

The trickle-down effects analysed in this chapter are limited to the interregional input–output spillover effects; other aspects of the trickle-down effects are outside our scope. Furthermore, an international comparison would be necessary for reaching any proper conclusions. Given these caveats, however, we can still draw some implications from our findings.

Trickle-down effects and regional disparities

Whether in terms of the impact of final demand on output or the simple output multiplier, we can obtain a similar picture about the interregional effects. About 10 per cent of the total repercussion effects induced by the coastal final demand goes to inland regions. Among them, the greater part goes to the central regions, especially to the Central region. On average in terms of sectors, about 20 per cent of total output in the Central region is induced by the final demands of the coastal regions. In some sectors such as mining and metal industry, up to 40 per cent of total output is induced by the coastal demands. From these facts, we can conclude that the Central region receives relatively large amount of spillover effects from coastal regions.[9] Evidence on the regional growth rate also seems to support the conclusion. Average annual growth rate of the central region during the period 1992–7 (e.g. from the Southern Tour Lectures of Deng Xiaoping to the time point being analysed) is 12.6 per cent, which is much higher than that of other inland regions (10.1% in the Southwest, 9.4% in the Northeast, and 8.5% in the Northwest).

Based on the 'Step Ladder' Theory, China's regional development strategy during the 1980s had an obvious tendency to favour the coastal regions. However, since the 1990s it has shifted to become more inland-oriented. An early focus on the new policy was the development of the Pudong New Districts in Shanghai. Following this, several cities near the Yangtze River and the capital cities of inland provinces were also opened up to foreign investments. Some ETDZs and High Technology Development Zones were established in several cities such as Wuhan. The development of Sanxia (Three Gorges) also started around this time. China launched the 'T-Letter Development Strategy', which aimed to spread growth from the coastal regions to the inland regions across the Yangtze River (Maruyama 1993; Kato 2003). Relatively strong spillover effects from the East Coast to the Central region imply that such a regional development strategy has actually started to work to a certain extent.[10]

Another important implication is that two regions identified as growth poles in the above analysis, East Coast and South Coast, are both located in the southern part of China. Though it is not large in magnitude, the mechanism transmitting trickle-down effects from the East Coast region to the Central region or from the South Coast to the Central and Southwest regions has been gradually formed. By contrast, in the northern part of China, the North Municipalities region has very few interregional output multipliers to the inland region, their spillover effect being limited solely to the coastal region. North Coast has the largest interregional output multiplier to Northeast. Therefore the North Coast ought to have become a growth pole for the Northeast region (see Table 8.5). Nevertheless, most of the total production in the Northeast region is induced by its own final demand of itself, rather than by that of the North Coast (Table 8.4). The Northeast region has a self-sufficient input–output structure. In addition, it has long suffered from problems arising from the dominance of state-owned heavy industries in the region. From this viewpoint, it might be said that the regional disparity problems in China need to be reconsidered from a *north–south*, and not solely from a coastal–inland perspective.[11]

Implications for regional development strategy

The spillover effects from coastal regions to western regions are only around 2–3 per cent and only about 10 per cent of the total output in the western regions is induced by coastal final demands (Table 8.4). This explains that spillover effects from the coastal regions to the western regions are very small and that reducing the regional disparities between them only through such small spillovers is very difficult. Brun, Combes and Renard (2002) found that a certain amount of spillover effects are transmitted from the eastern region to the central region, but that none are transmitted from the eastern region to the western region. Our conclusion is basically the same as theirs, although different methods are utilized.

Bearing this point in mind, we can evaluate the ongoing Western Region Development Strategy as a suitable and timely scheme for the balanced growth of regions within China. Because spillover effects from the coastal regions are unlikely to be significant, the formation of a strong industrial base within the western region is essential to acceleration of western growth.[12] Furthermore, several wide-scale infrastructure-building projects[13] in the strategy will undoubtedly strengthen spatial linkages between the western region and other regions and will improve investment conditions, all of which developments will lead to future increases in the spillover effects from the coastal regions.

However, this is a tentative evaluation. Because an overall evaluation of the policy should be made not only from an interregional input–output perspective, but also from other perspectives such as its effectiveness in inviting industry from outside regions. Since this point is related to other approaches on trickle-down effects, which have not been investigated in this chapter, it remains to be addressed in the future.

With regard to the policy of Western Region Development, there are some interesting findings to be observed in the spillover effects from the central to the western region. Besides considerable spillover effects to the western region, the effects from the Central to the western region are relatively large in relation to machinery industries, compared with the effects from the coastal region to the western region (see Table 8.6). Therefore, for the purpose of developing machinery industries in the western region, it may be effective to fully utilize the spillover effects from the Central region.

Finally, I would like to point out the limitation of the research in this chapter. Firstly, there are only eight regions in Multi-regional Input–Output Model for China. This regional definition might be seen as a restriction when attempting to understand interregional linkage structures. Any future work should pay careful attention to the classification of the Chinese regions. Secondly, I have made only primitive analyses by using an interregional input–output model, however, a coastal–central–western linkage structure might be identified clearly if a variety of structural analytical methods are applied. This is also left for future investigation. Finally, other aspects of the trickle-down effects will also be left for further investigation.

Notes

1. According to China's usual dichotomy of regions, the coastal region includes 11 provincial administrative districts (i.e. province, autonomous region, and municipality under central administration, hereafter 'province'). Those are Liaoning, Beijing, Tianjin, Shandong, Jiangsu, Shanghai, Zhejiang, Fujian, Guangdong, Hainan and Guangxi. The inland region includes 18 other provinces. There is also a trichotomy of regions in which all provinces are divided into three regions, namely, eastern region, central region and western region. The eastern region is interchangeably used with the coastal region. The central region includes Heilongjiang, Jilin, Inner Mongolia, Henan, Anhui, Hubei, Hunan, Jiangxi. The western region is composed of other provinces. But in the Western Region Development Strategy, which began in 2000, the western region is designated to include Guangxi and Neimenggu. In this chapter, I follow the latter definition of the western region. Note that in this chapter Liaoning is included in the central region because of the limitations of the data.
2. In this chapter, the (interregional input–output) spillover effects mean the impacts in one region that cause changes in another region just through interregional input–output linkages (Miller and Blair 1985, p. 121). Note that spillover effects *through technological and pecuniary externalities* are outside our concerns in this chapter.
3. Note that the definitions of the spillover effects in their papers are not same as that of this chapter. In Ying (2000), the definition of the term is same as the trickle-down effects developed by Hirschman. In Brun, Combes and Renard (2002), the term means the spillovers through supply-side and demand-side externalities.
4. As for the estimation methods in general, see Okamoto and Zhang (2003). More detailed information on the estimation methods and the data used is available in Hioki (2003a) and Zhang and Zhao (2002).
5. The patterns of spillover effects by region and by sector derived from the impact of final demand on output is almost the same as the results of output multiplier analysis. Therefore, I omit it in this chapter. See Hioki (2003b) for details.
6. Approximately 40 per cent of total production in the Mining and Metal Products sector in the central region is induced by coastal final demands. See Hioki (2003b) for details.
7. According to Richardson (1978), the concept of the growth pole has different meanings among researchers. Generally speaking, it usually implies the urban area where industries are concentrated bring strong spillover effects to the surrounding hinterland. In this chapter, we enlarge geographical coverage of the term and define it as the region where: (1) high economic growth is realized; (2) economic activity is relatively concentrated; and (3) there are strong spillover effects to the surrounding regions.
8. From the result of impact of final demand on output, spillover effects from coastal regions to inland regions are relatively large for sectors such as Metal Products, Mining and Chemical Products. See Hioki (2003b) for details.
9. Naughton (2002) indicates that the development of growth poles in the coastal region spreads to inland regions, such as Henan, Hubei and Anhui,

based on the growth rate of per capita GDP. Golley (2002) also expresses the same opinion from the findings of growth of regional manufacturing share of Anhui. This chapter may support these opinions from the aspects of an interregional input–output analysis.

10. In order to clarify this point, we have to compare with 1987 data, estimated by Ichimura and Wang (2003). However, because of differences in estimation methods, the results of such comparisons should be carefully interpreted. This is left to my further investigation.
11. Naughton (2002) proposed this perspective based on the result of his shift-share analysis.
12. To date, there are three important development areas: an economic belt along the Western–Longhai Railway and the Lanzhou–Xinjian Railway, the Nanning–Guiyang–Kunming area and the economic belt along the upper reaches of the Yangtze River (Office of the Leading Group for Western Region Development of the State Council, 'Circular of the State Council on Policies and Measures Pertain to the Development of the Western Region', 26 October 2000).
13. For example, projects such as 'Xiqi Dongshu' ('Gas Transport from West to East), 'Xidian Dongsong' (Electricity Transport from West to East), and 'Qing-zang Tielu' (Qinghai–Tibet railway construction) have been implemented during the Tenth Five-Year Plan period.

References

Akita, T. (2000) 'Decomposing Regional Income Inequality Using Two-Stage Nested Theil Decomposition Method', Paper Presented at the 6th World Congress of the Regional Science Association International in Lugano, Switzerland.

Akita, T. (2001) 'Regional Income Inequality in China: A Two-Stage Nested Inequality Decomposition Analysis', Mimeo.

Bao, S., G.H. Chang, J.D. Sachs and W.T. Woo (2002) 'Geographic Factors and China's Regional Development under Market Reforms, 1978–1998', *China Economic Review*, 13, 89–111.

Brun, J.F., J.L. Combes and M.F. Renard (2002) 'Are There Spillover Effects between Coastal and Noncoastal Regions in China?', *China Economic Review*, 13, 161–9.

Cai, F., D. Wang and Y. Du (2002) 'Regional Disparity and Economic Growth in China: The Impact of Labor Market Distortions', *China Economic Review* 13(2–3), 197–212.

Chen, B. and Y. Feng (2000) 'Determinants of Economic Growth in China: Private Enterprise, Education, and Openness', *China Economic Review*, 11, 1–15.

Chen, J. and B.M. Fleisher (1996) 'Regional Income Inequality and Economic Growth in China', *Journal of Comparative Economics*, 22, 141–64.

Chen, K. (1996) 'Kaikaku Kaiho Go Chugoku no Chiiki Kakusa' (China's Regional Disparity after the Reform), *Kokusai Kyoryoku Ronsyu (Journal of International Cooperation Studies)*, 4(1), 155–70.

Chen, K. (1998) 'Kaikaku Kaiho Igo Chugoku no Chiikikan no Kakusa to Jyuyou Hakyuryoku' (China's Regional Disparity and Interregional Spillovers after the Reform), *Kokumin Keizai Zasshi (Journal of Economics and Business Administration)*, 178(4), 61–72.

Chen, K. (2002) 'Chugoku no Chikukan Syotoku Kakusa to Syuseki no Keizai' (Regional Income Disparity and Agglomeration Economy in China), *Kokumin Keizai Zasshi (Journal of Economics and Business Administration)*, 186(3), 41–51.

Demurger, S. (2001) 'Infrastructure Development and Economic Growth: an Explanation for Regional Disparities in China', *Journal of Comparative Economics*, 29, 95–117.

Fan, C. (1995) 'Of Belts and Ladders: State Policy and Uneven Regional Development in Post-Mao China', *Annals of the Association of American Gegraphers*, 85(3), 421–49.

Fujita, M. and D. Hu (2001) 'Regional Disparity in China 1985–1994: The Effects of Globalization and Economic Liberalization', *Annals of Regional Science*, 35, 3–37.

Golley, J. (2002) 'Regional Patterns of Industrial Development during China's Economic Transition', *Economics of Transition*, 10(3), 761–801.

Hioki, S. (2003a) 'Chugoku Tachiikikan Sangyorenkan Moderu niokeru Moderu Sentaku to Chiikikan Koueki Suikei', (The Model Selection and the Estimation of Interregional Trade Flows in the Multi-regional Input–Output Model for China), in N. Okamoto (ed.) (2003), pp. 21–48.

Hioki, S. (2003b) 'Chugoku no Chiiki Kakusa to Enkai Chiiki kara Nairiku Chiiki heno Shintou Kouka' (China's Regional Disparity and the Trickling-down Effects from Coastal Regions to Inland Regions), Paper Presented at the 43rd Annual Meeting of Japanese Association for Comparative Economic Studies.

Hioki, S. (2004) 'Kogyoka no Kukanteki Sokumen' (Spatial Aspects of China's Industrialization), in H. Kato and K. Uehara (eds.) *Chugokukeizairon (Chinese Economy)*, Mineruba Shobo, ch. 6.

Hirschman, A.O. (1958) *The Strategy of Economic Development*, Yale University Press.

Hu, A., S. Wang and X. Kang (1995) *Zhongguo diqu chaju baogao (The Report of China's Regional Disparity)*, Liaoning Peoples' Press.

Hu, D. (2002) 'Trade, Rural–Urban Migration, and Regional Income Disparity in Developing Countries: A Spatial General Equilibrium Model Inspired by the Case of China', *Regional Science and Urban Economics*, 32, 311–38.

Huang, S. and H. Wei (eds) (2001) *Xibudakaifa yu dongzhongbu diqu fazhan (The Western Region Development and the East and Central Regions)*, Beijing: Jingjiquanlichubanshe, Appendix 2.

Ichimura, S. and H. Wang (eds) (2003) *Interregional Input–Output Analysis of the Chinese Economy*, Singapore: World Scientific Publishing.

Institute of Developing Economies–JETRO (2003) *Multi-Regional Input–Output Model for China 2000*, Statistical Data Series no. 86, Chiba: Institute of Developing Economies–JETRO.

Jian,T., J.D. Sachs and A.M. Warner (1996) 'Trends in Regional Inequality in China', *NBER Working Paper*, 5412.

Kanbur, R. and X. Zhuang (1999) 'Which Regional Inequality? The Evolution of Rural–Urban and Inland–Coastal Inequality in China', *Journal of Comparative Economics*, 27, 686–701.

Kato, H. (1997) *Chugoku no Keizaihatten to Shijoka (Economic Development and Transition to Market in China)*, Nagoya: Nagoya University Press.

Kato, H. (1999) 'Chugoku no Chiikikakusa, Kokunaishijotogo to Chiikiseisaku' (China's Regional Disparity, Market Integration and Regional Policy), *Kokumin Keizai Zasshi (Journal of Economics and Business Administration)*, 179(6), 77–96.

Kato, H. (2003) *Chiiki no Hatten: Series Gendai Chugoku Keizai 6 (Regional Development: Series Contemporary Chinese Economy 6),* Nagoya: Nagoya University Press.

Kimura, K. (2003) 'China's Regional Industrial Disparity from the Viewpoint of Industrial Agglomeration', in M. Kagami and M. Tsuji (eds), *Industrial Agglomeration: Facts and Lessons for Developing Countries,* Chiba: Institute of Developing Economies–JETRO, pp. 203–34.

Lin, Y. (2001) *Chugoku no Chiikikan Syotoku Kakusa: Sangyokozo, Jinko, Kyoiku Karano Bunseki (Regional Income Inequality in China: Industrial Structure, Population and Education),* Tokyo: Nihon Keizai Hyoron Sya.

Maruyama, N. (ed.) (1993) *Choko Ryuiki no Keizai Hatten: Chugoku no Shujika to Chiiki Kaihatsu (Economic Development in Chang Jiang Area: Transition to Market Economy and Regional Development),* Tokyo: Institute of Developing Economies.

Miller, R.E. and P. D. Blair (1985) *Input–Output Analysis: Foundations and Extensions,* Englewood Cliffs, NJ: Prentice-Hall.

Myrdal, G. (1957) *Economic Theory and Underdeveloped Regions*. London: Gerald Duckworth.

Nakagane, K. (1996) 'Chugoku no Chiikikakusa to Sono Kozo: Mondai no Seiri to Kongo no Tenkai ni Mukete' (Regional Disparity and its Structure in China: Survey and Toward Future Development) *Azia Keizai,* 37(2), 2–34.

Naughton, B. (2002) 'Provincial Economic Growth in China: Causes and Consequences of Regional Differenciation', in Mary-Françoise Renard (eds), *China and Its Regions*, Chelterham: Edward Elgar.

Ohashi, H. (2003) *Keizai no Kokusaika: Gendai Chugoku Keizai 5* (*Internationalization of Economy: Modern Chinese Economy 5*). Nagoya: Nagoya University Press.

Okamoto, N. (ed.) (2002) *Chugoku no Chiikikan Sangyokozo – Chiikikan Sangyo Renkan Bunseki (I) (Interregional Industrial Structure in China – Interregional Input–Output Analysis (I)),* Asian Input–Output Series no. 61, Chiba: Institute of Developing Economies–JETRO.

Okamoto, N. (ed.) (2003) *Chugoku no Chiikikan Sangyokozo – Chiikikan Sangyo Renkan Bunseki (II), (Interregional Industrial Structure in China – Interregional Input–Output Analysis (II)),* Asian Input–Output Series no. 63, Chiba: Institute of Developing Economies–JETRO.

Okamoto, N. and Y. Zhang (2003) 'Compilation Procedure of Multi-Regional Input–Output Model for China 2000', in Institute of Developing Economies, *Multiregional Input–Output Model for China 2000*, Statistical Data Series no. 86, Chiba: Institute of Developing Economies–JETRO, pp. 9–20.

Onishi, Y. (ed.) (2001) *Chugoku no Seibudaikaihatsu (Perspective of Inland Area Development Strategy),* Chiba: Institute of Developing Economies–JETRO.

Richardson, H.W. (1978) *Regional Economics*, Urbana: University of Illinois Press.

Theil, H. (1967) *Economics and Information Theory*, Studies in Mathematical and Managerial Economics vol.7, Amsterdam: North-Holland.

Tsui, K. (1993) 'Decomposition of China's Regional Inequalities', *Journal of Comparative Economics*, 17, 600–27.

Wang, S. and A. Hu (1999) *The Political Economy of Uneven Development: The Case of China*, New York: M.E. Sharpe.

Wei, H., J. Liu, M. Zhou, D. Yang and W. Hu (1997) *ZhongguoDiqu Fazhan: Jingji Zengzhang, Zhidubianqian yu Diquchayi (China's Regional Development: Economic Growth, Institutional Changes and Regional Disparities),* Beijing: Jingjiguanlichubanshe, ch. 9.

Williamson, J. (1965) 'Regional Inequality and the Process of National Development: A Description of the Patterns', *Economic Development and Cultural Change*, 13(4), 3–84.
World Bank (1997) *China 2020: Sharing Rising Incomes*, Washington, DC: World Bank.
Yang, D. (1990) 'Patterns of China's Regional Development Strategy', *The China Quarterly*, 122, 230–57.
Yang, D.T. (2002) 'What Has Caused Regional Inequality in China?', *China Economic Review*, 13, 331–4.
Yao, S. and Z. Zhang (2001) 'Regional Growth in China under Economic Reforms', *Journal of Development Studies*, 38(2), 167–86.
Ying, L. (1999) 'China's Changing Regional Disparities during the Reform Period', *Economic Geography*, 75(1), 59–70.
Ying, L. (2000) 'Measuring the Spillover Effects: Some Chinese Evidence', *Papers in Regional Science*, 79(1), 75–89.
Zhang, Y. and K. Zhao (2002) '2000 Nian Qiye Shengchan Touru Laiyuan he Chanpin Liuxiang Diaocha Fangfa (The Method of Firm Survey on Input Origin and Product Destination)', in N. Okamoto (ed.), pp. 73–82.
Zhang, Z., A. Liu and S. Yao (2001) 'Convergence of China's Regional Incomes 1952–1997', *China Economic Review*, 12, 243–58.

9
The Spillover and Feedback Effects between Coastal and Non-coastal Regions

Yaxiong Zhang and Kun Zhao

9.1 Introduction

Over the past two decades, China's economic development has been characterized as market-oriented reform. As part of a process of opening up to the outside world under the philosophy of the 'Step Ladder Development Policy', the coastal region, especially the south, enjoyed preferential economic policies and has achieved faster rates of economic growth than the Non-coastal regions. The Chinese government hopes that this will be a learning curve and provide the experience to introduce economic reforms to the interior regions, and, simultaneously, that the faster development of the coastal region could pass on to the other regions. While China is on a rapid growth path, there has been increasingly unbalanced regional development, particularly since the 1990s. As in the case of other large-scale economies, the Coastal (eastern) region of China grows much faster than the Non-coastal (western or interior) region, while the eastern region is much smaller than the western region. In order to develop the western region, in 1999 the Chinese government introduced a 'Western Area Development Strategy'. The regional development problem has become an important issue, and the study of the influence and interdependence of regional economies is becoming increasingly urgent.

The open door policy sees export demand as an important engine of China's economic growth. At the same time, the economic reforms introduces the market mechanism to economic development, and stimulates the enhancement of capital, service and commodity flows between regions. On the other hand, some regional governors have attempted to protect some local industries through intervening in interregional transactions. Poncet (2001) applied the 'border effects' method in measuring the magnitude of China's domestic market fragmentation and Chinese provinces' international integration between 1987 and 1997. Her research confirmed the successful promotion of a policy of opening up to international trade throughout the Chinese provinces. By contrast, the intensity of domestic trade flows in China's provinces decreased, so the reforms to promote domestic integration and the growing division of China's domestic market into cellular sub-markets failed. However, Poncet did not analyse the impacts of those factors on China's regional economic growth. Zhang and Felmingham (2002) used panel data for the period 1984 to 1998 to assess the impact of export expansion, inward Foreign Direct Investment, domestic investment and labour on the growth of China's eastern, central and western regions, and indicated that there were output growth spillover effects from eastern to central and western China and from central to western China. Using panel data from the period 1981–98, Brun, Combes and Renard (2002) also tested the interregional spillover effects between the Coastal and Non-coastal regions of China, but they found that spillover effects between these two regions were insufficient to ameliorate regional inequality in China in the short run.

The above analyses employed econometric models. However, in respect of regional economic analysis, the interregional input–output (IRIO) model is an effective tool. In the remaining parts of this chapter, section 9.2 will review and summarize the studies of the spillover and feedback effects in IRIO analysis, and section 9.3 will establish the methodology for the study of such effects between Coastal and Non-coastal regions in China. Then section 9.4 will show the empirical findings obtained using China's 2000 IRIO data compiled by the State Information Centre (SIC), China and the Institute of Developing Economies (IDE), Japan (IDE 2003). Finally, we will give some concluding remarks.

9.2 The spillover and feedback effects in IRIO analysis

In the IRIO model, the interregional transactions are separately recorded from the intraregional ones. Each sector's outflow is accordingly divided into sectoral intermediate inputs and the final demand of other regions. Supposing a two-region, non-competitive import-type IRIO model, the matrix form can be written as:

$$\begin{pmatrix} A_d^{11} & A_d^{12} \\ A_d^{21} & A_d^{22} \end{pmatrix} \begin{pmatrix} \tilde{X}^1 \\ \tilde{X}^2 \end{pmatrix} + \begin{pmatrix} Y_d^1 \\ Y_d^2 \end{pmatrix} = \begin{pmatrix} \tilde{X}^1 \\ \tilde{X}^2 \end{pmatrix} \tag{9.1}$$ [1]

where $A_d^{\alpha\beta}$ is the input coefficient matrix showing the per-unit requirements by sectors in region β from region α, $\tilde{X}^\alpha$ is the total outputs and Y_d^α is the final demand of region α. Thus A_d^{11}, A_d^{22} record the intraregional coefficients for region 1 and region 2, and A_d^{12}, A_d^{21} record the interregional coefficients between region 1 and region 2. The subscript d represents the domestic transactions.

Miller (1963) developed how to analyse the feedback effects by using the IRIO model. In his subsequent studies, Miller (1966, 1969) found some early results based on some numerical simulations of patterns on regional structure and trade, which suggested that the size of these feedback effects was likely to be quite small in practice. Miller's central contribution is to consider the analytical structure of the interregional linkages, which is instructive in examining the nature of the various multiplier, spillover, and feedback effects involved and their relationships with the method of multiplier decomposition analysis which subsequently has been developed and used in regional analysis (Round 1985; Sonis, Oosterhaven and Hewings 1993; Sonis and Hewings 1999), so that the potential interregional spillover and feedback effects can be clearly analysed by mathematic deduction in interregional IO models.

Arranging (9.1), we can obtain a form of Miller's model in the two-region case:

$$(I - A_d^{11})\tilde{X}^1 - A_d^{12}\tilde{X}^2 = Y_d^1 - A_d^{21}\tilde{X}^1 + (I - A_d^{22})\tilde{X}^2 = Y_d^2 \tag{9.2}$$

Solving the two equations for regional total output yields:

$$\begin{aligned} \tilde{X}^1 = {} & [(I - A_d^{11}) - A_d^{12}(I - A_d^{22})^{-1}A_d^{21}]^{-1}Y_d^1 \\ & + [(I - A_d^{11}) - A_d^{12}(I - A_d^{22})^{-1}A_d^{21}]^{-1}A_d^{12}(I - A_d^{22})^{-1}Y_d^2 \end{aligned} \tag{9.3}$$

and:

$$\begin{aligned} \tilde{X}^2 = {} & [(I - A_d^{22}) - A_d^{21}(I - A_d^{11})^{-1}A_d^{12}]^{-1}Y_d^2 \\ & + [(I - A_d^{22}) - A_d^{21}(I - A_d^{11})^{-1}A_d^{12}]^{-1}A_d^{21}(I - A_d^{11})^{-1}Y_d^1 \end{aligned} \tag{9.4}$$

This is the pioneer work undertaken by Miller. Both of (9.3) and (9.4) in the left-hand side show two terms, the first in (9.3) the total effect of final demand requirements, Y_d^1, on total output in region 1, including all inter-industrial and interregional effects, while the second represents the total output effect of final demand requirements in region 2, Y_d^2, which shows the spillover of output of region 1.

Miller's examination of feedback effects provided a new method of studying interregional economic relationships and influences, but his conclusion that the interregional feedback effects may be small has led to discussion about the necessities of compiling IRIO models while the focus is on one region. Greytak (1970, 1974) gave a different result from Miller's by using an eight-region, 23-sector interregional IO model of the USA, and he thought that the existence of feedback effects made the compilation of interregional or multiregional IO models necessary. Gillen and Guccione (1980) developed some interesting results on the maximum possible error that could be expected in certain IRIO models when interregional feedbacks were ignored using several inequality relationships on norms of matrices due to Charnes and Cooper (1961). And then Miller (1986) calculated the upper bounds of interregional feedbacks based on Gillen and Guccione's methods, and Guccione et al. (1988) calculated the least upper bound of interregional feedbacks, both of which showed that the interregional feedback effects may be quite small.

At that time, most of the studies focused on the size of interregional feedback effects, which appeared to be small, but the methodology about how to distinguish the spillover and feedback effects was not improved until Round (2001) factored out the term of the intraregional Leontief inverse in (9.3) and (9.4). The $\tilde{X}^1$ then is represented as in (9.5), which separated spillover, feedback effects explicitly following Miller's model:

$$\begin{aligned}\tilde{X}^1 &= \left[I - (I - A_d^{11})^{-1} A_d^{12} (I - A_d^{22})^{-1} A_d^{21}\right]^{-1} (I - A_d^{11})^{-1} Y_d^1 \\ &\quad + \left[I - (I - A_d^{11})^{-1} A_d^{12} (I - A_d^{22})^{-1} A_d^{21}\right]^{-1} (I - A_d^{11})^{-1} \\ &\quad \times A_d^{12} (I - A_d^{22})^{-1} Y_d^2 \qquad (9.5)\end{aligned}$$

For Y_d^1, if there were only one region, then the total output vector would be simply as in the single-region IO model, $(I - A_d^{11})^{-1} Y_d^1$. However, the IRIO model is successfully expanded to encompass interregional transactions. The requirements of region 1 from the various sectors in region 2 of per unit inputs are given by the elements in A_d^{21}; $(I - A_d^{22})^{-1}$ describes the total direct and indirect production to meet the unit demand for goods in region 2, then the total production of sectors in region 2 to meet the requirements from region 1 is given by $(I - A_d^{22})^{-1} A_d^{21}$; per unit inputs from region 1 to region 2 are represented by A_d^{12}, thus inputs from region 1 to sustain production within region 2 for region 1 are given by $A_d^{12}(I - A_d^{22})^{-1}A_d^{21}$; it is clear that $(I - A_d^{11})^{-1}A_d^{12}(I - A_d^{22})^{-1}A_d^{21}$ gives the total direct and indirect production to meet those inputs. As usual $[I - (I - A_d^{11})^{-1}A_d^{12}(I - A_d^{22})^{-1}A_d^{21}]^{-1}$, is the feedback multiplier to $(I - A_d^{11})^{-1}Y_d^1$. For Y_d^2, the second part on the left-hand side in (9.5), total per unit requirements for all sectors in region 2 to satisfy Y_d^2 are $(I - A_d^{22})^{-1}$; $A_d^{12}(I - A_d^{22})^{-1}$ indicates total interregional support from region 1 to sustain production activity in region 2, the spillover effect; as $[I - (I - A_d^{11})^{-1}A_d^{12}(I - A_d^{22})^{-1}A_d^{21}]^{-1}(I - A_d^{11})^{-1}$ shows all the requirements for production in region 1, it must therefore pre-multiply the expression for the direct inputs from region 1 to support activity in region 2. That is $[I-(I-A_d^{11})^{-1}A_d^{12}(I-A_d^{22})^{-1}A_d^{21}]^{-1}(I-A_d^{11})^{-1}A_d^{12}(I-A_d^{22})^{-1}$, which indicates the total outputs needed in region 1 to meet the demand, Y_d^2.

Following Round (1985) and based on a similar decomposition of a social accounting matrix (SAM) in Pyatt and Round (1979), Round (2001) also constructed a multiplier decomposition, which will be discussed in detail in the next section. As a result of these developments, the theory of how to distinguish and study the spillover and feedback effects by using the IRIO model was outlined for the first time. Sonis and Hewings (2001) explored a complementary vision of the role of feedbacks through the introduction of two additional notions – feedback loops and inter-regional hierarchies. Dietzenbacher (2002) has tried to consolidate the spillover and feedback multipliers with the linkage framework.

9.3 Methodology

Multiplier decomposition

As a demand-side model, (1) can be rewritten as:

$$\begin{pmatrix} \tilde{X}^1 \\ \tilde{X}^2 \end{pmatrix} = \left[I - \begin{pmatrix} A_d^{11} & A_d^{12} \\ A_d^{21} & A_d^{22} \end{pmatrix} \right]^{-1} \begin{pmatrix} Y_d^1 \\ Y_d^2 \end{pmatrix} = \begin{pmatrix} L^{11} & L^{12} \\ L^{21} & L^{22} \end{pmatrix} \begin{pmatrix} Y_d^1 \\ Y_d^2 \end{pmatrix}^2 \tag{9.6}$$

Round (2001) decomposed the Leontief inverse and rewrote model (9.6) in the following form, which is consistent with the total output expression, for instance, $\tilde{X}^1$ in (9.5):

$$\begin{pmatrix} \tilde{X}^1 \\ \tilde{X}^2 \end{pmatrix} = \begin{pmatrix} F^1 & 0 \\ 0 & F^2 \end{pmatrix} \begin{pmatrix} I & S^{12} \\ S^{21} & I \end{pmatrix} \begin{pmatrix} M^1 & 0 \\ 0 & M^2 \end{pmatrix} \begin{pmatrix} Y_d^1 \\ Y_d^2 \end{pmatrix} \tag{9.7}$$

where:

$$M^1 = (I - A_d^{11})^{-1}, M^2 = (I - A_d^{22})^{-1}$$
$$S^{12} = M^1 A_d^{12}, S^{21} = M^2 A_d^{21}$$
$$F^1 = (I - S^{12}S^{21})^{-1}, F^2 = (I - S^{21}S^{12})^{-1}$$

M accounts for the intraregional linkage, and S and F show the interregional spillover and feedback effects respectively. As the Leontief inverse consists of the intraregional and interregional linkages, following Round's decomposition, the model can be written as:

$$\begin{aligned}\begin{pmatrix}\tilde{X}^1\\ \tilde{X}^2\end{pmatrix} &= \begin{pmatrix}F^1 & F^1S^{12}\\ F^2S^{21} & F^2\end{pmatrix}\begin{pmatrix}M^1 & 0\\ 0 & M^2\end{pmatrix}\begin{pmatrix}Y_d^1\\ Y_d^2\end{pmatrix}\\ &= \begin{pmatrix}F^1M^1 & F^1S^{12}M^2\\ F^2S^{21}M^1 & F^2M^2\end{pmatrix}\begin{pmatrix}Y_d^1\\ Y_d^2\end{pmatrix}\\ &= \begin{pmatrix}F^1M^1Y_d^1 + F^1S^{12}M^2Y_d^2\\ F^2M^2Y_d^2 + F^2S^{21}M^1Y_d^1\end{pmatrix}\end{aligned} \tag{9.8}$$

We define $\begin{pmatrix}M^1 & 0\\ 0 & M^2\end{pmatrix}$ as intraregional linkage matrix, and $\begin{pmatrix}F^1 & F^1S^{12}\\ F^2S^{21} & F^2\end{pmatrix}$ as its interregional multiplier matrix. Where F^1S^{12} and F^2S^{21} show the total interregional spillover linkage matrix, F^1 and F^2 show intraregional linkage and total interregional feedback linkages. $\begin{pmatrix}F^1M^1 & F^1S^{12}M^2\\ F^2S^{21}M^1 & F^2M^2\end{pmatrix}$ shows another expression of the Leontief inverse in the two-region IRIO model, and $\begin{pmatrix}F^1M^1Y_d^1 + F^1S^{12}M^2Y_d^2\\ F^2M^2Y_d^2 + F^2S^{21}M^1Y_d^1\end{pmatrix}$ gives output-inducing effects classified by Y_d^1 and Y_d^2 with the multiplier decomposition.

Backward linkage and multiplier

Backward linkage reflects the induced output of all industries by the increase of one unit final demand in the jth sector. Total backward linkage in a single-region IO model is defined as:

$$TBL = \sum_i L$$

where L is the Leontief inverse. Similarly, we can define the intraregional and interregional total backward linkages. In the two-region

IRIO model, the intraregional backward linkages and the interregional backward linkages are as follows:

$$TBL^{11} = \sum_i L^{11}, TBL^{22} = \sum_i L^{22}$$

$$TBL^{12} = \sum_i L^{12}, TBL^{21} = \sum_i L^{21}$$

Since $\begin{pmatrix} L^{11} & L^{12} \\ L^{21} & L^{22} \end{pmatrix}$ is decomposed as $\begin{pmatrix} F^1M^1 & F^1S^{12}M^2 \\ F^2S^{21}M^1 & F^2M^2 \end{pmatrix}$, we can have:

$$TBL^{11} = \sum_i F^1M^1, TBL^{22} = \sum_i F^2M^2$$

$$TBL^{12} = \sum_i F^1S^{12}M^2, TBL^{21} = \sum_i F^2S^{21}M^1$$

Backward linkage is the column treatment indicating the gross total output increase under the one unit increase of each sector *j*'s final demand. Another characteristic of backward linkage measurement is the assumption of the one unit change of final demand, which is equivalent to the multiplier effect. In the context of IO analysis, various kinds of multipliers – such as value added, trade, income, employment and energy, etc. – can be derived by using additional vectors. They reflect the extra value of those vectors, or simply the output as required for unity increase of final demands or primary inputs. While in the IRIO model, the linkages from the interregional linkage matrix $\begin{pmatrix} F^1 & F^1S^{12} \\ F^2S^{21} & F^2 \end{pmatrix}$ do not correspond to with final demands or primary inputs directly. Alternatively, those linkages are equivalent to the multipliers regarding the increase of $(M^1Y_d^1, M^2Y_d^2)$, intraregional outputs. The F^1 reflects the extra value of region 1's output, which includes the intraregional and interregional feedback effects required by the increase in the region's final demand. Similarly, F^1S^{12} represents the spillover effect from region 1 to region 2 required by region 2's final demand. It is noticed that the interregional feedback multiplier is the difference between F^1 and I.[3]

We define the total interregional feedback backward linkages (*TBLF*) and total interregional spillover backward linkages (*TBLS*) as:

$$TBLF^{11} = \sum_i (F^1 - I), TBLF^{22} = \sum_i (F^2 - I)$$

$$TBLS^{21} = \sum_i F^2S^{21}, TBLS^{12} = \sum_i F^1S^{12}$$

Dietzenbacher (2002) set up the relations between the backward and forward linkages and the multiplier decompositions consisting of the intraregional, interregional spillover and feedback effects, which is different from Miller (1966), and distributed the feedback multiplier into intraregional effects and interregional spillover effects called home and foreign effects.

Output-inducing effect

When the sectoral structure of final demand is considered, the output-inducing effect can then be calculated under the given structure of final demand. The output-inducing effect reflects the total output induced of each industry by the given structure of final sectoral demands. It shows each sector's output increase, which is the row sum of the Leontief inverse weighted by the final demand structure. The output-inducing effect is calculated from the demand-side model, thus any increases in spillover and feedback effects are the results of respective increases in the final demands of the other region or the originating region. For instance, when the final demand of region 2 changes, the output of region 1 will be induced, which is called the spillover effect, while the changes in region 2's output to meet the demand of region 1 will lead to the change of the outputs, which flow to region 2, thus the effect will be fed-back to the output of region 1 – namely, the feedback effect.

Region 1's increase in output is measured by $F^1M^1Y_d^1 + F^1S^{12}M^2Y_d^2$. It is the product of the row-wise sub-matrix of $\begin{pmatrix} F^1M^1 & F^1S^{12}M^2 \\ F^2S^{21}M^1 & F^2M^2 \end{pmatrix}$ and $\begin{pmatrix} Y_d^1 \\ Y_d^2 \end{pmatrix}$. $F^1M^1Y_d^1$ includes the intraregional and interregional feedback output increase of region 1 induced by Y_d^1, and $F^1S^{12}M^2Y_d^2$ represents the interregional spillover effect from region 1 induced by Y_d^2. Correspondingly, region 2's output increase is measured by $F^2M^2Y_d^2 + F^2S^{21}M^1Y_d^1$.

9.4 Empirical studies

Data

The empirical studies are based on an analysis using the Multi-regional IO model for China 2000 (IDE 2003), which was compiled under a collaboration between SIC and IDE. The model was constructed from provincial IO tables for 1997 and related the provincial statistics of China. In the model, there are eight regions, including thirty administration districts (provinces) of China except Tibet.[4] The method of regional division was based on the three-region-belt division (eastern, central and western) from East to West, in which the western region division is consistent with the strategy of Western Area Development, and connected with the six economic zones division which is still popular from north to south. Thus, the 12 provinces in the west were divided into the Southwest region and the Northwest region, including six provinces respectively, and the Northeast region still comprised Heilongjiang, Jilin and Liaoning. Then ten provinces left in the eastern belt were divided into four coastal regions, and six provinces left as the newly classified Central region.[5]

With regard to the sector classification, the model records 30 sectors, which are based on the 40-sector classification of the National Input–Output table. Eleven service sectors excluding the transport and warehousing sector and the wholesale and retail trade sector – were aggregated into service sectors because of insufficient data for the interregional service flows, so that only 30 sectors were left in the multi-regional IO model.

In order to study the spillover and feedback effects between the Coastal and Non-coastal regions of China, the eight-region model was aggregated into a two-region model, in which the four coastal regions were merged into the Coastal region (region 1), while the other four regions were merged into the Non-coastal region (region 2). We also made

Table 9.1 Sector classification

Code	*Sector classification*
1	Agriculture
2	Mining
3	Food products
4	Textile and clothing
5	Wooden products
6	Paper and printing
7	Chemical products
8	Non-metallic mineral products
9	Metal products
10	Machinery
11	Transport equipment
12	Electronic products
13	Other manufacturing products
14	Electricity, gas and water supply
15	Construction
16	Trade and transport
17	Services

some aggregations of the sector classifications, and some sectors in the 30-sector model were aggregated into a 17-sector model, which is shown in Table 9.1. The output and final demand structures of the Coastal and Non-coastal regions are listed in Table 9.2.

Backward linkages and output multipliers

As the expression of the intermediate input structure, the Leontief inverse can be treated as the total sectoral production technology matrix. Consequently, the column sum of the various linkage matrix (backward linkage) reflects the total technology input for sector *j*. Table 9.3 shows the results of the calculated intraregional and interregional linkages and multipliers, and they are normalized by the averages in Table 9.4. Table 9.3 shows that the averaged $M^1, F^1 - I$ and F^2S^{21} are 2.2788, 0.0178 and 0.1337, while the averaged $M^2, F^2 - I$ and F^1S^{12} are 2.2747, 0.0193 and 0.1468, respectively. Clearly, the Non-coastal region tends to display a higher dependence on the Coastal region's technology transfers (as the direct and indirect intermediate inputs for the production).[6] As the regional technology transfer, the spillover effect shows the movements from the relatively high technology region to the lower one, while the feedback effect is the second round technology interdependence between the Coastal and Non-coastal regions. Both spillover multipliers of Coastal and Non-coastal regions are clearly larger than the corresponding feedback multipliers (7.51 and 7.61 times). As the multiplier regarding the increase of $(M^1Y_d^1, M^2Y_d^2)$, the interregional spillover and feedback effects contribute more output to the Non-coastal region than to the Coastal region.

At the industry level, metal products (9), electricity, gas and water supply (14), wooden products (5), non-metallic mineral products (8) and construction (15) sectors in the Non-coastal region spill over their technologies extensively to the Coastal region, while metal products (9), electricity, gas and water supply (14), wooden products (5), construction (15) and machinery (10) sectors, etc. process the stronger feedback effects of the technologies from the Coastal region to the Non-coastal region. As backward linkages and multiplier effects, those industries also contribute greatly to the gross total output of the Coastal region. Electronic products (12), transport equipment (11), machinery (10), textile and clothing (4) and metal products (9) sectors, etc. in the Coastal region spillover their technologies to the Non-coastal region, while those sectors in turn spill over their technologies from the Non-coastal region back to the Coastal region as a second round technology transfer. Similarly, these industries

Table 9.2 The output and final demand structures of Coastal and Non-coastal regions

	Coastal region				*Non-coastal region*				*Ratio*	
Sector	*Total output (1)*	*Share*	*Final demand (2)*	*Share*	*Total output (3)*	*Share*	*Final demand (4)*	*Share*	*Total output (3)/(4)*	*Final demand (4)/(2)*
1	1,027.32	9.02	416.24	13.24	1,440.41	16.76	672.38	19.75	1.402	1.615
2	242.35	2.13	3.35	0.11	440.49	5.13	8.20	0.24	1.818	2.446
3	654.74	5.75	299.32	9.52	724.52	8.43	417.05	12.25	1.107	1.393
4	1,167.41	10.25	146.87	4.67	369.25	4.30	165.51	4.86	0.316	1.127
5	122.38	1.07	17.60	0.56	101.74	1.18	28.76	0.84	0.831	1.634
6	307.67	2.70	24.77	0.79	134.24	1.56	14.88	0.44	0.436	0.601
7	1,136.51	9.98	52.95	1.68	694.53	8.08	63.15	1.85	0.611	1.193
8	417.90	3.67	33.84	1.08	462.84	5.39	44.71	1.31	1.108	1.321
9	738.74	6.48	15.84	0.50	537.09	6.25	20.39	0.60	0.727	1.288
10	516.13	4.53	180.59	5.74	306.54	3.57	136.10	4.00	0.594	0.754
11	293.92	2.58	121.58	3.87	237.46	2.76	91.70	2.69	0.808	0.754
12	839.50	7.37	129.02	4.10	206.14	2.40	62.57	1.84	0.246	0.485
13	283.33	2.49	30.42	0.97	155.81	1.81	25.47	0.75	0.550	0.837
14	249.96	2.19	27.83	0.89	193.14	2.25	24.21	0.71	0.773	0.870
15	969.02	8.51	905.21	28.79	769.53	8.96	737.87	21.67	0.794	0.815
16	876.77	7.70	116.60	3.71	734.71	8.55	152.16	4.47	0.838	1.305
17	1,548.79	13.59	725.59	23.08	1,083.52	12.61	757.74	22.26	0.700	1.044
Total	11,392.45	100.00	3,143.91	100.00	8,591.97	100.00	3,404.54	100.00	0.754	1.083

Source: Data from the Multi-regional IO model for China 2000.

Table 9.3 The regional and interregional feedback and spillover linkages and multipliers

	M^1	$F^1 - I$	F^2S^{21}	M^2	$F^2 - I$	F^1S^{12}
1	1.7773	0.0067	0.0588	1.6808	0.0077	0.0661
2	2.0177	0.0123	0.0977	1.9672	0.0127	0.1000
3	2.4127	0.0102	0.1004	2.2547	0.0090	0.0888
4	2.6548	0.0127	0.0909	2.4624	0.0199	0.1947
5	2.4603	0.0231	0.1864	2.3347	0.0169	0.1340
6	2.4330	0.0140	0.1040	2.3858	0.0199	0.1712
7	2.3219	0.0200	0.1550	2.4042	0.0212	0.1716
8	2.3000	0.0215	0.1723	2.4162	0.0163	0.1281
9	2.4388	0.0381	0.2648	2.5819	0.0288	0.1806
10	2.3533	0.0217	0.1465	2.5135	0.0309	0.1999
11	2.5556	0.0202	0.1329	2.5642	0.0296	0.2052
12	2.4854	0.0208	0.1363	2.4035	0.0426	0.2997
13	2.1888	0.0180	0.1280	2.2125	0.0189	0.1383
14	1.9645	0.0274	0.2318	2.0780	0.0113	0.0951
15	2.3691	0.0230	0.1694	2.4562	0.0188	0.1279
16	2.0202	0.0067	0.0506	1.9788	0.0115	0.0949
17	1.9866	0.0061	0.0467	1.9746	0.0121	0.0997
Total	38.7400	0.3025	2.2725	38.6692	0.3281	2.4957
Average	2.2788	0.0178	0.1337	2.2747	0.0193	0.1468

contribute greatly to the gross total output of the Non-coastal region as a result of the interregional multiplier effect.

The patterns of the two regions' technology transfer are clearly different. The horizontal axes in Figure 9.1 indicate the ratios of the two regions' sectoral total output (Non-coastal region to Coastal region for (a) and (b), Coastal region to Non-coastal region for (c) and (d)), while the vertical axes are the associated spillover or feedback effects. Figure 9.1 shows the clear pattern that the spillover or feedback effect initiated from the Coastal region is becoming stronger the more developed the industries are in terms of the sectoral output ratio. But (a) and (b) of F^2S^{21} and $F^1 - I$ from the Non-coastal region do not show a similar pattern. This indicates that although some industries' spillover effects to the Coastal region are strong, the Non-coastal region does not successfully transfer its advanced technologies to the coastal region. The gross total output of the Non-coastal region to the Coastal region is 0.754, with only agriculture (1), mining (2), food products (3) and non-metallic mineral products (8) sectors' total output being greater than those of the Coastal region. On the other hand, the products of material or intermediate goods production industries must be widely distributed as intermediate transactions.

Table 9.4 The normalized regional and interregional feedback and spillover linkages and multipliers

	M^1	$F^1 - I$	F^2S^{21}	M^2	$F^2 - I$	F^1S^{12}
1	0.7799	0.3771	0.4400	0.7389	0.3979	0.4503
2	0.8854	0.6911	0.7310	0.8648	0.6605	0.6810
3	1.0587	0.5744	0.7513	0.9912	0.4641	0.6049
4	1.1650	0.7161	0.6797	1.0825	1.0299	1.3259
5	1.0796	1.2963	1.3947	1.0264	0.8779	0.9128
6	1.0676	0.7854	0.7780	1.0489	1.0298	1.1659
7	1.0189	1.1242	1.1597	1.0570	1.0977	1.1691
8	1.0093	1.2102	1.2889	1.0622	0.8427	0.8725
9	1.0702	2.1429	1.9809	1.1351	1.4938	1.2301
10	1.0327	1.2173	1.0956	1.1050	1.6035	1.3615
11	1.1215	1.1340	0.9943	1.1273	1.5337	1.3980
12	1.0906	1.1681	1.0195	1.0567	2.2097	2.0418
13	0.9605	1.0116	0.9572	0.9727	0.9787	0.9418
14	0.8621	1.5427	1.7337	0.9135	0.5841	0.6480
15	1.0396	1.2907	1.2669	1.0798	0.9737	0.8709
16	0.8865	0.3748	0.3788	0.8699	0.5955	0.6461
17	0.8718	0.3433	0.3497	0.8681	0.6271	0.6793
Total	17.0000	17.0000	17.0000	17.0000	17.0000	17.0000

This evidence supports the view that most of the industries in the Non-coastal region still do not have any technological advantage. Put another way, in terms of material and intermediate inputs, some industries do not successfully spill over their products to the Coastal region exclusively.

Normalized backward linkages are listed in Table 9.5. The average intra- and interregional backward linkages of the Coastal region (F^1M^1 and $F^2S^{21}M^1$) are 1.7752 and 0.2248, while those of the Non-coastal region (F^2M^2 and $F^1S^{12}M^2$) are 1.7579 and 0.2421. Though the average interregional backward linkages are small, only the intraregional backward linkages of textile and clothing (4) sector in the Coastal region and metal products (9) sector in the Non-coastal region are greater than 2.[7] This is more evidence to show that the interregional linkage plays an important role in the regional economic development. The intraregional backward linkages are mainly determined by the intraregional linkage matrix M^1 and M^2, while the patterns of the interregional backward linkages are quite similar to the interregional spillover linkage matrix F^2S^{21} and F^1S^{12}. Figure 9.2 shows the degrees of the corresponding linkages. It is clear that the curves of F^1M^1 and F^2M^2 almost superpose with M^1 and M^2 respectively. Conversely, the lines of $F^2S^{21}M^1$ and $F^1S^{12}M^2$ are quite similar to those of F^2S^{21} and F^1S^{12}. Thus, this shows that the spillover effect is

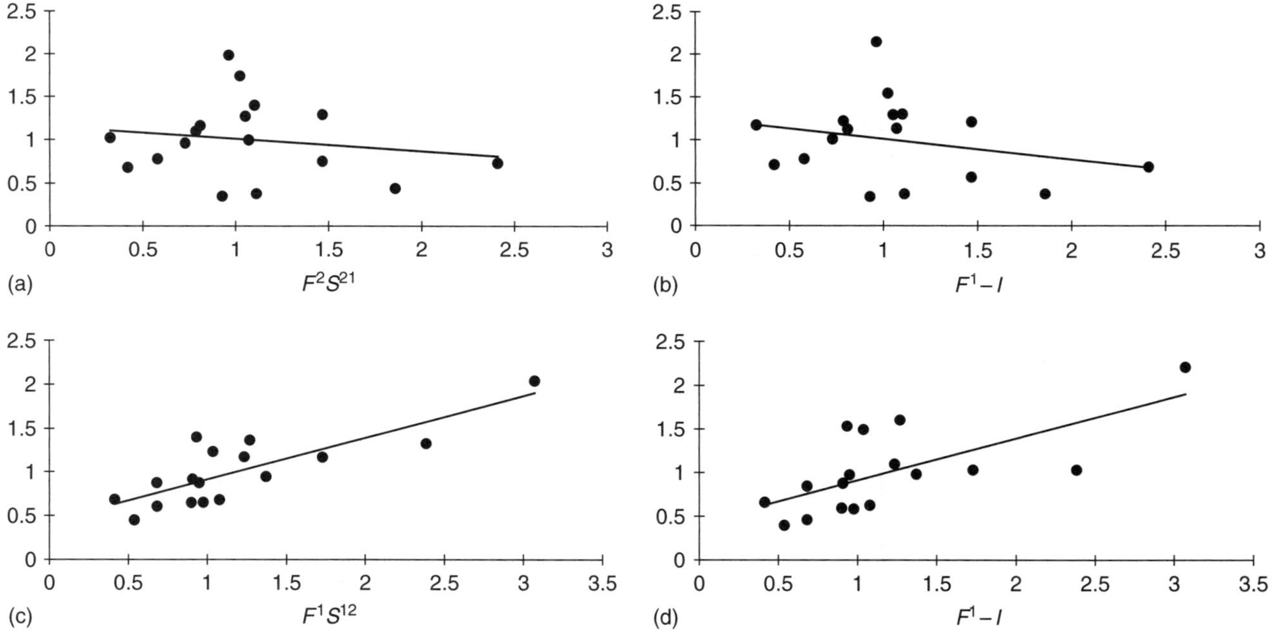

Figure 9.1 Patterns of technology transfer

Table 9.5 The normalized intraregional and interregional backward linkages (output multipliers)

	F^1M^1	$F^2S^{21}M^1$	*Total*	F^2M^2	$F^1S^{12}M^2$	*Total*
1	1.3737	0.1042	1.4778	1.2884	0.1081	1.3965
2	1.5673	0.1697	1.7370	1.5152	0.1728	1.6880
3	1.8678	0.1778	2.0456	1.7295	0.1643	1.8938
4	2.0598	0.1961	2.2559	1.9012	0.2976	2.1988
5	1.9197	0.2810	2.2007	1.8015	0.2327	2.0342
6	1.8909	0.2078	2.0988	1.8434	0.2727	2.1161
7	1.8096	0.2424	2.0520	1.8582	0.2692	2.1275
8	1.7945	0.2589	2.0534	1.8641	0.2372	2.1013
9	1.9211	0.3790	2.3001	2.0039	0.3022	2.3061
10	1.8403	0.2665	2.1068	1.9549	0.3231	2.2780
11	1.9965	0.2720	2.2686	1.9945	0.3435	2.3381
12	1.9415	0.2638	2.2053	1.8796	0.3968	2.2763
13	1.7064	0.2179	1.9242	1.7105	0.2332	1.9437
14	1.5370	0.2656	1.8026	1.5988	0.1750	1.7738
15	1.8526	0.2838	2.1363	1.8984	0.2479	2.1462
16	1.5627	0.1174	1.6801	1.5226	0.1675	1.6901
17	1.5369	0.1180	1.6549	1.5199	0.1714	1.6914
Total	30.1782	3.8218	34.0000	29.8847	4.1153	34.0000
Average	1.7752	0.2248	2.0000	1.7579	0.2421	2.0000

stronger than the feedback effect, which cannot shift the pattern of the intraregional linkage, as the second round interregional linkage effect.

Output-inducing effects

Backward linkage is the column sum of the Leontief inverse as output multiplier is under the assumption of one unit increase of one given sector's final demand. It shows the gross total output increase for all sectors under one unit increase of the given sector's final demand. The output-inducing effect derived in equation (9.8) takes into account the structure of the final demands. It is the row-wise sum of the Leontief inverse and shows each sector's total output increase under the given structure of the final demands.

Table 9.6 shows the contributions of two regions' spillover and feedback output-inducing effects to the sectoral total outputs. The Coastal region's spillover and feedback effects' contributions are 9.66 per cent and 1.21 per cent to region's gross total output, while the Non-coastal region's spillover and feedback effects contribute 9.64 per cent and 1.33 per cent respectively. It shows that the interregional spillover and

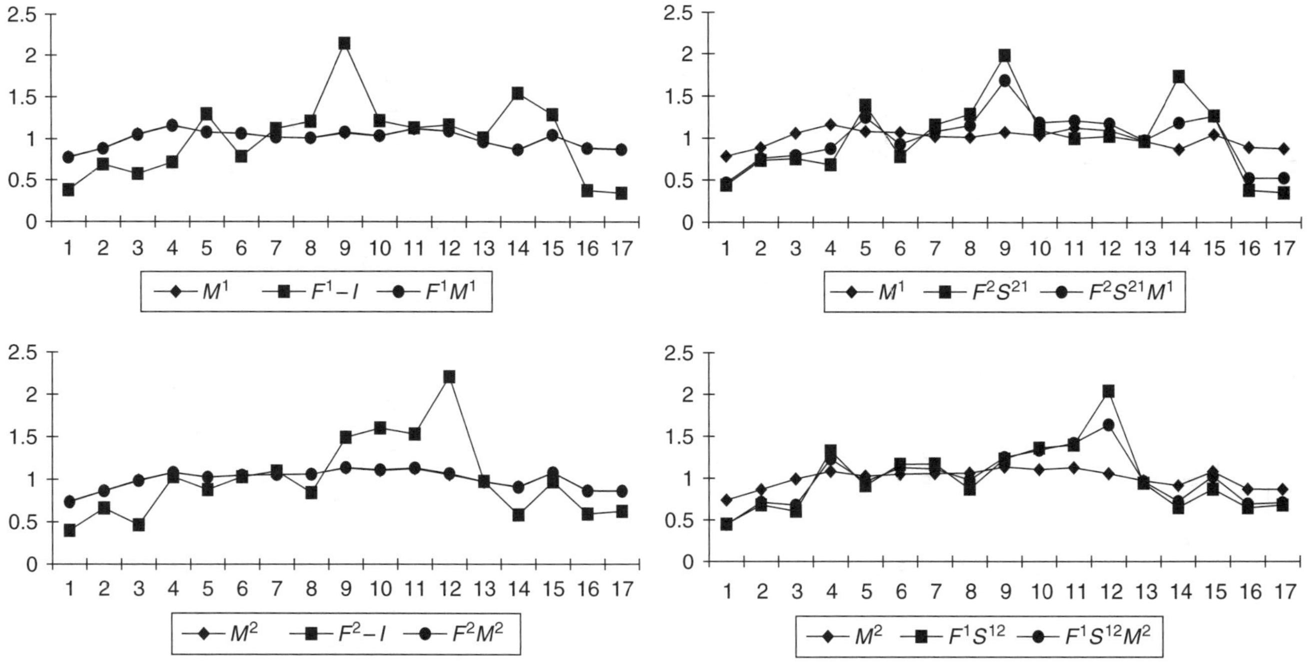

Figure 9.2 Patterns of linkages
Note: –◆– is behind –●– in top left and bottom left parts of the figure

Table 9.6 The feedback and spillover output inducing effects (%)

	Coastal region			*Non-coastal region*		
	Feedback	*Spillover*	*Total*	*Feedback*	*Spillover*	*Total*
1	0.35	4.22	4.57	0.35	3.33	3.68
2	3.39	21.60	24.98	4.06	26.38	30.44
3	0.43	5.82	6.26	0.43	4.49	4.92
4	1.05	10.07	11.12	0.86	5.57	6.43
5	1.14	10.29	11.43	1.32	13.67	14.99
6	1.71	15.81	17.52	1.33	10.06	11.39
7	2.81	21.87	24.68	2.64	16.51	19.15
8	0.72	7.30	8.02	1.05	12.23	13.28
9	2.53	16.83	19.36	3.48	24.02	27.51
10	1.08	8.13	9.21	0.97	7.03	8.00
11	1.17	9.27	10.44	0.94	6.74	7.68
12	1.27	11.49	12.76	1.11	8.19	9.29
13	1.92	14.18	16.10	2.37	16.53	18.90
14	1.56	11.38	12.94	2.19	15.32	17.51
15	0.06	0.50	0.57	0.06	0.43	0.49
16	1.84	14.40	16.25	1.78	12.86	14.65
17	0.61	4.80	5.41	0.59	4.21	4.79
Average	1.39	11.06	12.45	1.50	11.03	12.54

feedback linkages contribute significantly to regional economic development. The geographical sizes of two regions are different, but the economic sizes are quite similar. At the same time, the regional final demands are even nearer, where the ratio of Y_d^{22} to Y_d^{11} is 1.083. It becomes the basic reason why the magnitudes of the corresponding inducing effects are quite close between the two regions.

At the sector level, in the Coastal region, the sectoral contribution ratios of the spillover effects in chemical products (7), mining (2), metal products (9), paper and printing (6) and trade and transport (16) sectors, etc. are greater. The feedback effects in mining (2), chemical products (7), metal products (9), other manufacturing products (13) and trade and transport (16) sectors contribute strongly to sectoral growth; in the Non-coastal region, the spillover output-inducing effects in mining (2), metal products (9), other manufacturing products (13), chemical products (7) and electricity, gas and water supply (14) are significant, while the sector which have the strongest feedback effects are the same as those with strong spillover effects.

Table 9.7 The contributions of feedback and spillover output inducing effects (%)

	Coastal region			*Non-coastal region*		
	Feedback	*Spillover*	*Total*	*Feedback*	*Spillover*	*Total*
1	0.03	0.39	0.42	0.05	0.46	0.51
2	0.08	0.53	0.62	0.23	1.50	1.73
3	0.03	0.38	0.41	0.04	0.37	0.40
4	0.06	0.56	0.62	0.03	0.20	0.24
5	0.01	0.11	0.12	0.02	0.18	0.20
6	0.04	0.33	0.37	0.02	0.16	0.18
7	0.24	1.85	2.09	0.20	1.23	1.43
8	0.03	0.29	0.32	0.06	0.68	0.74
9	0.18	1.18	1.36	0.24	1.69	1.93
10	0.05	0.41	0.47	0.04	0.26	0.29
11	0.03	0.28	0.31	0.02	0.17	0.19
12	0.07	0.63	0.70	0.02	0.17	0.19
13	0.04	0.29	0.32	0.04	0.30	0.34
14	0.04	0.31	0.35	0.06	0.40	0.46
15	0.01	0.05	0.06	0.01	0.04	0.04
16	0.17	1.30	1.46	0.17	1.23	1.40
17	0.10	0.76	0.86	0.09	0.61	0.70
Total	1.21	9.66	10.86	1.33	9.64	10.97

Table 9.6 only shows the feedback and spillover effects' contributions to the growth in sectoral output, while the percentage contributions to regional gross output are listed in Table 9.7. In the Coastal region, the spillover and feedback effects of the chemical products (7) sector contributes 2.09 per cent to regional gross total output, trade and transport (16), metal products (9), service (17) and electronic products (12) contribute 1.46, 1.36, 0.86 and 0.70 per cent respectively to the gross output. Different from sectoral contributions, mining (2), paper and printing (6) and other manufacturing products (13) decrease their rank of the contribution, while service (17) and electronic products (12) sectors' effects become more important. In the Non-coastal region, the metal products (9) sector contributes 1.93 per cent – which is the highest of all sectors – to gross total output by the spillover and feedback effects. The mining (2), chemical products (7), trade and transport (16) and non-metallic mineral products (8) sectors contribute 1.73, 1.43, 1.40 and 0.74 per cent respectively to the gross output. The other manufacturing products (13) and electricity, gas and water supply (14) sectors decrease their rank of the contribution, while trade and transport (16)

and non-metallic mineral products (8) sectors' effects become more important.

The Coastal region's feedback effect and the Non-coastal region's spillover effect are induced by Y_d^{11}, while the Coastal region's spillover effect and the Non-coastal region's feedback effect are induced by Y_d^{22}. It is easy to know that the value of gross total output induced by Y_d^{22} is 1,214.78 billion RMB, which is larger than that by Y_d^{11}, 966.11 billion RMB. Figure 9.3 shows the relations of the regional final demands with the corresponding output inducing at the industrial level. The horizontal axes in Figure 9.3 indicate the ratios of the two regions' sectoral final demands (the Non-coastal region to the Coastal region for (a) and (d), the Coastal region to the Non-coastal region for (b) and (c)), while the vertical axes indicate the spillover or feedback output inducing accordingly. Figure 9.3 shows the clear pattern that the spillover or feedback effect initiated from the Non-coastal region's final demand is becoming stronger as the ratio of the Non-coastal region's final demand is increasing. But the output induced by the Coastal region's final demand in (b) and (c) do not show such a pattern. The productions induced by other sources, such as imports, would have met the demands for the outside region which supplied goods and services in Coastal region. Further evidence is provided by the fact that most of the manufacturing and machinery industries' induced output of spillover or feedback outputs, especially by Y_d^{11}, are quite small.

9.5 Concluding remarks

In terms of the our interregional analysis, the spillover effect is direct, whereas the feedback effect is indirect. Miller developed the methodology on feedback effect analysis by using the IRIO model. Following Round (2001), the IRIO model's Leontief inverse is decomposed to intraregional linkage and its interregional multiplier matrix, then the interregional spillover and feedback effects are discussed, and their backward linkages are defined. Backward linkage is the column-sum while the output-inducing effect is the row-sum of the Leontief inverse weighted by final demand structure.

For two regions, the interregional spillover and feedback effects play an important role in regional economic development. The spillover effects are clearly stronger than the corresponding feedback effects in terms of linkage, multiplier and inducing effect.

The patterns of the various linkages and output-inducing effects are clearly different at the sectoral level. The sectors which process the

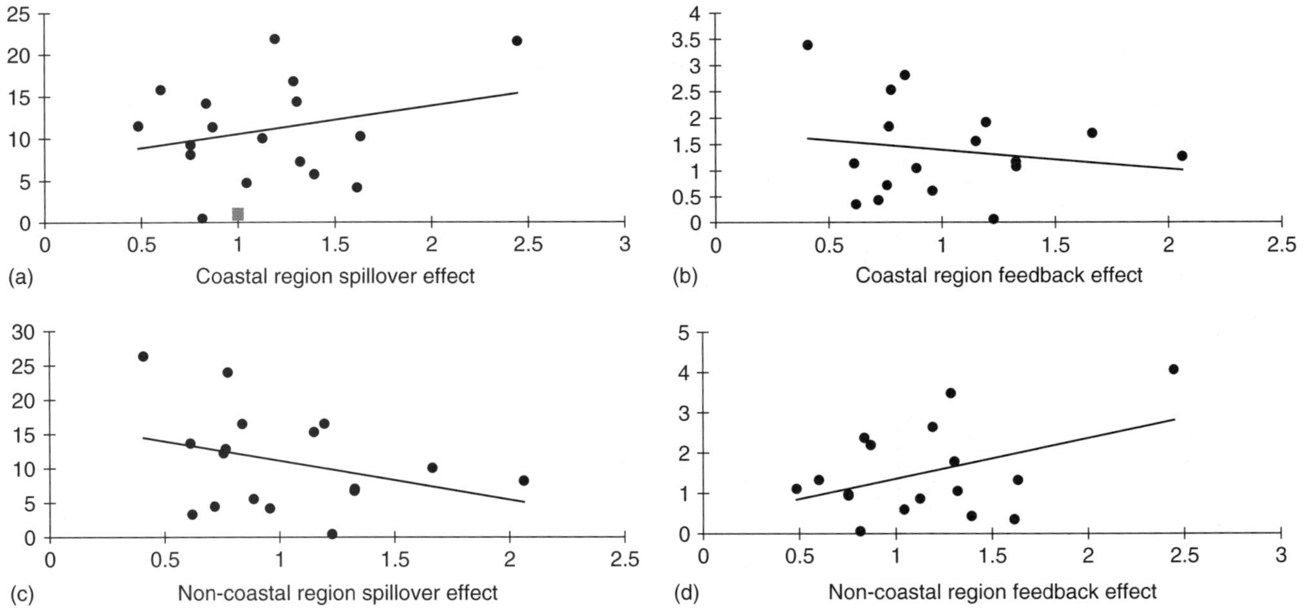

Figure 9.3 Patterns of inducing effects

strongest linkages and multipliers are mainly concentrated on manufacturing, while the material and services sectors tend to show larger output-inducing effects. As the multiplier, the interregional spillover and feedback effects for the Non-coastal region are stronger than that for the Coastal region. Similarly, the gross total output induced by the Non-coastal region's final demand is larger than that induced by the Coastal region's.

The spillover effect initiated from the Coastal region to the Non-coastal region is the most important in that not only does it transfer the advanced technologies to the Non-coastal region, but it also supplies production to meet the demands of the Non-coastal region. Thus the development of manufacturing in the Coastal region, and especially the high-tech sector, is beneficial for the wide economic growth of the whole nation, while the Non-coastal region could make better use of its advantages in materials and resource. On the other hand, the Non-coastal region does not show either the considerable technology transfer effect to the coastal region or the output inducing effect initiated by the coastal region's demands.

The geographical sizes of the two regions are quite different, but their economies are similar in scale. This is the main reason why the magnitudes of the total linkages and inducing effects between the two regions are quite close. As a result, in this study we cannot assess the different picture of the intraregional, feedback and spillover effects between small and large economies as discussed in Dietzenbacher (2002).

Notes

1. The import matrix is not explicitly expressed here, as this study focuses on the regional issue domestically. Under this circumstance, the export demand is ignored also, so the total outputs are reduced to $\tilde{X}^{\alpha}$.
2. Strictly speaking, the regional final demand is $\begin{pmatrix} Y_d^{11} \\ Y_d^{21} \end{pmatrix} + \begin{pmatrix} Y_d^{12} \\ Y_d^{22} \end{pmatrix}$. In terms of equation 9.6, the calculation process is the same whether taking into account Y_d^{21} and Y_d^{12} or not, thus for simplified discuss the interregional spillover and feedback effects, we ignore those interregional flows and define: $\begin{pmatrix} Y_d^{1} \\ Y_d^{2} \end{pmatrix} = \begin{pmatrix} Y_d^{11} \\ 0 \end{pmatrix} + \begin{pmatrix} 0 \\ Y_d^{22} \end{pmatrix}$
3. Miller (1966) and Miller and Blair (1985) define the interregional feedback-inducing output effect as $[(I - A^{11})^{-1} - A^{12}(I - A^{22})^{-1}A^{21}]^{-1} - (I - A^{11})^{-1} = \tilde{F}^1$. Round (2001) shows $\tilde{F}^1 = (F^1 - I)M^1$.
4. Tibet has not compiled any input–output tables to date.
5. The region is to be defined as the Northeastern region (Heilongjiang, Jilin and Liaoning), the North Municipalities region (Beijing and TianJin), the

North Coast region (Hebei and Shandong), the East Coast region (Jiangsu, Shanghai and Zhejiang), the South Coast region (Fujian, Guangdong and Hainan), the Central region (Shanxi, Henan, Anhui, Hubei, Hunan and Jiangxi), the Northwestern region (Inner Mongolia, Shaanxi, Ningxia, Gansu, Qinghai, Xinjiang) and the Southwestern region (Sichuan, Chongqing, Yunnan, Guizhou, Guangxi and Tibet). Taiwan, Hong Kong and Macau are excluded.

6. In an input–output context, technology is usually embodied in commodities transacted among industries. If a certain industry inputs the commodities for production, it means that this industry purchases the technologies embodied in those commodities. This refers to the technology transfer to that industry in this chapter.
7. As the normalization is weighted by the sectoral average, including both each of the 17-sectoral intra- and interregional backward linkages, the normalized sectoral average is approaching 2.

References

Batten, D.F. and D. Martellato (1988) 'Modelling Interregional Trade with Input–Output Systems', *Richerche Economiche*, 42(2), 204–21.

Brun, J.F., J.L. Combes and M.F. Renard (2002) 'Are the Spillover Effects Between Coastal and Noncoastal Regions in China?', *China Economic Review*, 13, 161–9.

Charnes, A. and W.W. Cooper (1961) *Management Models and Industrial Applications of Linear Programming*, vol. 1. New York: Wiley.

Dietzenbacher, E. (2002) 'Interregional Multipliers: Looking Backward, Looking Forward', *Regional Studies*, 36(2), 125–36.

Dietzenbacher, E. and J.A. van der Linden (1997) 'Sectoral and Spatial Linkages in the EC Production Structure', *Journal of Regional Science*, 37(2), 235–57.

Gillen, W.J. and A. Guccione (1980) 'Interregional Feedbacks in Input–Output Models: Some Formal Results', *Journal of Regional Science*, 20(4), 477–82.

Greytak, D. (1970) 'Regional Impact of Interregional Trade in Input–Output Analysis', *Papers Regional Science Association*, 25, 203–17.

Greytak, D. (1974) 'Regional Interindustry Multipliers: An Analysis of Information', *Regional and Urban Economics*, 4, 163–72.

Guccione, A., W.J. Gillen, P.D. Blair and R.E. Miller (1988) 'Interregional Feedbacks in Input–Output Models: The Least Upper Bound', *Journal of Regional Science*, 28(3), 397–404.

Liew, C.K. and C.J. Liew (1985) 'Measuring the Development Impact of a Transportation System: A Simplified Approach', *Journal of Regional Science*, 25, 241–57.

Lundqvist, L. (1981) 'Applications of A Dynamic Multiregional Input–Output Model of the Swedish Economy', *Papers Regional Science Association*, 47, 79–95.

Miller, R.E. (1963) 'Comments on the "General Equilibrium" Model of Professor Moses', *Metroeconomica*, 40, 82–8.

Miller, R.E. (1966) 'Interregional Feedback Effects in Input–Output Models: Some Preliminary Results', *Papers of the Regional Science Association*, 17, 105–25.

Miller, R.E. (1969) 'Interregional Feedback Effects in Input–Output Models: Some Experimental Results', *Western Economic Journal*, 7, 41–50.

Miller, R.E. (1986) 'Upper Bounds on the Sizes of Interregional Feedbacks in Multiregional Input–Output Models', *Journal of Regional Science*, 26(2), 285–306.

Miller, R.E. (1998) 'Regional and Interregional Input–Output Analysis', as chapter 3 in W. Isard, I.J. Azis, M.P. Drennan, R.E. Miller, S. Saltzman and E. Thorbecke, *Methods of Interregional and Regional Analysis*, Aldershot: Ashgate, pp. 41–124.

Miller, R.E. and P.D. Blair (1985) 'Input–Output Models at the Regional Level', In *Input–Output Analysis: Foundations and Extensions*, Englewood Cliffs, NJ: Prentice-Hall, pp. 45–99.

Poncet, S. (2001) 'The Magnitude of Chinese Provinces' Internal and Interregional Trade Integration. Is Chinese Provinces' Greater International Openness Threatening China's Domestic Market Integration?', paper presented at the 3rd International Conference on the Chinese Economy, *Has China Become Market Economy?* CERDI (le Centre d'études et de recherches sur le développement international), Clermont-Ferrand, France.

Pyatt, G. and J.I. Round (1979) 'Accounting and Fixed Price Multipliers in a Social Accounting Matrix Framework', *The Economic Journal*, 89, 850–73.

Round, J.I. (1985) 'Decomposing Multipliers for Economic Systems Involving Regional and World Trade', *The Economic Journal*, 95, 383–99.

Round, J.I. (2001) 'Feedback Effects in Interregional Input–Output Models: What Have We Learned?', in M.L. Lahr and E. Dietzenbacher (eds), *Input–Output Analysis: Frontiers and Extensions*, New York: Palgrave, pp. 54–78.

Sonis, M. and G.J.D. Hewings (1999) 'Miyazawa's Contributions to Understanding Economic Structure: Interpretation, Evaluation and Extensions', in G.J.D. Hewings, M. Sonis, M. Madden and Y. Kimura (eds), *Understanding and Interpreting Economic Structure: Essays in Honour of Kenichi Miyazawa*, Heidelberg: Spring-Verlag, 13–51.

Sonis, M. and G.J.D. Hewings (2001) 'Feedbacks in Input–Output Systems: Impacts, Loops and Hierarchies', in M.L. Lahr and E. Dietzenbacher (eds), *Input–Output Analysis: Frontiers and Extensions*, New York: Palgrave, pp. 71–99.

Sonis, M., J. Oosterhaven and G.J.D. Hewings (1993) 'Spatial Economic Structure and Structural Changes in the EC: Feedback Loop Analysis', *Economic Systems Research*, 5, 173–84.

Zhang, Q. and B. Felmingham (2002) 'The Role of FDI, Exports and Spillover Effects in the Regional Development of China', *The Journal of Development Studies*, 38(4), 157–78.

10

Conclusion: Spatial Structure and Regional Development in China

Nobuhiro Okamoto and Takeo Ihara

10.1 The interregional input–output approach to China

Recent studies on the regional development of China have shown that regional disparity has become a significant problem, and this has led many policy makers and researchers to pay attention to the issue of how we might develop the underdeveloped regions of the nation. It should be noted, however, that most of the approaches to date have focused on the situation in specific regions, rather than considering interregional interdependency. Therefore, in order to add something substantial to these previous studies, we felt the need to consider the interregional feedback effects and/or spatial interactions quantitatively. This was the main reason why we compiled the full-scale interregional input–output model for China as a useful analytical tool for considering spatial economy. We have also analysed the current regional economy in China by using this sort of interregional input–output approach.

When we reviewed the empirical implementation of an interregional input–output analysis on regional economic issues in China, this revealed that there have been few compilation works and few applications of an input–output analysis to the regional economy as it actually exists in China. In this regard, through careful and earnest discussions within our study group, we achieved the following consensus: First, we have to explain the limitations of an input–output model, together with its underlying assumptions so as to extend its model for further study works. Secondly, we also have to show how to compile and estimate a body of full-scale interregional input–output data which can then be used as the basis for further empirical investigation. In the light of this, let us make some additional comments.

With regard to the first point, we dare to admit that in the current circumstances an input–output model arouses considerable scepticism, although it should be regarded as the most fundamental and useful framework for grasping the real economic structures in a simple and consistent way. Upon closer investigation, it becomes clear that many of the criticisms relate to the strong technical assumptions that lie behind an input–output model. Therefore, in order to cope with such current circumstances to become better off, we outlined, in Chapter 2 (Ihara), the basic structure of an input–output model in more detail, together with an explicit acknowledgement of its qualifications and limitations, in order to clarify the relative advantage of the model. We, then, also explained the contemporary frontiers on an input–output model for further research.[1]

As for the second point, we dare to say that we still suffer from the severe restrictions on the available interregional input–output data for China. Under these conditions, we have to address such problems as how we could obtain or estimate reliable interregional input–output data in China. Eventually, in Chapter 3 (Okamoto and Zhang), we clarified the non-survey methods of estimating regional and interregional input–output data and production accounts (i.e., total outputs) in the region concerned, we have estimated interregional input–output coefficients and the related Leontief inverse matrix.[2]

10.2 The results of our study

Using our interregional input–output model, which was developed with our estimated data, we have tried to analyse various regional development problems in China. More specifically, we have employed the data from our Multi-Regional Input–Output Model for China (CMRIO) (Institute of Developing Economies 2003). According to our CMRIO model, the regional breakdown in China has been carried out correctly. Therefore, our empirical studies of the regional development of China have been basically conducted subject to this sort of regional definition. However, the regional definition and/or division for China have been widely discussed in the literature. As a result, many other methods of dividing up the regions of China have been proposed.

Therefore, in Chapter 4 (Li and Hou), these regional divisions for China were investigated in some depth, together with some additional explanations of our regional breakdown by eight regions. For further reference, we have undertaken some comparative analyses of the social and economic development of eight regions from such viewpoints as basic conditions, GDP and structure, infrastructure, opening to the outside world, market scale and residents' consumption, development potential and economic activities. As a result, we have found that: (1) there is a considerable difference between the regions in terms of geographical scale, size of population and the degree of wealth. Namely, the Northwest region is the largest, the Central region is the most heavily populated and the East Coast region is the richest. (2) In terms of overall characteristics, the East Coast region has the strongest economic power as well as industrial activity, and it has the most promising market potential. By contrast, the Northwest region faces the greatest struggle in trying to develop, because it is sparsely populated, has small local markets, and is very inconveniently situated.

Then, what kind of factors brought about above-stated differentials in regional development in China? This is the question considered, in Chapter 5 (Kanazawa). As a result, it emerged that the coastal region (i.e., North Municipalities, North Coast, East Coast, South Coast) has been developing through intermediate demand, while the interior region (i.e., Central, Northwest and Southwest) has been developed by the final demand factors, with its comparative advantage of construction and agricultural sectors. These findings have significant implications for the Western Area Development Strategy (see Table 10.1).

It should be noted that natural resource allocation across the regions in China might also have significant implications for their development. Natural resources are principally concentrated in the Central and Western regions. On the other hand, sea resources are concentrated in the East Coast and South Coast regions, where manufacturing industries are a dominant sector. Thus, a particular spatial linkage in China has been formed. More specifically, coal, oil, natural gas, metal ore and agriculture resources tend to flow from the Central and Western regions to the East Coast and South Coast, while manufacturing products tend to flow from the coastal region to the Central and Western regions. These differences between regional economies eventually generate the transaction of resources and goods over the regions. In this regard, the spatial linkage structure in China has been clarified, in Chapter 6 (Pan and Liu), which shows us the interregional interdependency of space economy. Namely, the Northeast and Southwest regions have the smallest connection to their outer regions, while the Northwest region has the largest one. In addition, it should be noted that the East Coast, South Coast and North

Municipalities regions have more backward linkages but fewer forward linkages. On the other hand, the North Coast and Central regions have more forward linkages but fewer backward linkages. Therefore, we might consider that the North Coast and Central regions take the role of suppliers of natural resources, providing intermediate goods to such regions as the North Municipalities, the East Coast and the South Coast, which is regarded as an already developed region in China.

Judging from the spatial aspects of an economic activity, the majority of industry seems to be concentrated in the East Coast and South Coast regions, and hence its industrial agglomeration in these regions might lead to the achievement of high rates of development. With the progress of spatial economics or new economic geography, it is generally recognized that the spread of development from core industrialized economy (i.e., East Coast and South Coast) might be caused by the relocation of a manufacturing sector. The movement of a manufacturing sector might depend upon the wage differentials and linkages among sectors. If the wages are given, the linkages among sectors will be important for the movement of industry from the agglomerated region to another region. Those sectors with few linkages will move quickly from the region, because it is not necessary for them to supply the intermediate goods to sectors in this region. In order to understand the possibility of movement of manufacturing sectors in a heavily concentrated region, the intraregional/interregional linkages in the East Coast and South Coast regions have been measured, in Chapter 7 (Okamoto), where the industry is agglomerated. As a result, we established the following: (1) that although the linkage structure in the South Coast is relatively simple compared to that in the East Coast region, the electric and telecommunications sector is a core of linkage in the region, and, even more, intraregional linkage of this sector is quite strong within the region; (2) the East Coast region seems to have relative advantages for developing with the existence of various sectors, which had been already established during the planning period. Therefore, the linkage structure among machinery industries has been forming significantly in terms of directions, volumes and technical relations. Thus, this region might be regarded as the major beneficiary from the agglomeration economies.

So far, we have considered the spread of development from the core to the periphery of the region largely from the viewpoint of the movement of the industrial sectors. However, if we consider the regional disparity in the context of Myrdal, Hirschman, Wiliamson, then the 'trickle-down' or 'polarization' effect might become the most important concept. Therefore, in Chapter 8 (Hioki), the regional disparity was discussed intensively in the context of the trickle-down effect, which can

Table 10.1 Regional development in China

	Characteristics (Ch. 4)	*Differential factors (Ch. 5)**	*Spatial linkages (Ch. 6)*
Northeast	Relative high per capita GDP Relative high infrastructure of railway transport	Crude oil and natural gas Urban household consumption	Relative average linkage to outside region
North Municipalities	Largest population density Highest per capita GDP	Tertiary industry Intermediate inputs	Large backward linkage to outside region
North Coast	Relative high value added of primary sector Relatively open economy	Primary industry Developed by outflows	Large forward linkage to outside region
East Coast	Largest GDP share	Most of sector Pulled by exports	Large backward linkage to outside region
South Coast	Most open economy	Most of sector Pulled by exports	Large backward linkage to outside region
Central	Largest population	Agriculture Pulled by outflows	Large forward linkage to outside region
Northwest	Largest land area Smallest per capita GDP	Agriculture, trade and transport Pulled by domestic demand	Largest linkage to outside region
Southwest	Highest proportion of employment in primary sector Least urbanization	Agriculture, food products Pulled by domestic demand	Smallest linkage to outside region

Notes
* Upper: comparative advantage sector.
Lower: its factor.

be measured by the repercussion of final demand and output multiplier. The analysis finds, that around 10 per cent of the total repercussion goes to the interior region. Therefore, we can evaluate that the 'Step Ladder' policy to some extent worked well as a sound regional development policy. On the other hand, the East Coast and South Coast regions are playing very important roles in promoting growth in China. In addition, the North Municipalities region seems to have only a very small trickle-down effect to other regions, and the North Coast region plays the role of being a growth pole for the Northeast region.

Chapter 9 (Zhang and Zhao) focused on the same issues as mentioned above. The questions it aimed to consider were as follows: Are there spillover effects between Coastal regions and Non-coastal regions? If any exist, how should we measure their effects? Although some studies have tentatively attempted to reveal spillover effects by using an econometric model, an interregional input–output model should be regarded as the most appropriate and effective tool to measure feedback and spillover effects between the core and the periphery of the region. We have discussed the methodology on feedback and spillover effect analysis in the context of input–output framework. And we have clarified the fact, by our method for the case of two regions, that the interregional spillover and feedback effects play very important roles in regional economic development. It should be noted that the spillover effects are clearly stronger than the corresponding feedback effects in terms of linkage, multiplier and inducing effect. In addition, with regard to the multiplier, the interregional spillover and feedback effects for the Non-coastal region seem to be much stronger than that for the Coastal regions. Similarly, gross total output induced by the Non-coastal region's final demand seems to be larger than that for the Coastal region's. Therefore, we can state that the development of the manufacturing industries – especially the high-tech sector – in the Coastal region, might get the benefit from the nation-wide economic growth, while the Non-coastal region could better utilize the advantage in terms of both materials and resources. On the other hand, the Non-coastal region does not show the consistent technology transfer effect, and even the output-inducing effect, which was initiated by the Coastal region's demands (see Figure 10.1).

Keeping those findings in mind, what conclusions can we draw confidently from the empirical studies detailed in this book? Our key findings can be summarized as follows:

(1) The Northeast region, which is considered to be a heavy industrial area, has a self-sufficient structure with relatively few spatial

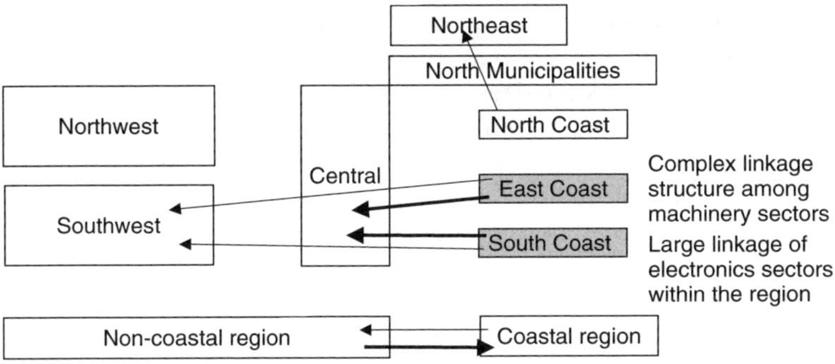

Figure 10.1 Spatial structure in China

Notes
Shaded boxes show industrial agglomeration region.
Arrows show trickle-down or spillover effect.

linkages to other regions. By contrast, the East Coast and South Coast regions are regarded as the development centre or growth poles of the Chinese economy, in which industry is highly concentrated, and their economic activity has a certain amount of spillover effects to both the Central and Southwest regions. The Central and North Coast regions might occupy the economic position as suppliers of both materials and intermediate goods, to support the development of the coastal region. However, the Northwest region is dependent to a considerable extent on other regions.

(2) From the viewpoint of regional development policy, it is very important to consider the spatial interactions between different regions. From our results so far, we may conclude, as some policy implications, that the Northeast region should form more intensive spatial linkages with the North Coast and North Municipalities regions, while the Northwest region should introduce more investments of new industry into the associated region.

10.3 Some concluding remarks for further study

As Dietzenbacher and Lahr (2001, p. 1) mentioned, in the recent literature input–output analysis has been used as one of the major tools in applied quantitative economics. This input–output technique is widely used for the analysis of all sorts of economic issues, such as structural economics, development economics, regional economics and regional science among others. Input–output research fell out of favour during the

1970s and 1980s, but, following the development of economic theory in the new growth theory, new trade theory and spatial economics, it is very natural that the next step of research on these topics should be a positive and empirical work in both multi-sectoral and multi-regional framework. Thus, it should be noted that input–output analysis has experienced a strong revival in the 1990s.

In China, the uneven development of the regional economies has been a subject of considerable interest in the late 1990s, and some studies have tried to approach this issue from the aspects of endogeneous growth theory (Jian, Sacks and Warner 1996; Raiser 1998; Yao and Zhang 2001) and also from the aspect of spatial economics (Fujita and Hu 2001; Kimura 2003). Therefore, in accordance with the historical development of an input–output research, the empirical studies on regional development in China have been needed for their multi-sectoral and multi-regional aspects. In this context, an interregional input–output model has been particularly required by regional economists. To meet their expectations, and also to satisfy this potential demand for interregional input–output model, we have compiled the full-scale Multi-regional Input–Output Model for China, always appreciating the severe data restrictions.

In addition, this book has tried to consider spatial structure and regional development in China, based on an interregional input–output approach that has used our estimated data to the fullest possible extent. As already summarized in this book, not only could we obtain very meaningful information on regional development problems in China, but we could also explain how to utilize new frontiers of interregional input–output analysis. Therefore, we are convinced that this book may serve to deepen the understanding both of regional development in China and of the possibilities for interregional input–output analysis in general. Finally, we are looking forward strongly to working together to conduct further empirical studies on spatial structures and/or regional developments based on our shared analytical methods and interests.

Notes

1. Then, we, in turn, applied our own analytical methods to such areas as the analysis of inter-industrial linkages (Chapter 7), the spatial structural analysis (Chapters 6 and 8), the decomposition technique for structural change (Chapter 5), and the multipliers (Chapter 9), so as to provide in-depth analysis of the development of the regional economies of China.
2. Through the empirical study of a comparison of the estimated model and the original provincial/interregional table, we can conclude the following: (1) that we can use national technical coefficient for regional economic

analysis instead of using the regional one if the region concerned has a relative large GDP, and that the regional input coefficient estimated by the location quotient approach might also be useful for regional impact analysis: (2) but regarding interregional input coefficient estimated by the same method, the result was not so good, especially in respect of interregional transaction parts because the location quotient method does not measure cross-hauling between regions.

References

Dietzenbacher, E. and M.L. Lahr (2001), 'Introduction', in M.L. Lahr and E. Dietzenbacher (eds), *Input–Output Analysis: Frontiers and Extensions*, New York: Palgrave.

Fujita, M. and D.P. Hu (2001) 'Regional Disparity in China 1985–1994: The Effects of Globalization and Economic Liberalization', *Annals of Regional Science*, 35(1), 3–37.

Institute of Developing Economies–JETRO (2003) *Multi-Regional Input–Output Model for China 2000*, Statistical Data Series no. 86, Tokyo: Institute of Developing Economies–JETRO.

Jian, T.L., J. Sachs and A. Warner (1996) 'Trends in Regional Inequality in China', *China Economic Review*, 7, 1–21.

Kimura, K. (2003) 'China's Regional Industrial Disparity from the Viewpoint of Industrial Agglomeration', in M. Kagami and M. Tsuji (eds), *Industrial Agglomeration: Facts and Lessons for Developing Countries*, Tokyo: Institute of Developing Economies–JETRO.

Raiser, M. (1998) 'Subsidizing Inequality: Economic Reforms, Fiscal Transfers and Convergence across Chinese Provinces', *Journal of Development Studies*, 34(3), 1–26.

Yao, S. and Z.Y. Zhang (2001) 'Regional Growth in China under Economic Reforms', *Journal of Development Studies*, 38(2), 167–86.

Index

Notes: f = figure; n = note; t = table; **bold** = extended discussion or heading emphasized in main text.